DI017332

Cruising the Easy Way

Books by Bill Robinson

The Science of Sailing
New Boat
A Berth to Bermuda
Where the Trade Winds Blow
Expert Sailing
Over the Horizon
The World of Yachting
The Best from Yachting *(Editor)*
Better Sailing for Boys and Girls
The America's Cup Races *(co-author)*
Legendary Yachts
The Sailing Life
The Right Boat for You
Great American Yacht Designers
America's Sailing Book
A Sailor's Tales
Cruising: The Boats and the Places
South to the Caribbean
Where to Cruise
Islands
Caribbean Cruising Handbook
Eighty Years of Yachting
Cruising the Easy Way

BILL ROBINSON

Cruising the Easy Way

W · W · NORTON & COMPANY
NEW YORK LONDON

Copyright © 1990 by Bill Robinson.
All rights reserved.
Printed in the United States of America.

The text of this book is composed in Avanta, with the display set in
Palatino. Composition by Vail Ballou. Manufacturing by Maple Press.
Book design by M. Franklyn Plympton.

First Edition
Library of Congress Cataloging-in-Publication Data
Robinson, Bill, 1918–
Cruising the easy way / Bill Robinson.
p. cm.
Includes bibliographical references.
1. Sailing.   2. Yachts and yachting.   I. Title.
GV811.R5814   1990
797.1'24—dc20   90-32717

ISBN 0-393-02847-X
W.W. Norton & Company, Inc.
500 Fifth Avenue, New York, N.Y. 10110
W.W. Norton & Company, Ltd.
37 Great Russell Street, London WC1B 3NU

1   2   3   4   5   6   7   8   9   0

Contents

CONTENTS

Photographs appear following page 112

PROLOGUE

One Day

Why we cruise

~~~~~~

The first evidence of the new day was a gentle bobble of wake as the utility launch from the Bitter End Yacht Club went by, starting its daily rounds. There had been no rain squalls during the night, so the hatch was open and I could see a patch of clear blue sky through it. So far, so good, and my ritual check out the companionway to the cockpit gave more evidence that it was going to be a good day.

The sun was still behind the hill inshore of us, but its golden light suffused the hills two miles away to the westward across Gorda Sound, and a few minor clusters of cumulus rimmed the horizon. The breeze was fitful in the lee of the hill, but farther out on the sound it riffled the water to a darker blue. Off to the north, the boats anchored behind Saba Rock between the tip of Virgin Gorda and Prickly Pear Island were riding evenly, bows to the eastward and flags standing well in the trade wind. Yes, it was a good day, and we would be out in it soon.

There was no hurry, though. It had been a pleasant evening of dinner ashore at Bitter End, the yachting-oriented resort complex, comparing notes with other cruising sailors over coffee (laced with spiced rum in the Bitter End tradition) on the beachfront terrace afterwards, and a nightcap, dubbed a *"chapeau,"* short for *chapeau de la nuit* in our best fractured French, in the cockpit of *Brunelle*, our CSY37 cutter. We were tied up at the Quarterdeck Club, the small marina maintained by the Bitter End, after a day of beating our way eastward in Sir Francis Drake Passage against the trades from the previous day's

Sailing westward into the afternoon sun in Sir Francis Drake Channel

anchorage at Trellis Bay, Beef Island, through the heart of the British Virgin Islands where we based *Brunelle* for nine seasons.

There was no special plan for the day. As usual in BVI cruising, we would gauge the weather, gauge how we felt, get underway after a leisurely breakfast, and choose the day's schedule as we went along. Any number of anchorages were there for the visiting for a lunch stop and/or overnight. Jane did her usual balancing act with poached eggs while I set up the portable table in the cockpit, and we watched the day build to bright sunshine over the usual breakfast fare. On the Out Island 41 across the slip, the charterers were stirring for their cockpit breakfast, looking as though they had had a later night than ours at the Bitter End. Around the anchorage there were signs of life on the big fleet of boats riding to the Bitter End's bright, shocking pink moorings, or at anchor.

The Bitter End, Virgin Gorda

Jack Haight, my one-time college roommate, and his wife Debbie, frequent cruising companions, pitched in to do the dishes before heading up the path to the Bitter End gift shop for some postcards, and I did my routine chores of paying the dockage, checking battery water and lube oil levels, and removing the sail cover from the main. When everyone had been to the head (ashore at the Quarterdeck Club), put on sunburn cream, and found novel, knitting, or cruising guide, I announced that we were "in all respects ready for sea" and the lines were cast off. I had been running the engine for a while to charge the refrigerator, timing it so that the required hour would end at about the time we cleared the marina and made sail. This was accomplished on a turn to windward through the anchorage, the "noise" was killed to grateful sighs, and we headed dead downwind under main, westward to the narrow pass between Mosquito Island and Anguilla Point at the western end of Gorda Sound.

The depth in the pass is about six feet, and charter yachts are warned against using it, but, with our 4'10" draft, we have always made it without trouble. As the trade built behind us, we swooped by the native settlement at Gun Creek, where the houses string upward in a single line from the waterfront to the heights of Bay Hill, and the real estate development at Leverick Bay, where one of the small cruise ships that ply the Virgins was alongside the pier. The color of the water changed dramatically from deep blue to pale green as we came onto the shallows at the pass, and we dipsy-doodled through the best water, judging depth by color. The squiggles in our course were needed to miss the shallows making out from Mosquito Island and the large reef, just out the western side, where ocean swells set up breakers. Several boats have been wrecked on this reef over the years.

Outside in deeper water, we ran along the heights of Mountain Point and I checked and commented on my favorite tree, an oddly comical umbrella-shaped one standing in solitary splendor in the last saddle between the hills that undulate out to the rocky western terminus of Virgin Gorda. This tree has been there in all the years we have cruised the BVI, growing a bit thicker as the years pass, but always amusing to me in its solitary, picaresque dignity.

Around the stark low end of Mountain Point, where Atlantic swells build a restless surge over the harshly rugged rocks, we jibed to port and set roller-furling jib and staysail for the reach down Drake Passage.

To port, tucked in behind Mountain Point, was the thin ribbon of white sand at Long Bay, where we sometimes stop for snorkeling and beachcombing without much company, but we had not yet been underway long enough to stop.

Usually as deserted as Long Bay, Savannah Bay is the next anchorage south on Virgin Gorda, also proscribed for bareboats because of its protecting reef. Sometimes we thread our way in there for a lunch stop, but now the sailing was too good to stop. A string of boat traffic headed to and from Gorda Sound stretched out before us, almost like cars on a highway. In either direction, it was a fast reach and the boats made a lively sight as the northbound ones swished by us. While we caught up to one or two smaller boats on our tack, we had an 80-foot, professionally crewed ketch gradually overtake us on our course. Her charterers lolled around the deck in luxurious indolence as she worked by us.

Once out from under the bulk of 1,359-foot Gorda Peak just to windward, we felt the increased heft of the wind swooping across the low saddle behind Savannah Bay, and *Brunelle* surged happily up to hull speed. Little Dix resort, tucked into its own bay, disappeared quickly behind Colison Point and the ominous boil of its nearby reef, and the forest of masts at Virgin Gorda Yacht Harbour came next to view. A steady stream of boats was negotiating its narrow L-shaped entrance in both directions.

The Haights had not seen The Baths, the fabulous collection of house-sized boulders at the southern tip of Virgin Gorda, so we decided to make that our lunch stop. We had come 10 miles in just under two hours, a normal pre-lunch run in the BVI, so we doused sail and threaded our way under power through the anchored fleet of perhaps 40 boats. They were bobbing and swaying gently in the surge that is always present here to some extent, confining it to lunch-stop status, and I found room, not always easy to do, in my favorite spot to drop the hook here, a patch of clear sand a bit north of the main beach. Much of the bottom off The Baths is grassy, and there are a few coral heads, but this spot has good holding ground, and *Brunelle* settled into place with no fuss. Sometimes the surge is too high for a safe dinghy landing on the beach, but it was not bad today, and Jack and I put the Avon inflatable over from its resting place to starboard of the mast on *Brunelle*'s raised deck, an easy chore. We do not carry an outboard, so Jack, an old Princeton 150-pound crew member, took to the oars and rowed Debbie in to the beach, already well lined with dinghies, between two of the highest boulders.

There was steady dinghy traffic back and forth all the while, and more boats moved in to join the anchored fleet. While the Haights explored the strange pools and caverns in among the great tumble of rocks and did some snorkeling on the reef just offshore, Jane and I had

a Scrabble game (I don't like to leave the boat untended in an anchorage like this, and we have seen The Baths often over the years), and
then she set about getting lunch. I don't ask what's for lunch. I just
ask, "What are we having with celery today?" Jane's favorite way to
put a lunch together is to chop celery into small bits and then make a
salad of it with shrimp, salmon, tuna, or chicken, which always seems
to suit.

When the Haights came back, wildly enthusiastic over their shore
excursion, they washed off the salt under our deck shower, a black
plastic bag left in the sun to warm and then hung from a halyard strung
between the mast and shrouds. A cooling concoction took care of another
kind of saltiness—in the throat—before getting to the celery-mix-of-
the-day, and it was time to sail some more.

One of the features that makes a BVI cruise so rewarding is the wide
choice of harbors that are always within easy reach. Here, we could
duck the two miles back to Virgin Gorda Yacht Harbour if we wanted
more marina amenities or had to attend to food, fuel, or water resup-
ply, but we had had a marina the night before, so no supplies were
needed. Downwind of us there was a choice of a five-mile run northwest to Marina Cay or Trellis Bay, both good anchorages with good
restaurants, and Marina Cay has rental moorings if we felt too lazy to
anchor. We had already been to Trellis Bay on the way east, spending
a hilarious evening at The Last Resort, with its excellent buffet dinner
and the inimitable songs and patter of the proprietor, Tony Snell.

Another choice was Cooper Island, also with a restaurant and rental
moorings, about the same distance due west. Across from it on Tortola, Maya Cove offered an excellent but crowded anchorage, and a
few miles west of it, Road Town, the "metropolis" of the BVI, was a
major supply, transfer and entertainment spot. Nanny Cay's snug marina
would be only a couple miles more. Peter and Norman islands, with
a choice of anchorages, were also in easy reach, a run of eight to 10
miles. There were so many choices that we could set off without making a decision. There was enough south in the breeze by now, and it
was at a perfect 12-knot velocity, to set the Flasher, our poleless spinnaker that makes downwind sailing so much more fun. It was soon up

and drawing in all its multicolored splendor, and we swept westward at a good clip. To port, the strange jumble of rocks called Fallen Jerusalem, an extension of the boulders at The Baths, slid swiftly by, then Ginger and Cooper islands. As the sun lowered over the bow, plating Drake Channel a glittering silver, it was time to choose a destination. We all decided we had had enough "civilization" after eating ashore the previous two nights, so we opted for splendid isolation. This is easier said than done in the BVI, but there were a couple of possibilities. We would try Key Bay on the south side of Peter Island, little known to the bareboat fleets and a lovely spot if there was no southerly surge. If the surge proved too much, it was a quick jaunt to Little Harbour on the north side of Peter or across to the Bight of Norman Island, one of the most popular BVI anchorages.

Rounding to the southward off Salt Island, where a tiny native village, whose few inhabitants still tend the salt flats, makes an interesting day stop, we handed in the Flasher and set the double headsail rig. To starboard were the stark bluffs of Dead Chest Island, supposedly the site of the "yo, ho, ho and a bottle of rum" myth, and to port a gaggle of moored boats marked the favorite diving spot of the area, the 120-year old wreck of the steamship *Rhone*, a hurricane casualty. Now the Caribbean Sea itself was under our keel, and *Brunelle* rose and fell to the open swells. A very dry boat, she handled the whitecaps nicely on the way to Carrot Rock, which has never looked like a carrot to me. It was sending up the breaking seas into white sheets of spray as we rounded it and headed on the opposite jibe the mile or so into Key Bay, named, I guess, because a small key (cay) stands off its eastern point. The little island affords extra protection behind it in about 20 feet of water, with several patches of clean sand for the choosing between the darker grassy areas.

The surge was negligible, and we were delighted to settle in at anchor after a fine sail. We had the next thing to splendid isolation, as there was only one other boat, and she was well off at the other end of the bay several hundred yards away. No one else came in as the sun went in back of clouds over the blue bulk of St. John in the American Virgins, five miles to the west. It sent great shafts of light through holes

A sunset to end a perfect cruising day

in the clouds, suffusing them with swiftly changing sunset hues of gold, pink, and red. Off to the east, cumuli out in the open Caribbean were a delicate salmon, reflecting the late sun.

The swimming ladder was quickly dropped for pre-cocktail swimming, and happy hour lived up to its name in the approaching dusk. One of our favorite cruising dinners, going back to when it was the only thing I knew how to cook on my first cruises in the '30s, is corned beef hash and peas—quick, easy, and always satisfying—and this seemed like a good night for that.

As night filled in, the only lights we could see were on the other boat, and a glimmer or two on St. John, which seemed isolation enough in one of the most popular cruising grounds in the world, and a quarter moon cast a thin path of light across the water as it followed the sun behind the mountains of St. John. Some tapes, first Ella Fitzgerald and then Glenn Miller, went well with *chapeaux* as we watched the moon disappear.

And so it was a day on which nothing much had happened, and yet everything that had happened had been delightful. It, and many others like it, could be called the "perfect cruising day." In essence, it was the reason why we cruise, and why all the planning, organizing, coping with problems, and working out of practical details are very much worth the effort. Behind the result, before the easy cruising, there must be a great amount of preparation.

Part I

Organization

I

Choosing a Boat

The basics

~~~~~~

Putting it all together for a "perfect cruising day" doesn't just happen. The days when everything goes right can only be the product of thought and preparation, of the working out of many details and compromises.

It is an absolutely valid cliché about cruising boats that every boat is a compromise, or we would have one stock design instead of the multiple choices available in sail and power. My experience as owner of four cruising auxiliaries between 24 and 42 feet, and frequent cruiser under the OPBYC (Other People's Boats Yacht Club) burgee, almost all under sail, has been that every time I board a boat to cruise, I am instantly aware of the truth of the cliché. Every inch of every boat, from bow to stern, is made up of compromises of some sort, and they must be balanced in evaluating and choosing a boat.

The first consideration is the type of cruising to be done, ranging from marina-hugging in apartmentlike powerboats to world-girdling passagemaking of the hairiest chested variety. The boat must be suited to the purpose in the best way possible. For most of us, the bulk of cruising is done, of course, in local waters for weekends and vacations, and the dream of far horizons can be answered, in a way, by chartering in more exotic areas. More and more people, however, are taking off for extended cruising over long periods of time. They may be retirees released at last from the daily grind and taking advantage of newfound free time, but many cruising sailors are doing this at an early age, not waiting for the "golden years" before they bust loose.

And so these are the starting considerations in choosing a boat:

3

Cost, both of purchase and operating
Suitability to area
Suitability to those who will be using her
Comfort in relation to performance
Looks vs. function
Rig
Draft (governed by hull form)

And so the compromises that affect an individual situation must be considered and met as well as possible. The first one, naturally, is a personal matter. It is folly to fall in love with a boat that will be a financial burden, crimping plans right from the start. Cost is not just the price tag on the boat itself. Unless the vessel is fully found, the cost of outfitting her must be considered, and then the running cost of operating expenses, maintenance, and insurance. For those who cut all ties from house and home, these can be considered cost-of-living expenses, not just the price of recreational pleasure.

Many long-distance voyagers and live-aboards still in their vigorous years supplement their income by interrupting continuous cruising and taking temporary jobs in different areas. Perhaps the top skill in making this sort of arrangement possible is to be a good mechanic. They are in demand everywhere, and an enterprising sailor can do quite well as a free-lance mechanic. I am the opposite, always in need of help for anything more complicated than changing a light bulb, and I have been delighted to hire such free-lancers in out-of-the-way harbors when trouble developed. The fully retired of a more elderly stripe might find it harder to get temporary work, and the whole project should thus be suited to the retirement budget. Nonetheless, it is always helpful to be a do-it-yourselfer.

Balancing Compromises

There are other basic compromises to balance: comfort and ease of handling vs. performance; looks vs. function; rig; draft; construction method; use of space for specific purposes; total number of berths possible for the actual living space. These are major, but each boat has many more minor ones throughout the layout. Bill Lapworth, one of the 20th century's most successful yacht designers, has had a basic rule in designing boats of any size: Boats are for people. Whether it was a Cal-20 or a 60-footer, he has kept this in mind as a rule of thumb, and his boats as a result are always comfortable to be aboard, above and below decks, for the right number of people. Some designers have ignored this, scaling the proportions of a good-looking 40-footer down to a 24-footer that might be lovely to look at but would be about as comfortable as a dog kennel.

It is surprising how often a love affair with a boat's looks ends up in ownership of an unsuitable choice. People who sail on shallow bays or inland waters end up owning husky cruisers such as a replica of Joshua Slocum's *Spray* or a Tahiti ketch for sentimental reasons, and severely limit their use. Other sailors have taken off on world voyages in cockleshells that should be confined to inland waters. Sometimes they make it, sometimes they don't. My own boats have been chosen for function and have not always been the most beautiful boats around, but "handsome is as handsome does," and function comes first for me. The reverse of this is the practice of completely ignoring looks in an attempt to get full headroom in a 20-footer, for example, with a monstrosity as a result. And, as an aside, hotshot ocean racing boats built to beat the International Offshore Rule measurement can sometimes come out looking like a nightmare distortion of a decent sailboat.

Powerboats are even more likely to suffer distortion in the interests of space and accommodations, often seeming to be higher than they are long, or giving the impression that someone forgot to append the after half.

Accommodations

Accommodations and layout should make sense in relation to how the boat is to be used. A family with young children, doing mostly weekending, can benefit from the practice some builders have of cramming as many bunks as possible in a minimum space. Everyone knows everyone and the situation can be kept well in hand. If several adult couples try to fit into the same layout, chaos can result, with someone suddenly realizing that he is brushing somebody else's teeth instead of his own. If the plan is to have guests aboard frequently this should be considered, with privacy a governing factor. If a live-aboard couple wants as much room as possible for themselves and guests be damned, a completely different type of layout should be chosen. I have seen a 50-footer that was laid out expressly for one couple, with a great big stateroom and a roomy lounge, and only one head, where the only sleeping space for guests brash enough to remain overnight was a convertible settee in the main lounge.

Offshore passagemaking calls for very different bunks from the kind of coastal cruising in which stops are made every night. In fact, offshore passages call for special considerations in every department, and an entirely different breed of boat.

To Race or Not To Race

In the "good old days," a cruising boat and an ocean racer were one and the same. In fact, the basic philosophy of the early ocean races such as the Bermuda Race, the Transpac, the Mackinac, and the occasional transatlantic race, was to prove that cruising sailboats could safely venture offshore. Today, the breeds are mutually incompatible, and the cruising boat owner who wants to race has a difficult time of it. The IOR made it impossible for a well-found, comfortable cruising boat to do well in offshore racing, which led to the development of the IMS (International Measurement System) in an attempt to rate all types of boats for distance racing. It has allowed some older cruising boats to be competitive, but as soon as designers start turning out boats for the IMS, the well-rounded boat will again be in trouble.

At a level below the grand prix ocean racing events, it is possible to combine cruising and racing when a rating formula like PHRF, (Performance Handicap Rating Formula), which rates boats on the basis of past performance of the type, is used. Many clubs use this for local racing, and the term cruiser/racer is no longer an anomaly. This is a solution that many owners are comfortable with. Another solution is to own a boat that has one-design racing as a class, a growing trend in many areas, as more and more sailors become fed up with the complexities of rating systems and the rapid obsolescence they foster. Because so many IOR boats have to be quickly discarded like so many squeezed out toothpaste tubes, the trend has been to PHRF and one-design.

It is still a fact that the amenities that make a boat right for cruising, such as bow-chocked anchors, big refrigerators, extra heads and well-built, solid lockers, bulkheads and other below-decks fittings, are all wrong for getting the ultimate speed potential out of a boat. However, the extra fractions of knots that eliminating these features accomplishes are really not that important, so performance ratings and one-design racing can be thoroughly rewarding. For ultimate speed, choose a high-tech catamaran like the San Diego Yacht Club's America's Cup defender in 1988, but expect no other useful purpose to be served. A cruising boat owner needs a well-rounded boat.

Multihulls

And speaking of catamarans, there are multihulls that are used for cruising, and they have some fanatical devotees. Circumnavigations have been made in catamarans and trimarans, and they can obviously be made to go faster than monohulls if that is the intent. In general, they are cheaper to build than monohulls of similar overall length, and they can be fitted out with cruising amenities quite easily.

That's the good news. The bad news is that they have one serious, basic safety flaw: they can capsize. Once capsized, they cannot be righted. Other drawbacks are the need for strong construction of the connections between the hulls, as failures are common here, and the amount of space they take up in mooring areas and marinas. If all yachts were multihulls, marinas would require much more space than they do now for the same number of boats. Also, multihulls are extremely sensitive to excess weight, which means that every ounce of cruising amenities

There are many choices to make, such as center cockpit vs. aft cockpit, single
stick vs. divided rig

added has a direct effect on performance. As a naval architect once described it to me, trying to make a comfortable cruising boat out of a multihull while retaining its good sailing qualities is like going on a diet of cheese and laxatives. As I have said, they do have their devotees; I am not one of them. For sailing fast, yes; for cruising, no.

Choice of Rig

Rig is of course one of the major considerations in choosing a cruising boat. Later on, I will go into the different ways of handling sail, and the nuances of various rigs. First, however, comes the basic choice. By far the greatest number of cruising boats are single stickers, which is only natural. Divided rigs have their adherents, and often with good reason, but they are in the minority.

In my opinion, a divided rig on a boat under 40 feet overall is not necessary or advisable. There may be certain areas, circumstances, and special purposes where a ketch, yawl, or schooner this small has strong points, especially in cat-rigged boats, but not as a general rule. The extra stick gets in the way of the cockpit; extra sails, spars and rigging cost money; and sailing performance is not usually as efficient as on a single-masted boat in this size range.

The advantages of a divided rig are in the smaller size of each sail, which makes for ease of handling; the greater number of sail combinations possible, both in crowding on sail and in reducing it by stages; and the heavy weather practice of using two very small sails, such as jib and jigger (mizzen). All these advantages become much more obvious and helpful the larger the boat is, while the bigger a single-masted boat is, the harder it is to handle the main and headsails. In the 40-foot size range the choice of rig is wide open, and either single mast or divided rig can be easily handled, but if a cruising boat is bigger, the divided rig has more appeal and usually makes more sense.

Divided rig almost always means ketch nowadays in the cruising boat field. The yawl, with its minimum mizzen mast, was mainly developed as a rule beater under some ocean racing rating formulas of

9

the past. Some sail area was "unpaid for" on yawls, which made them attractive for ocean racing, but for cruising, the larger mizzen of a ketch makes more sense. In that favorite heavy weather tactic of divided-rig sailors, jib and jigger, there is better control and power with the larger mizzen. I must say that I have had some delightful heavy weather sails jogging along on a reach under that combination, with everything nicely under control, and good speed, while the wind howled. In light air, it is fun to add a mizzen staysail and feel the extra power, but all this only makes sense in larger boats.

The schooner is a rig that still delights traditionalists, and it has its points, especially in its power off the wind. It is not as easy to shorten to a two-sail combination in a schooner as in a ketch, nor is the balance as good. Schooners have never been noted for their windward ability, and this is particularly true in smaller ones. When a big schooner is barreling along on a broad reach in a good blow, however, there is a wonderful feeling of controlled power. One of the most exciting sails I have ever had was in the replica schooner *America* (108 feet LOA), hitting 14 knots on a broad reach in a 30-knot breeze in the Baltic.

A modern version of the schooner, developed in Europe but now seen in all waters, has a rig of two masts of equal height with equal marconi sails. This is a fairly efficient sailing rig, with easily handled sails, and several easy combinations for reducing sails in a blow. For this rig to be efficient, however, the boat should be in the 50-foot range or larger.

With a single stick, the choice is between the single or double headsail rig—sloop or cutter in the traditional terms—and there are many nuances and variations here that I will go into in detail in the chapter on sail handling. I will discuss the variations of cat ketches, cat schooners, plain catboats, unstayed rigs, and all their variations at that time. My remarks about size of boat in relation to rig do not necessarily hold true in these special categories.

As we go into greater detail in the chapters to come, we can study all the compromises, and the many, many details, that go into these considerations.

II

Pitfalls and Booby Traps

Features to avoid

~~~~~~

Vital to the success of a cruising boat is its layout in the cockpit and below decks, the relation between them, the accommodations provided, and how they suit the people who are to use them. The variations are endless, and there are compromises every inch of the way. It is important to analyze requirements ahead of time, and it is also important to be on the lookout for booby traps: practices and features that are a mistake.

Before going into an analysis of various layout solutions, it is helpful to be aware of some practices, often fairly prevalent, that detract in some way from the functions of a cruising boat. I have mentioned such sins as crowding in too many bunks and scaling down a good-looking boat to too small a size, and both of these can be quite damaging. We once were loaned an outboard cabin cruiser for publicity purposes that was 22 feet overall, and was advertised as a "four-sleeper." This she was, technically, as there were four bunks in an upper-lower configuration, but this gave her much too much freeboard, and my feet stuck out over the end of a bunk by eight or 10 inches. Also, there was not room to stow as much as a toothbrush in the cabin.

In contrast, the first cruising boat we owned, *Mar Claro*, a 24-foot Amphibi-Ette sloop, suited our family, as it then consisted, quite well. She had a big double berth forward that could accommodate Jane and daughters Martha and Alice, then 13 and 10, with plenty of space, while son Robby, 15, and I had the bunks in the main cabin that were kept good and roomy by extending them under the cockpit. The head-

A glamorous looking boat may have features that make her
difficult to operate

Mar Claro

room problem was solved by a convertible hood. While this saddled us with such nicknames as "the floating covered wagon," it was a very practical solution. The hood could be removed to make two-thirds of the boat a cockpit for day sailing, but even better, by rolling up the sides, we had in effect a Navy top or a Bimini. We never had more than four adults cruising, and she was a good solution for the family at the time. She was not as eye-pleasing as the aforementioned scaled down 40-footer might be, but she was a lot more usable. I know of few other 24-footers that could have accommodated our family as well.

She was built in 1958, and since then there has been more thinking put into solutions of space in smaller cruising boats, those roughly 30-feet and under. Pop-top hatches have done what our hood did for headroom. "Hideaway" galleys on a shelf that can be pushed out of the way when not in use can save a great amount of space. Portable ice chests can mean more room for proper bunks, and, while most people want enclosed heads, a head tucked under a bunk with a pull curtain for privacy can also be a space saver.

Bunks: How Many?

Again, the size of bunks is more important than the number of bunks. People in 24-footers are no smaller than those in 45-footers, and skimping on bunk space ruins a boat for them. The business of how many a boat sleeps can go to extremes in either way, like the 50-footer for two mentioned in the first chapter, or a 29-footer we once cruised in that only had bunks for three, or, conversely, a more modern 29-footer that was a "seven-sleeper." Perhaps refugee boat people would have appreciated this layout, but it was ridiculous for a recreational cruise for anyone except a family with five small children, if you can even picture that scene. Jane and I were very comfortable by ourselves, and, as always happens, the extra bunks became handy stowage catch-alls.

Space for stowage is a problem on almost any size boat, and unused bunks traditionally come into play for this. The ingenious placement of lockers, shelves, bins and cupboards is always helpful, and a solution we had on our Amphibi-Ette, the rigging of bunks nets like those once used in railroad sleeping cars, worked pretty well until the nets got so full that they practically took over the bunk space. Then Jane would have an inventory reduction session with the net's owner. Lack of good stowage space is something that should be analyzed carefully.

Cockpits and Walkthroughs

Another mistake that I have seen all too frequently is the slighting of cockpit space in favor of more room below. In almost all kinds of cruising except Arctic explorations and long passages in the Roaring Forties, the majority of a cruising crew's time is spent in the cockpit, and they should be comfortable while there. There should be good leg room, comfortable seats, ease of moving about, and elbow room for handling sails. In other words, a boat is not well suited for cruising unless there is a balance between proper, full-size bunks and a comfortable, liveable cockpit, with both areas designed for the same number of people. Obviously, a seven-sleeper 29-footer could not fit all seven in the cockpit while sailing.

There seems to be a fad for walk-through accommodations in center-cockpit boats. To me, this gimmick is a negative one in anything under about 45 feet. The cockpit has to suffer, as on a 41-footer we cruised in with plenty of space below, but a narrow, knee-bumper of a cockpit, with seats too high for good back support. Another cockpit sin is failure to provide a good helmsman's seat. On a 44-foot charter bareboat we once sailed, the helmsman sat on a flat, athwartships seat, with the frame of the after companionway right in the middle of his back. Leaning back provided an uncomfortable poke from the frame, and a wheel trick was a tiring chore instead of fun.

Controls and Instruments

Also in the helmsman's department, placement of engine controls is often done with no thought for easy access. I have seen them down at foot level, which is awkward, and even unsafe, in maneuvering for a mooring or a marina slip. Sometimes they can only be worked by reaching through the steering wheel, not easy to do while turning the wheel at the same time. The fad for large steering wheels, which makes sense on an ocean racer for precise touch and control, is a nuisance on cruising boats, not only for reaching the controls, but also for moving about the cockpit. The 41-footer with the walk-through also had an oversize wheel, and it took an adagio dance to squeeze by it in the narrow, cramped cockpit. As for type of control, I much prefer the single-lever gear and throttle, placed where it can be reached around the wheel, not through it. In the cockpit and engine department, two Australian-built boats we cruised in had, for some unfathomable reason, the engine instruments placed in the cabin, a not very helpful situation.

Two other items that are sometimes placed below, with no way for them to be worked from the cockpit, are depth sounders and VHF radios. If a skipper has to choose between staying at the wheel and going below to work either of these instruments in a tight situation, it can be a serious problem. Shouting instructions and reports between the skipper and a second party at the instruments below is not very satisfactory.

There has been other evidence of poor thinking below decks on boats we have used over the years. None would be terribly damaging by itself, but they amount to annoyances that can take away from the pleasure of being on board. Poor galley arrangements, for example, can have a bad effect on the cook's morale, and the cook's morale is vital to that of the whole crew.

Galley Errors

On one 30-footer, the galley ran athwartships all the way across the after end of the cabin, with the companionway ladder crossing it in the middle. The cook would suddenly be interrupted by a shoe in the face, or the ladder user would step in the salad bowl. It was not a handy setup. On a 37-footer with a roomy main cabin, the galley counter ran fore-and-aft right in the middle of the cabin, with an L connecting it to the port bulkhead. The stove was against the bulkhead, and the refrigerator was forward of the stove. Only one person could work in the narrow space between the counter and the stove, cutting down on cooperative help, and access to the ice during meal preparations was difficult, causing conflicts.

I have seen a setup on another boat where the sink was outboard of the stove, and a singed armpit was the price of using the sink when the stove was lit. This boat also had the icebox in behind the stove, making things doubly awkward.

Access to ice is often a problem, and vessels that have a wet bar away from the meal preparation area make things a lot easier. Just getting into the icebox or refrigerator can sometimes be a problem. A hinged top that can be propped or strapped up is a great help, but I have cruised in a boat with the galley area fore-and-aft along the starboard bulkhead, where it was impossible for one person to get something out of the refrigerator when the boat was heeling on starboard tack. It was a big open cabin, with no way to brace one's back, so one hand had to be used to hold on, and the other had to prop up the refrigerator top. The top was in the middle of a wide expanse, too far from the outer edge for even one's head to prop against it, and too far from the bulkhead for a shock-cord strap to hold it. This expanse was also so wide that Jane, who is a normal sized five-foot-four female could not reach the shelves along the bulkhead. No motion-study analysis had been made in this area.

Bunk Size and Placement

I have mentioned bunk size, which is important no matter the size of the vessel. An area in which bunk size is often skimped is the forward cabin, where the bunk tapers down toward the bow. I have seen many examples where anyone over five-foot-eight ends up with cramped calves and toenail gashes on the ankles when bunking *à deux*. Overhead space is also important in the V-berth for getting in and out. I have been in a "luxury" crewed charter yacht that had upper and lower bunks in the guests cabins, and it was physically impossible to turn over in the lower bunk. In this setup, Jane and I spent the cruise sharing the single upper bunk. (We were younger then!)

Quarter berths that extend under the cockpit seats are an efficient use of space as long as they are full-length and a normal-sized adult can get in and out without gymnastics. We have on one occasion been consigned to what I call a pigeonhole bunk, in this case a double extending under the cockpit, with the only access across the top end. The rather low overhead extended all the way to the head of the bunk. It was a cool-weather cruise, and the bunk was cozy for snuggling and sharing body heat until one of us had to get up during the night. This would call for a contortionist act that usually included a knee in the face of the dormant companion, both in and out. On a 37-foot, aft-cabin boat, the double bunk was right in the middle of the cabin. Sleepers' heads had to be at the forward end, as the other end was under the after deck, with no room for anything but feet. This meant that there was no headboard, and pillows kept dropping onto the cabin sole, often interrupting sleep. This bunk also could not have reading lights, an amenity that live-aboards particularly appreciate. Good reading lights are often ignored in cabin layouts. I happened to be writing up the cruise in this boat and mentioned the difficulty with the bunk, and it was changed in later versions of the model. I was shown the new setup, in which the bunk was set athwartships across the after end of the cabin, at a subsequent boat show and was told, with a touch of asperity, by the builder, that it was "the Bill Robinson Memorial Bunk."

The Head

It is amazing to me how people who obviously spend a lot of time around boats fail to realize nuances like those above. Perhaps they are too busy building them ever to go sailing in them. The same complaint also applies to heads. First of all, if there are two heads in a boat, an amenity I strongly endorse in boats larger than 35 feet or so, it is a nice touch to have them on opposite sides of the boat. In this way, there is always a leeward head when the boat is heeling. Using a windward head while either standing or sitting can be a difficult balancing act.

Adequate room in a head is another problem. Some we have cruised with were just too small for a normal six-foot male, not to mention someone more outsize. I have seen several different cases in which a male could not stand up straight in front of the toilet, making the usual function another gymnastic feat. In the fairly common practice of having a shower in a head, some thought in placing items so that every fixture in the place doesn't simultaneously take a shower can make a difference. There is a growing trend to building in a separate shower stall, which is a good idea if the space can be allocated.

All these examples of impractical thinking may not be very obvious on a cursory inspection of a boat's cabin, but they become quite evident when lived with, so it helps to think about them in advance in evaluating a boat. Of course, if everything else is just what is desired, a single nuisance item can be endured, but it helps to be aware.

Engine Installation

A feature that affects layout, comfort, and convenience is engine installation. Engine access for normal maintenance and for more serious repairs is vitally important, but a feature frequently ignored. There are so many variations that it is not possible to go into details here, but it is a subject that should be carefully considered. Not only is access to the engine important, but it is also important to study how location of the engine affects the general layout. In smaller boats, outboard power is an excellent solution, either on a bracket or in a well, as this is a great saver of space that can be allocated to accommodations. Recent development of smaller diesel engines has also been a great boon. Practically no cruising auxiliaries have inboard gasoline engines anymore, and diesel is now much more practical for small boats than in times past. The safety factor of a diesel is extremely important. Insulation of the engine compartment for noise and heat is a must.

Cockpits: Center or Aft

One of the basic choices in the layout of a cruising auxiliary is between center-cockpit and aft-cockpit configurations, and there is no clear-cut answer here. Both types have strong devotees and obvious advantages. Our four boats have equally represented both types, and I am pretty much evenly divided in preference. Both types have worked well in the given boat.

I would say that the choice does not become a factor below 35 feet or so, although there are smaller boats that have used the center-cockpit layout, with a tiny after cabin, holding just a double bunk, tucked behind the cockpit. The only advantage here is in privacy gained while actually sleeping. One has to have something of a dog kennel or caveman mentality to be happy in a cabin like this.

Opponents of center cockpits claim that the location of the cockpit forward of the stern exposes the crew to more spray, which is occasionally true if the hull shape is a wet one. Only once or twice in our own center-cockpit boats have we been in conditions where we would definitely have been drier if we had been in the stern, and the larger the boat, the less likelihood there is of the center location being prone to drenchings. The people in it are higher above the water than in an after cockpit, which is some protection against spray, and forward visibility is better than in most aft-cockpit boats. There are those who prefer to be closer to the water and to the feel of it flowing by, which is possible in an after cockpit, as is the ability to see the whole boat before them.

The real advantage in a center-cockpit arrangement comes in the interior layout, where it is much easier to provide privacy in the sleeping cabins. The separate aft cabin with its own head is a little world apart, and there is not that feeling of too-close community living that prevails when everyone on board is in one area. The practice of joining the areas with a walkthrough passage below decks defeats this advantage in a way. In miserable weather, it can be nice to come to breakfast without having to put on foul weather gear, but that is a small benefit compared to what is often a waste of space, and, as pointed out, a detriment to the comfort of the cockpit.

In a center-cockpit boat without walk-through, the engine area under the cockpit can be roomy and convenient, a real advantage. This is one of the good features of our newest boat, *Helios*, a CSY 42. Walk-through layouts usually take space away from the engine compartment. It may be easy to check the passageway side of the engine but almost impossible to get at the other side.

It is sometimes difficult to grasp the nuances of the details that make a difference until they are lived with over a period of time, and it might be helpful here to analyze the features of our own boats. In *Tanagra*, our Morgan OI 36, we lived aboard close to a year, and in the nine years we owned *Brunelle*, the CSY 37, we lived in her about four years of total time, long enough to become quite used to her. *Helios* is in charter service, and we have not yet spent enough time in her for the same sort of familiarity, though there are a few features worth mentioning.

III

Living with Compromises

How our own boats worked out

Day-to-day living over a period of time is the best way to find out what works and what does not work in the way of layout features, but sometimes a compromise that may not be the best becomes so familiar, and is coped with so routinely, that it comes as a surprise to realize that there might be a better way. What we have learned from our own boats does help, however, in pointing the way to what to look for.

Helios: CSY 42

As for *Helios,* in our brief acquaintance measured in a few weeks, we have become aware that the emphasis is on special amenities for the bareboat charterer, rather than for extended living aboard. These amenities include a microwave oven, an entertainment center of TV, tape deck, and radio, and an inverter that changes 12-volt battery power to 110-volt to handle them. Amenities make a great hit with charterers. An innovation topsides is a hardtop permanent Bimini with a cloth extender. The hardtop contains a permanent light fixture, convenient for evening use without having to rig a portable light, since so much time is spent in the cockpit in southern waters. The mainsail has full battens and lazyjacks, handy when dousing sail, as it settles down on the boom under control without the immediate need for furling or tying stops. A drawback is the necessity to have the boat or the boom

21

Our latest choice of boat: a CSY 42

absolutely head-to-wind when hoisting the sail to keep the battens from fouling against the lazyjacks.

Tanagra: OI 36

Tanagra, the Morgan Out Island center-cockpit 36, was a model that suffered an unjust reputation for poor sailing qualities because it was associated in people's minds with the OI 41, the most widely used charter boat of the '70s and early '80s. The 41 was designed to attract newcomers from powerboating at a time of fuel shortages, when many were switching to sail, and it was roomy and comfortable, a fine platform for chartering pleasure as long as there was no need to go to windward with any speed or efficiency. She had a beamy shallow hull, with a full-length, shallow keel, and she made considerable leeway and had to be coaxed carefully through tacks. We cruised in one for a week in the British Virgins when the design was new, and I can attest to this problem from personal experience. Reaching and running, fine; to windward, no go.

When people heard we owned an OI, they would nod sympathetically with the 41 in mind, and make tactful comments about accommodations, but the 36 had an entirely different hull configuration. Back in the '60s, the Cruising Club of America rule was the rating rule in effect for ocean racers, and Morgan had a 38-footer built to the CCA rule that was a successful competitor in many events. When it became outdated when the IOR replaced the CCA Rule for ocean racing, the mold was adapted to the Out Island mode, with the long overhang aft chopped off to accommodate the after cabin of a center-cockpit layout. She was therefore a good performer on all points of sail. Our local Morgan dealer in New Jersey held an Out Island regatta for his customers for a couple of years, and we left the 41s far behind on windward legs, far enough, in fact, to make up for their better speed on reaches, where they gained speed on a longer waterline.

Tanagra: Interior

The after cabin in *Tanagra* was extremely roomy for a 36-footer. In fact the bunk was so big that our son, his wife, and two small children once spent the night in it when we had an overflow crowd aboard. The head was also roomy, and it was on the opposite side of the boat from the forward head, a pleasant amenity I have mentioned. The cockpit was of adequate size, with easily handled controls and steering, and, naturally, good forward visibility. The engine space under the cockpit was large for a boat of this size, but there was a problem in getting at the far side of the engine from the entrance area, as it involved crawling across the engine, not a good move when it had been running.

The main cabin had a fore-and-aft galley for the length of it on the starboard side, an easy arrangement for more than one person to perform galley or bar chores at the same time, and there was a convertible dinette to port. This was really only big enough for seating four people, but otherwise adequate. The convertible dinette is an efficient use of space for times when you have more than four sleeping aboard, but the toe-smashing business of making it up as a bunk at bedtime can be a bit of a nuisance, especially at the end of an evening "happy hour," and a nuisance again to remake in the morning. *Tanagra* did not have mechanical refrigeration, but the big icebox was well insulated, and a couple of large bags of cubes would last a week, even in the Bahamas.

The forward head was not as large as the after one, and was just barely big enough for the average male. It was the forward cabin, which could be two singles or, with a filler piece, a double, that was hampered by constrictions of the center cockpit layout caught up with a 36-foot overall length. The bunks just were not long enough or wide enough, and average adults ended up with toenail-slashed ankles at the narrow forward end.

This drawback, plus the rather confined size of the main cabin, led Morgan to produce an alternate layout in the 36 that was fine for in-port entertaining, but a bust otherwise. The roomy aft cabin remained the same, but in the main cabin, the head was placed against the after bulkhead with the galley opposite, and there was a roomy saloon with bench berths on each side of a drop leaf table, but they were not wide enough to be good berths. The forward cabin was a travesty, a tiny crawl-in that was only big enough for kids or midgets.

Tanagra: Above Deck

On deck, there was no good place for a dinghy. I have seen an OI 36 with stern davits for a small dinghy, not a good solution in my book. We had an eight-foot Avon inflatable, and it could be carried athwartships on deck at the stern or forward of the mast, a bit awkward either way, but at least manageable.

The boom was high enough so that the Bimini could be kept up while sailing. This takes some getting used to in the inability to look straight up at the sails, but sun protection is an important feature in southern cruising. This was our first boat with a roller-furling headsail,

Tanagra

and I took to it immediately as a great convenience for shorthanded cruising, which we did often, as a couple. Once, with the engine kaput, we had to make a downwind landing into a marina slip, fortunately in moderate air, and as we approached it, people from surrounding slips came dashing over expecting a crash landing, but I gradually rolled up the jib until only a handkerchief was left, killing it completely as we settled gently into the slip. This was the kind of roller furler that was on its own stay, not the headstay, which had its advantages. A regular jib could be hanked on the headstay, allowing a change to a genoa or working jib if desired. One time, we were beginning to be overpowered in an increasing breeze, and, when I tried to roll the jib in to douse it, it rolled so tightly in tension that there was a good section of sail left exposed when all the furling line was off the drum. This is sometimes a problem with roller furling, and if the sail is on a grooved headstay it can be an awkward one. In this case, I simply freed the halyard and dropped the whole thing on deck, and we were out of trouble.

And so *Tanagra*, in sum, had more advantages than disadvantages. She sailed satisfactorily, she was comfortable for us to live aboard in the aft cabin, and we could take quite a few visitors, though in somewhat cramped conditions. She had very good tankage: 100 gallons of water on the pressure system and a spare 75-gallon tank under the forward bunk that only worked by hand pump, a good backup. She held 60 gallons of diesel, good for almost 400 miles under power, and she could make almost seven knots with her 40-h.p. Perkins 4-108. Our reasons for moving on to *Brunelle* were that she was not that comfortable for guests, and, because we wanted to operate in the Caribbean, I felt her construction was a bit on the light side. In sum, her compromises came out to a plus for the way we were using her at the time.

Brunelle: Construction

Construction quality was one of the reasons we chose *Brunelle*. It is difficult for a layman to analyze fiberglass construction, as it all looks pretty much the same to the casual eye. There have to be very obvious weaknesses in accompanying features, like shoddy joiner work, flimsy hardware, poor backing and seating for deck fittings, and weak hatches to tip off poor construction, unless the buyer is capable of analyzing thickness of mat, layup methods, joining of superstructure and hull, and other technicalities. It happened that CSY had a set of photos of a 44 that had been battered about in The Baths, that curious conglomeration of boulders on the beach in Virgin Gorda. A careless charterer had put her aground there, and she bounced around the rocks in the surf for several hours before being pulled out. The only damage, supported by photos, was to rudder and propeller. The hull maintained integrity except for cosmetic scratches, and this was convincing on construction quality. Later, it was reassuring to have professionals working on board comment on just how high the quality was. It was also grim confirmation to see the remains of another brand of fiberglass boat that had gone on the rocks at Prospect Reef outside Road Town,

Tortola. In a few hours, nothing was left but tattered sheets of glass strewn along the waterfront in rather small pieces.

A technical treatise on fiberglass construction this is not, but it is important to get some sort of professional opinion on construction methods if at all possible.

As I have said, *Brunelle's* features added up to what we wanted in a boat for our purpose: extended cruising in the Caribbean in a boat we could handle as a couple but could be comfortable in with guests aboard. It is instructive, therefore, in analyzing her features, to realize that just about every inch of her, above and below decks, represented a compromise of some sort. In four years of living in her and with them, we became rather familiar with them, and learned to appreciate them.

Brunelle: Interior

Brunelle's forward cabin was well thought out in that the bunks were full-size in width and length and did not narrow down to that ankle-slashing little V at the foot end. They could be used as singles or could be made into a double with a filler piece. There was a good storage bin under them, good shelf space on each bulkhead, ample drawer space and a hanging locker. We were not apologetic in putting guests there, and in fact we sometimes used it ourselves when alone.

There were compromises, though. The storage bin was awkward to get at and the filler piece had to be moved around depending on its role of the moment. It was hard to make up the bunk with it in place. It was also hard to make up the bunk and to get in and out of it, because, to maximize its size, it was raised quite far off the cabin sole. There were lumps and bumps when the filler piece was in place for making it a double. As mentioned, the head should have been on the opposite (starboard) side since the after head was to port. This was the only thing I could class as a mistake in the way she was laid out.

The dinette in the main cabin did not convert to a bunk, a plus in my book, because the extra berths were instead achieved through a settee to starboard that easily made into an upper and lower. However,

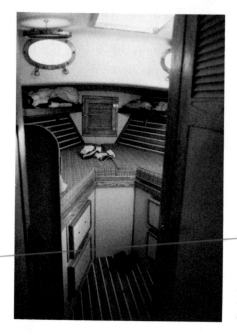

A typical compromise: To get sufficient bunk space in *Brunelle*'s forward
cabin, it had to be high off the deck

the dinette table was not comfortable for more than three people. We
probably could have solved the problem of adding a leaf to it, but we
never did, as in all the time we spent aboard, we only ate below about
two dozen times, preferring the cockpit unless the weather was terrible.
In a more northern area, with more time below, we would have had
to put more thought into this compromise. There was good stowage
area here in bulkhead lockers (one used as a liquor locker) and shelves,
and the spaces under the dinette and settee were used for the two 100-
gallon water tanks. The 54-gallon fuel tank was in the bilge under the
main cabin sole, with a sump and bilge pump forward of it.

The after cabin was to port opposite the galley, so that the open
space between its bulkhead and the refrigerator was a bit narrow. This
gave a feeling of confinement on coming below decks, but the positive
compromise was that it was close enough for bracing against when
working in the area while heeled on starboard tack. It was an angled
approach to the main cabin from the companionway steps, and the

angled area of bulkhead was used as a hanging area for foul weather gear, right above the dry-garbage basket. This was all quite an efficient compromise.

The after cabin was minimum size, but we ended up using it as our own because it had the VHF radio in it and what rather laughingly passed for a navigation table, as well as the electricity panel of switches and breakers. The bunk was a settee that made up into a double, and, once I learned the contortionist sequence of steps, it was my job to make and unmake it each evening and morning. We had a minimum-space head, and a hanging locker with a chest of drawers beneath it, and there was stowage space under the bunk, as well as a Constavolt for keeping the batteries charged when on shore power. It ran hot and managed to warm the bunk up a bit if left on during the night. Since our navigation was all piloting and eyeballing, I never used the nav table as such, and it became a catch-all desk for books, writing materials and other paraphernalia. When I wanted to spread a chart, it was just as easy on the refrigerator top or dinette table, or right in the cockpit. This cabin was all compromise, but it served, and we became very much at home in it.

Brunelle: Galley

There was little of compromise about the galley area, which had been well thought out. The refrigerator, with three large compartments, one a freezer, was just aft of the settee, with cupboards along the bulkhead behind it for plates, utensils, dry stores, and crockery. The lift-up lids of the refrigerator compartments could be held up by shock cord, making access easy. The compartments were deep, too deep for Jane to reach the bottom, but wire dishwashing baskets wedged in place kept the contents accessible. The refrigerator, whose compressor worked off the main engine for one hour a day, did not make ice, but of course kept it as long as needed in the freezer. It only worked on 12-volt so could not be run on shore power, which I suppose was a compromise of some sort.

There was enough work space on top of the refrigerator, an easily maintained, rough plastic surface, for two people to work together on galley chores or bartending.

The four-burner propane stove, with oven, was just aft of the refrigerator and made cooking much easier than the pressure alcohol stoves we had had before. It was protected by an elaborate system of safety switches, and the tanks were all the way aft under the helmsman's seat, vented through the transom. The stove was gimballed for underway use, and the only difficulty we ever had with it was in getting the oven to light.

The rest of the galley ran athwartships along the after end of the cabin, with a small working space outboard and then a two-basin sink inboard of that. Next to it were the companionway steps, a curved, two-step arrangement that we dubbed our "circular staircase" and which made cabin access much easier than a steep ladder. Dishwashing was done at the steps, which were used for stacking the dishes for drying. This sometimes made for arguments from someone who wanted to use the companionway.

The only other compromise in the galley was the handling of garbage. A bin under the work space next to the sink was intended for garbage, but this proved awkward, and we used the bin instead for stowage of pots and pans. We rigged a bracket for a Rack-Sack garbage bag set up inside the door of the locker under the sink for wet garbage, and dry garbage went in a topped basket against the bulkhead just forward of the companionway steps. It was perhaps a bit uncouth, and another compromise to have a garbage can be the first item sighted by someone stepping below, but it was handy. A custom extra we were glad we ordered was ports over the sink and in the after cabin: better ventilation, and communication with the cockpit.

Brunelle: Above Deck

To continue the compromise theme on deck, starting at the bow, the bow-chocked anchor, wrong from a weight distribution point of view, was very easy to handle. She had come from the builder's yard with a 25-lb. plow, but I changed this to 35 lb. and I'm glad I did. For backup we kept the 25-pounder and for a lunch hook or for fore-and-aft anchoring, we had a 15-lb. Danforth. Actually, the regular anchor was so easy to use that we only used the Danforth the few times when we did a fore-and-aft job. A 16-ft. shot of chain gave the anchor good extra weight and bite. I had ordered a power anchor windlass, but the first time I used it (with the engine running, as required) it blew its breaker, and I said the hell with it and never bothered to use it again. In different circumstances, such as in the Pacific islands where harbors are deep and coral heads abound, and all-chain rodes are *de rigueur,* a windlass is a must. In our operations, I never missed the power windlass, and I finally gave its rusty remains to a mechanic who was working aboard. Not only is stowage handy with a bow-chocked anchor but the mess of bringing a muddy one on deck is avoided. I found the plow to be the best all-around compromise after having had experience with old fashioned Navy (also called yachtsman's) anchors, Northills, kedges, and Danforths. It is weakest on hard, grassy bottom (but what anchor isn't?) but it works well on most types of bottom. If you are dragging, it is usually a slow process, not the sudden all-out release that happens when a Danforth is fouled or pulls out, so bearings must be taken and checked after all seems secure.

The raised-deck compromise that made for such a marvelous amount of gunwale-to-gunwale headroom below deck was a two-edged feature topsides. It is a disadvantage in the way a boat looks, and extra climbing is needed when trying to move about the deck quickly, but it does provide a great amount of extra flat space on deck, solving the dinghy problem for us with a good untrammeled spot to starboard of the mast, where we stowed our Avon inflatable. Most charter boats simply tow a rigid dinghy, but we did not want a rigid dinghy being towed while making interisland passages, and wrestling one aboard would have been a real chore. I could launch and retrieve the Avon easily by myself, without worrying about halyard lifts and davits. It was not the greatest rowboat in the world, in fact rather clumsy, but it served us well for 13 years on two boats with very minor maintenance and repairs. I

What to do about the dinghy? Our inflatable worked out well and stowed handily on deck in a one-man operation

decided not to use an outboard because of the problem of maintenance and of gas can stowage, and we got along fine, with minimum inconvenience.

Designed for tropical use, the CSY 37 was fitted with six sturdy hatches. They did break up deck space except for the area where we stowed the dinghy, but they really kept the cabins cool. Only problem was in rain squalls when there would be a mad dash to get them down, and there were no Dorade-type vents to supplement ventilation below. It could get a bit close there in protracted rain, and at night we made a practice of closing all hatches except the ones right over occupied bunks, so that those could be quickly closed, with no need to rush around to the others when a squall hit.

The cockpit was a prize feature of the CSY 37 design, and much appreciated, since 95 percent of waking hours were spent in it. It had roomy seats with good backs, easy access to winches, a good helmsman's seat and steering-and-engine-control station, and a handy portable table that could be rigged on the binnacle. It also had a sturdy Bimini, which was never lowered while we were aboard. A dodger curtain could be rigged on the forward end of the Bimini, but we only used it once, crossing the Gulf Stream from Miami to Bimini in dusty going. In colder areas it would have been much appreciated. A little flap on the after end of the Bimini gave extra protection to the helmsman. As already mentioned, it is a problem to get used to not seeing the sails by directly looking up, but they can be checked with a little neck-craning, and through a see-through in the Bimini, and the protection from the sun is absolutely mandatory in southern waters.

Cockpit stowage was good in two deep lockers, which also contained the batteries. There was room for our sail inventory, dock lines, and so forth, but not for fenders, which were usually lashed on the foredeck while underway. There was no lazarette or after deck, however, which was one reason I did not want an outboard. I don't know where the gas can could have been properly stowed.

Brunelle: Engine Installation

Brunelle's engine was a Westerbeke 4-108, rated at 40-h.p. which gave us about six knots in smooth water and was extremely efficient with fuel. There was very easy access through a big hatch in the cockpit sole, and it was simple to do routine chores like checking the lube oil and cooling-water level. A compromise here, which made the tri-cabin aft cockpit layout possible, was V-drive gearing. The forward end of the engine faced aft, and the V-drive was located under the "circular staircase." It was a very efficient use of space, but when work had to be done on the stuffing box, it was an extremely confined area for a normal-size man. Bobby Velasquez, owner-manager of Bobby's Marina, Philipsburg, Sint Maarten, who is a husky 200-lb. (plus) six-footer, took one look at the setup and said "I'll have to send a boy to work there. I wouldn't fit." Whenever anyone did work on it, groans and grunts were a continuous accompaniment to the job.

The refrigerator compressor was attached to the main engine and worked off it via a belt, and was also easily accessible for maintenance and repairs. The tank for hot water, which worked off the engine or when on shore power, was tucked away to starboard in the engine compartment and was a problem to remove and replace when the original one corroded.

One problem with the engine compartment was noise. When it was running, the cockpit hatch reasonated a bit, and the Bimini reflected the noise back down. No insulation had been provided by the builder, so we added a foam type that was covered by silver foil. It worked well for a couple of years but the foam then began to disintegrate, and all of it eventually had to be removed. I never got around to a replacement solution, though I should have, as the noise level was high.

It took a while for us to solve the swimming ladder problem. The first one I bought, a light plastic one that tied onto lifeline stanchions, was absolutely useless as it curved down under the turn of the bilge and made climbing out a Herculean feat of strength. For a while we had a rigid wooden ladder that was lashed on at the gate in the lifeline amidships, a nuisance to rig and unrig, but a good ladder, but we finally ended up with a permanently installed folding metal ladder on the transom that was a joy.

Brunelle: Rig

Which brings us to the rig, which was certainly a compromise, but an ideal one for our purposes. The 265-square-foot mainsail (which is incidentally, exactly the same area as the sail on the 18-foot Sanderling catboat we daysail at home), was perhaps a bit small for light weather areas, but fine in trade wind sailing. CSY, incidentally, offered a taller rig, and we saw some in Long Island Sound waters.

It was easily raised and doused, and a custom addition we ordered that was a great help was a gallows frame for the main boom. The main had jiffy reefing that I could do single-handed in a couple of minutes, another great help for shorthanded cruising.

The greatest joy was the foretriangle; a high-cut roller furling jib (some people call it a Yankee), and a club-footed staysail. In a full-sail breeze this made a good combination for going to windward, with a good slot between the sails when they were properly trimmed. A single overlapping genoa would have no doubt given her better windward ability, and we did have one, but we only rigged it once. She sailed well enough with it, but the fuss of tacking it when shorthanded was not worth it, and the flexibility of the double headsail rig was terrific, especially when combined with the ease of jiffy reefing.

When the time came to shorten sail and still keep sailing well (usually a bit over 20 knots of wind), the first step would be to single-reef the main—I never did double-reef it. Next would be to douse the staysail, and, finally, to furl the jib and reset the staysail. In a couple of passages, we went through this procedure and *Brunelle* handled it beautifully. We were once caught in a 40-plus-knot squall and simply rolled up the big jib and carried on under main and staysail. Sometimes as lunch hour neared and we were carrying a full set of sail in a strong breeze, heeling well, we would reduce to what we called "the cocktail rig" by simply rolling up the jib and continuing under main and staysail. She would straighten right up to a comfortable angle of heel for happy hour and lunch making and would continue to make respectable progress.

For downwind sailing we had another compromise, a poleless spinnaker. Its manufacturer, Ulmer, calls it a Flasher, and other sailmakers have different trade names for the same idea. In breezes under 15 knots with the wind anywhere from a hair forward of the beam to 15 degrees off the quarter, it added great fun and zip to downwind work without the fuss of gear for a poled spinnaker.

And so *Brunelle* was a vast bundle of compromises that, in sum total, gave us a boat that we were extremely happy with over extended use, and she was a very capable performer. Something different might have been done, and have been moderately acceptable, at almost every one of the points of compromise, but they balanced out well. In analyzing and choosing a boat, they must all be considered.

IV

Practical Arrangements

Mail, finances, supplies,
repairs, seasonal layups,
maintenance, medical concerns, red tape

There is a rosy-hued dream that a life of cruising is one of carefree abandon, freed from all mundane considerations of the nitty-gritty of the daily grind. In a way, this is almost true, as "the real world" does fade to unreality when the immediate world is the confines, measured in feet, of a sailboat chasing distant horizons. I have had the feeling, when plowing across trackless trade wind seas, with nothing but charging blue, white-capped waves to the limits of visibility, that there really was nothing else in the world but the sun, wind, stars, and moon, and this small collection of fiberglass, Dacron, and aluminum. Cruising *is* an escape, which is perhaps its major fascination, but the fact remains that there is a whole big world over the horizon, with its cities, towns, mountains, highways, banks, airports, hospitals, supermarkets, and post offices. Escape can never be total, and, to some degree, the cruising sailor must continue to deal with the realities of that world.

For the vacation sailor, off for a couple of weeks, responsibility can be totally forgotten for the time being, only to be faced again on that Monday morning awakening back in the rat race. It is a different prospect for those who take off for longer periods, either a few months at a time or as a permanent way of life. There is no longer the daily involvement to handle, but certain practical arrangements have to be arrived at. Not many cruising sailors can follow a *Kon-Tiki*-like self-sufficiency forever. Boats do not generate food, fuel, maintenance, or the means of financing them. Family and friends are not completely forgotten, and the empty horizon finally does produce a port where, to some extent, contact with that "real world" must be established and maintained. This chapter, then, addresses how to handle the practicalities that must be faced, no matter how many ties have been physically or symbolically cut. Naturally, each individual situation will be a bit different, with its own problems and solutions, but there are some generalities that might help to point the way.

Finances and Mail

Basic, of course, is the question of finances. No matter how thin might be the shoestring that holds an operation together, some provision must be made for the cash and credit needed to continue operations. Credit cards have made this problem a lot simpler in many parts of the world, but hard cash is still a necessity, and the use of credit cards presupposes the use of the mails, coming and going. I am not talking now about money earned by working while cruising, which is a solution, often rather hit-or-miss, for the voyagers who are off on their boats forever-and-a-day. As pointed out before, transient employment is a good supplementary source for those with special skills, especially mechanics.

The first question is what to do about receiving mail. Unless income is all of the kind that can be sent directly to a bank account, which is increasingly easier to arrange now, incoming checks must be deposited. If the cutting of ties has been complete, there may not be many bills to pay, but usually there are some obligations left over, and, if credit cards are used, their payments must be kept up. The best arrangement is to have a relative or close friend take on these duties, or, if no one is available in this way, to pay a professional individual or service to do this. Incoming mail to the boat can be forwarded either to a permanent drop, if operations are confined to one area, or to prearranged spots. Marinas or clubs in the major harbors popular with voyaging sailors will hold mail for pickup, and this can be arranged in advance once an itinerary is established.

When we operated in the Caribbean for months at a time, I opened a joint checking account with my daughter, who lived near our stateside home. She took care of our banking and bill paying, and she forwarded important mail to our base at Village Cay Marina, Road Town, Tortola, BVI. We also had guests coming down frequently, and they acted as couriers for any mail that could not wait until we got back home. Of course the piles of magazine and junk mail that would greet us when we did come back were rather daunting. Mail service in and out of the Caribbean is not the swiftest and not predictable, so we did not depend on it too seriously.

In cosmopolitan areas like the Caribbean, Europe, or the more populous ports of the south Pacific, credit cards are a means of cashing checks or buying travelers checks from local banks or American Express offices. There are comparatively few areas in the Caribbean where the dollar is not accepted, eliminating the need for exchanging to local currency. In the BVI, the dollar is the official currency anyway. Paper money is much more popular and acceptable than American coins. In

A full service marina like Village Cay in Road Town, Tortola, makes a good base for practical arrangements

moving around the Caribbean, I tried to keep a good supply of American singles on board. Making change for larger bills is often a problem in the islands, but George Washington's picture is very popular. In getting a supply of one-dollar bills, I was once given all brand-new bills, and they caused quite a stir when I used some in a chandlery in Sint Maarten. The clerk fingered them with great skepticism and curiosity, and I guess he thought I had made them myself. He said he had never seen new ones before.

If one port is to be used as a base for a length of time, it might be a good idea to open a local account. Banks are ubiquitous in all the Caribbean islands, with branches of U.S., British, Canadian, and some European banks.

Radio and Telephone

Aside from the subject of mail, there is communication by radio and telephone, and this can be handled in various ways, depending on the area. For far-ranging world cruisers, ham radio is the best solution. I am not a ham operator, but I have cruised with owners who are, and it is a marvelous means of keeping in touch no matter where the location. Of course it takes time and study to acquire a ham license, but it is well worth the effort for those who intend to be otherwise out of touch for long periods of time. It is by far the most effective safety measure in getting help quickly for operational or medical emergencies, and, through the helpful worldwide network of ham operators, patches can be made to any telephone for personal communication with family or business connections.

Single sideband radio is also usable for long range communications, though nowhere near as satisfactory as ham. *Brunelle* was equipped with SSB at commissioning, but it was never installed properly, and I found, through daily experience in the Caribbean, that it was no help in that area anyway. Most of the Caribbean is in the 809 telephone area code and direct telephone connections can be made throughout the world from most islands. However, in the French islands, which are on their own system, telephoning is possible but not so simple. For example, collect calls take extra time, and U.S. credit cards are not accepted, so paying cash in advance is the best way. Telephone centers are usually in post offices.

The VHF radio is the "party line" of areas like the Caribbean, an indispensible item for ship-to-ship and ship-to-shore operations. Most of the islands have marine operators who can place land calls to anywhere in the world, and one never feels out of touch. In more distant cruising, out of range of VHF (line of sight to the horizon), SSB and ham provide the best answers.

Operating Costs

Back to the question of finance. It is always an interesting question as to what costs are like in various cruising areas. Most U.S. areas are comparable, though we found, when we were cruising in the states a few years ago before basing in the Caribbean, that the farther away we got from the metropolitan areas of the Northeast or of South Florida, the better prices were. We based *Tanagra* in Oriental, North Carolina, one winter, and marina fees and maintenance costs were appreciably lower than at home in the New York-New Jersey-Connecticut region.

In the Caribbean, marina fees average a bit less than in the U.S. and labor costs are a lot less in most areas. In places like Road Town, or English Harbour, Antigua, the piers are swarming with young men eager to do maintenance chores on boats for a daily fee about the same as an hourly labor rate in most U.S. yards. Sometimes the quality of the work matches the price, but we have had generally good luck when we did take on someone from the "Hey, Skip; you got any work for me?" brigade.

European costs are similar to American ones, though the same rule of thumb about distance from metropolitan areas applies, and some countries, like Greece, still have remarkably reasonable prices for labor and services, except in the fancier marinas catering to large power yachts.

Food prices vary, and in that respect, the continental U.S. comes out better than any island location. It is always a shock, when buying food in a Caribbean market and recoiling from the prices in comparison to home, to realize that the natives have to pay the same prices, too. As a counter, liquor prices are appreciably lower because of absence of taxes, but beer and wine do not have the same advantage. They average about the same as stateside.

The most expensive place I have ever seen for food and liquor prices, restaurant meals, and just about everything, is French Polynesia, especially Papeete, Tahiti. For example, a fifth of gin was $32 in 1988, and I paid $34 for two paperback novels and a newspaper. We did not do much food marketing there, but what little we saw was also very expensive.

It is some help on food costs to shop at native open-air markets. Jane got rather adept at this in the Caribbean, where she learned to buy locally grown items like christophene, a form of squash, tanya, a potato substitute, and local fruits. Fish is another good buy, but in many tropical areas it is risky to eat fish you catch yourself. The native professional fishermen know where to fish, but inexperienced visitors cannot be sure that the fish they catch is not infected with ciguatera, a poison that causes very debilitating illness originating from a fungus on reefs. Some areas, such as the lower Caribbean, are relatively free of ciguatera, but it is found in many Pacific areas, and in the northern Caribbean. Local advice is needed before doing any fishing. Even large fish that are not reef feeders can be infected with it from eating smaller fish that are reef feeders. No such problem exists in colder northern waters.

Aside from food, there is always a question of availability of marine supplies in the farther reaches of the world, but this, too, is no longer the problem it once was. Almost anywhere in the world where yachts are found is sure to have a chandlery, and we found in nine seasons in the Caribbean that most routine marine supplies, from fuel and water to hardware, paints, tools, and the general run of gadgets, were generally available. Major heavy items, such as a replacement for the hot water tank, had to come from the states, as did most engine spares.

We stocked up on Westerbeke spare parts from the distributor in New Jersey when we were home for the summer, but things like alternator belts, filters, and gaskets were generally available. One odd problem developed that took some time to solve. In repairing the engine V-drive, European-measure bolts for the flange were used in American-measure holes and did not fit perfectly, resulting in their shearing off after a short time. The mistake was made twice before a different mechanic figured out what had been done.

Repairs and Maintenance

As I have already said, it helps a great deal to be your own mechanic when off in foreign waters. Many owners are good at this, but I am not. First of all, most manuals are not made for layman's use, and I found our engine manual to be about as helpful as a diagram of the digestive system of a llama. It was great on where to get spare parts in Madagascar, but the best use I ever made out of it was to figure out that mechanics changing the lube oil in Fort de France, Martinique, had put too much in. Then I had to remember how to say "too much oil" in French, and I finally got the idea across by repeating "*trop de huile*" like a broken record.

I have written at other times about what I call the Friendly Yacht Service Co., my favorite way of getting repairs made when I have a problem and am not close to professional help. If I am at a marina or in a anchorage with other boats, I find a likely soul and make my approach. It is never as direct as, "Hey, can you fix my water pump?" I start out more deviously with a question like, "Have you ever had trouble with your water pump?" or "Do you know anyone who works on water pumps?" Sometimes I get a shrug and a vacant stare, but quite often there is a satisfying "Oh; having trouble, Bill? Mind if I take a look at it?"

This has worked well on occasion, and once, when we had a dead engine in Portsmouth, Dominica, of all out-of-the-way places, after a fruitless day of my trying to find a mechanic, a young man swam over from a nearby boat to ask if we knew anyone sailing to Europe. I said I didn't, and gratuitously added a grumpy, "And we're not going anywhere either with a dead engine," just to vent my spleen. In a few minutes his skipper dinghied over, said he'd heard I had trouble, was a mechanic, and would be glad to look at it for $10 an hour if that was OK. I quickly agreed, and in 10 minutes he found that we had water in the cylinders. The anti-siphon valve in the exhaust had frozen open, and we had sucked in water by reaching fast at a good angle of heel. The 10 minutes was well worth $10 to me, and we all had a beer to celebrate.

Later, incidentally, our boatkeeping mechanic who took care of *Brunelle* over the summer layup made an alteration to prevent this from happening again. He added a fitting that put a flow of engine cooling water through the valve to make sure that it never froze, and the water was then ejected in a thin stream through a small opening in the topsides. It was a rather odd sight, and we nicknamed it our urinator.

Although there are isolated harbors where no mechanic can be found, most harbors and almost every marina in the Caribbean have at least one resident mechanic. Over the years we had service good and bad in several languages from boat owners moonlightning, auto mechanics doubling their trade (one who came aboard in St. Barts got seasick in the gentle harbor surge), a couple of frauds, and some very good ones.

Yachting centers like St. Thomas, Road Town, Philipsburg, English Harbour, Fort de France, Castries (St. Lucia), Kingstown (St. Vincent), and St. George's (Grenada) all have good services of all kinds from general mechanics to specialists like refrigerator men. Sail repairs are generally available in the same places, and we once had a fine job done on a rip in the staysail by a furniture upholsterer on the French side of St. Martin for a very nominal fee. Given the greater distances between yachting centers in the Pacific, it is easier to be isolated from professional help, but help is available in the ports where yachts are found, and Europe, of course, presents no more problems than the continental U.S.

Leaving the Boat in Layup

One problem faced by part-time cruising people in foreign waters is what to do with the boat when she is laid up and out of use. Our son operated a Westerly Tiger 25-foot sloop in Europe for five summers on schoolteacher vacations, and he would simply look for a yard to leave her for the winter when it was time to go back to school. He had good luck doing this and found good professional help in Sete, in the south of France, Malta, Trieste, and Patras, Greece. Europe abounds with boatyards, and operations are, of course, seasonal, even in the Med, so there is no problem in finding a storage yard. Our son's adventures were in the early '70s, and prices were generally quite reasonable in the yards they found, but inflation has no doubt had its effect, and prices similar to U.S. yards should be expected except in out-of-the-way, relatively primitive areas.

Our one season of taking *Tanagra* south from New Jersey to North Carolina for winter storage worked out well. We had good fall cruising in the Chesapeake and the Carolina sounds on the way there, and a delightful cruise on the Neuse River and out to Cape Lookout in March, when the weather was like August in New England, as an extra dividend. Also, as mentioned, prices were very reasonable.

We operated *Brunelle* in the Caribbean from December to late April or May each winter and then left her out of commission for the summer, and this was accomplished in several different ways. The first year, she was hauled out in dry storage at Tortola Yacht Services in Road Town, and incidentally survived Hurricane David with no problem. After that, except for one summer, she was in wet storage at Village Cay Marina in Road Town at a discounted rate contracted by paying for the whole season ahead of time that came out to just under $200 a month (from 1980 to 1986).

For $50 to $60 a month, varying over the years, we had a professional boatkeeper who opened the boat and aired her once a week, turned over the engine, and made sure the dock lines and so forth were secure. This is a completely protected marina, and *Brunelle* survived Hurricane Klaus in her slip with no damage. The boatkeeper also did what repair and maintenance chores there were at reasonable labor rates, took her to Tortola Yacht Services for an annual haulout before we came down in late fall, and had her ready to go when we arrived. That particular boatkeeper is no longer active, but there are several services available. TYS's prices for haulout and bottom painting were comparable to stateside rates.

In the one season that we did not leave her at Village Cay, she spent the summer at Sint Maarten, with Robbie Ferron, who at present writing is still in business as a boatkeeper. He had roughly the same fees as in Road Town, but dockage was free as he put her at anchor in perfectly protected Oyster Pond, checking her as necessary. The boat was stripped of equipment to prevent looting, and Robbie did the usual seasonal maintenance chores and had her ready to go when we arrived. This too was a satisfactory arrangement, although we prefer the BVI as a full-time base.

One problem with leaving a boat over the summer in the Caribbean, at least at a marina, is that of crawly visitors. Cockroaches abound, managing to find their way aboard at some time, and fumigation is a must in getting ready to start out again.

There are other good bases for seasonal layup, such as St. Thomas, Virgin Gorda Yacht Harbour, and Antigua, where many owners leave their boats securely moored to the mangroves on the east side of English Harbour, sometimes with a boatkeeper to tend them. Farther south, the French islands and St. Lucia and Grenada all have all-weather facilities for seasonal layup.

In the Pacific, long-distance voyagers usually find a layup spot during the hurricane season of January into late March. Papeete used to be a favorite, but rules have been changed restricting the length of stay by foreign boats, preventing this. American Samoa has come into use for the hurricane layover, with boats tucked away at the head of Pago Pago Harbor. Some cruisers go down to New Zealand and Australia to avoid the hurricane belt.

Moving Between Areas

There are owners who want to keep their boat in commission all year. On the West Coast this can mean a junket to Baja California, which is a long pull down the Mexican coast, but it can be broken up with occasional stops, and marina facilities are increasing in such spots as Cabo San Lucas and Mazatlan. The Mexican government has recently permitted charter operations to be run by non-Mexicans, and bareboating is now possible in the upper Gulf of California.

On the East Coast there is steady seasonal traffic north and south, both to Florida and the Bahamas, and to the Caribbean. If enough time is available, the Intracoastal Waterway can be a rewarding cruise in itself. Many powerboat owners hire delivery crews who speed the boats over the route in as little time as a week, and it is even possible to make an outside run between inlets in good weather, especially south of Morehead City, North Carolina. For slow speed auxiliaries it is a longer pull, and 65-foot mast restrictions in several places limit the size of boat that can do it. We did sections of it in *Tanagra* several times and always enjoyed the adventure.

There is a marked difference between heading south in the fall and north in the spring because of the variation in daylight hours. About nine hours is the maximum running time in the fall, while this can be stretched to three or four hours more in the spring. Although I have pushed through for as much as 85 miles on a northbound day when trying to keep a tight schedule, an average of a 50-mile days in either direction is a much better kind of schedule. Navigation on the ICW is by statute miles, incidentally, and those used to figuring speed in knots get a feeling of greater accomplishment operating by statute. One of the tougher sections of the trip is the Jersey coast, where there is no Waterway at all for the 24-mile stretch from Sandy Hook to Manasquan Inlet, and the inland sections of it from there to Cape May are rather shallow and jammed with local traffic on weekends. When negotiating the Jersey Coast by sail, it is a smart idea to pick a good northwester when leaving Sandy Hook, and to use the local "trade wind" of an afternoon southwester when coming up the coast. When a cold front northwester comes through, it usually lasts long enough to get most of the 110-mile stretch of open coast covered, eliminating a slog into the usual southwester. Coming north, it is important to avoid any chance of a northeaster, which makes this stretch of water very uncomfortable and makes it unwise to duck into any of the few inlets for shelter. They are tough to negotiate in a strong onshore wind.

Those who go offshore to the Caribbean face a different set of problems. From the Northeast, there are several routes to choose from, starting with a direct shot all the way to St. Thomas, or Antigua, for example. Not many elect to make the trip nonstop, and alternate routes include a passage to Bermuda and then on to the Caribbean; a coastal passage via the ICW as far as Morehead City, North Carolina, and then straight down; the ICW to Florida and an island-hopping passage from there. The most popular way is via Bermuda, with the Morehead City route a close second. The island-hopping route after the ICW adds a tremendous amount of distance, as it really involves negotiating two sides of a triangle. And speaking of triangles, no attention or credence should be paid the whole-cloth nonsense about the "Bermuda Triangle." It is a made-up ghost story.

Timing the Passage

More important than the route is the timing. The best time to be at sea in either direction is May and June, but very few people are heading south at that time of year. The obvious time to go is the autumn, which presents problems, and narrows the choice down to a small period of time. Coming north in the spring is a lot easier, as May and June are the obvious months.

Going south in the fall by the popular Bermuda route is asking for a rough trip. Starting too soon means that it is hurricane season, and starting too late means exposure to winter gales. In either case, the Gulf Stream is no place to be. This narrows the choice of time to late October, although hurricanes are still possible then, and there is another phenomenon I have dubbed "the Election Day storm." Sometime between the third week in October and mid-November there is traditionally a nasty storm along the Atlantic coast. In the more than 40 years I have lived on the Jersey shore, this has been true almost every year, and sometimes right on Election Day itself. On one exception, I remember saying on Dec. 1 that we had not had such a storm that year, and it blew 80 knots the next day! Year after year, this storm, which very often forms in the Carolinas when frontal systems clash and then buzz-saws up the coastline, has wreaked havoc on boats taking the Bermuda route. Sometimes it forms further south and can disrupt the Morehead City route, too. The best defense is a very careful check of weather reports and the location and progress of fronts, choosing a time when a frontal system has just passed, with westerlies behind it. Often, however, this type of storm forms very rapidly, with little warning, and is hard to predict.

In comparing notes with sailors who had come down to the Caribbean by either of these offshore routes, there was almost unanimous agreement that it had been a nasty, rough trip, the price to be paid for using a boat both north and south.

The "Thorny Path"

We took the island-hopping route with *Brunelle*, since she was built in Florida. This has been dubbed the "Thorny Path" because it is usually almost entirely to windward, and it can be a rough slog for someone who is pressed for time and pushing on as quickly as possible. We took from January to May to get from Tampa to Tortola, cruising the Bahamas and Turks and Caicos in leisurely fashion and picking our weather. We were then lucky enough to have the trades quit, leaving a flat calm to power through, for two of the normally ruggedest stretches, Caicos to Puerto Plata, Dominican Republic, and Puerto Plata to Samana along the unforgiving north coast of that rugged land. We did have the trades on the nose from Samana to San Juan. (This trip is described in detail in my book *South to the Caribbean*.)

48

An alternative to the island-hopping route, which is followed by delivery crews taking new charter bareboats from Florida to the Virgins, is to pick a time of westerlies to leave Florida and head straight through the Bahamas and due east into the Atlantic until meeting the trades, and then veer in a southeasterly direction toward the islands. There is usually windward work involved in this.

And then there are people who ship their boats back and forth by freighter, avoiding all these choices. It is expensive, but perhaps not a lot more than the actual underway expenses of a passage when meals, transportation, and other operating expenses are taken into account. It is not, however, a hassle-free method and can be rather rough on the boat.

Once we got *Brunelle* south we were very happy to leave her there and do our northern sailing at home in our catboat, or in OPBs (Other Peoples' Boats).

Medical Concerns

One other practical consideration in long-range cruising is what to do about medical problems, or, in many cases, medical routines. In a subcategory of this, perhaps the worst problem is dental trouble, as it is so often unpredictable and unpreventable. First aid kits do provide treatment for some types of dental problems, at least for temporary relief, but it is good planning to have a thorough dental check up, complete with all work that seems at all necessary, before taking off into the blue. The standard of dentistry is not very high in places like the Caribbean islands, and dental chairs are few and far between in the vast reaches of the Pacific. We were fortunate to be in Anguilla when Jane developed an abcessed tooth, as it is a British colony and has the British system of public health services. The dental clinic, manned by a young Welshman, took efficient care of her for a tiny fee. It is probably best to "plan" your toothaches for British islands, or in the larger cities of other nations.

The same holds true of hospitals. We have had two experiences with

49

hospitals in foreign ports, one on the Greek island of Rhodes that was unbelievably bad, and one at Road Town, Tortola, where everything was beautifully handled. A small clinic in the native settlement of Gun Creek, Virgin Gorda, was also very helpful and efficient, but standards in many areas are not as high.

It is important to have a good medical manual aboard and to work with a doctor in assembling a good first aid kit that includes various antibiotics and other remedies that can be administered by a layman. For those on continuous medication for such things as high blood pressure, it is important to have an adequate supply for the entire length of the trip, as availability of drugs varies greatly. In French areas, for example, everything seems to have a different name from standard English-language items. I once forgot to take blood pressure pills to the BVI, fortunately for a short visit, as the medication I take was not available at all. Instead, the doctor I saw in trying to get a prescription said, "You are on vacation. Just stay calm."

A corollary of this is always to keep medication with you in hand luggage when travelling to a cruising area. Checked baggage can go astray, and it is often next to impossible to get the same prescriptions filled in a strange place. We experienced this problem once before learning our lesson.

A long shot that might work, if a doctor is not available, is to ask for medical help from a cruise ship doctor if one happens to be in the area. This is nothing to depend on, but I have seen it work once or twice.

Government Formalities

In moving about in foreign waters, a cruising sailor inevitably must be prepared to cope with the rubber-stamp brigade that mans the world's customs and immigration offices. It is a nuisance, but a fact of life. Requirements vary dramatically, but, in an era in which political tensions are not lessening in many parts of the world, and in which emerging nations, many only recently independent, make a strong show of their newfound dignity, there are very few areas where formalities do not have to be observed. Also, conditions change, and it is important to check in advance on the latest requirements. For example, France instituted visa requirements after a period of heightened world terrorism several years ago, catching many visitors unprepared, especially in the French islands of the Caribbean. The significant fact that Martinique and Guadeloupe and their satellites are departments of France, not colonies, came as a surprise to cruising sailors who arrived without visas. As a practical matter, visas can usually be arranged on arrival, but it is better to prepare in advance.

It is essential to have passports. Now that U.S. passports are good for 10 years, there is not the recurring worry over their imminent expiration, which used to happen to voyagers off in remote areas. Even where passports are not required, they are about as good a means of identification as there is.

There is always the temptation to forget the whole thing and take one's chances of not being checked, and it is true that this is quite easy to do in some areas. It is not worth the risk of very unpleasant repercussions if things go wrong. We once made a hurried run from St. Vincent to the BVI with long daily passages that started at dawn and ended at sunset, with no plans for visits ashore. It was also over a weekend partially, and we were never able to check in to any customs and immigration office in any of the stops till we got to the BVI. No one was the wiser.

Before that, the first time we arrived in Puerto Rico, it was early evening when we arrived at the Club Nautico in San Juan, and I dutifully went to the telephone, where a list of numbers for checking in was posted. I tried every one of them, with no answer, and it was not until the next morning that we could check in. If we had been illegal aliens, we could have been breakfasting in New York by the time the official finally appeared.

We learned in San Juan that it pays to be middle-aged squares. Our procedure was perfunctory and over with in five minutes, without a glance below decks, but another boat that had been on the same route and arrived soon after we did had a very different experience. Her crew consisted of three young people in their 20s who were perfectly good citizens as far as we could tell in seeing them in several ports on the way, but they had long hair and beards and wore cutoff jeans and sweatshirts, and they were given a two-hour going over that went as far as examining their peanut butter jars for "controlled substances." Anyone contemplating entry anywhere with contraband aboard should be well forewarned, as the result of official discovery is confiscation of the boat.

The question of guns aboard is a problem in going through customs in most areas. We have never had a gun aboard (or at home), as I think that they lead to more troubles than they solve, but a great many owners do not feel secure without firearms. If there are firearms aboard, it is important to admit to them before they are found in a search, as this can lead to all sorts of trouble. Local regulations should be obeyed.

In times past, we have cruised in the Mediterranean and in Scandinavia with no formalities between countries, but, again, latest requirements should always be checked ahead of time while making cruise plans. Foreign boats visiting U.S. waters must deal with rather stringent regulations if they are not from a country with reciprocal agreements.

V

Guests Aboard

How to fit the right ones in

~~~~~~

Having guests aboard has always been one of the most rewarding aspects of owning a cruising boat. Over the years we have made this a continuing activity with both family and friends, and it has been perhaps the best way to establish and develop relationships that are deep and lasting. From infancy to adulthood, and especially through the often difficult teens, with our children and now our grandchildren, it has been one of the best ways of all to establish communication and shared pleasure in the family, and much of our family "togetherness" over the years has been fostered by cruising. The next chapter will discuss cruising with children, while friends as guests will be covered here, but there is of course some overlap in the way things are organized.

In checking back over *Brunelle's* logs, I find that we had close to 70 individuals as sleeping guests aboard over her nine seasons, many of them as frequent repeaters, and 99 percent of the visits were successful. We did take a "hitchhiker" once for a couple of days as a favor to a friend, and we were glad to get rid of him, but in all the other cases, the guests were previous acquaintances, and we did not invite them lightly. There are some people who are great fun to be with at a club dance or dinner party on shore who would not be compatible on a boat, and it is important to analyze what makes compatability afloat before asking someone to join you on a cruise.

Experienced sailors like Neil and Connie Lindeman make good guests aboard

No Experience Needed

It is not necessary that guests be sailors, and many of ours were not. In fact, it is sometimes harder to fit an experienced sailor, who has his own way of doing things, into your own systems and practices. As long as a nonsailing guest expects this type of "roughing it" and does not demand Waldorf-Astoria service, and understands about sensible clothing, shoes, and luggage, there should be no problem. If they get the word that it is perfectly all right to do nothing until told, things can go smoothly. Then, when they are told, it should be in terms that they can understand, not necessarily in technical nautical language.

As for experienced sailors, my policy when a guest on someone else's boat is not to do anything unless ordered (barring emergencies) and then to try to do it the way the skipper does it himself. It is amazing how many little procedures there are on a cruising boat that can be

54

done perfectly correctly in different ways: just the way lines are cleated and coiled or the way Jane and I use hand signals between me on the bow and Jane at the wheel while handling the anchor.

If there is an opportunity, it can be a help to go over things when a guest sailor comes aboard so that there is familiarity with the skipper's methods. One thing that bothers me, for example, is how a line is coiled after it is cleated, such as a halyard. I prefer a coil that is held onto the cleat by one loop of the line so that it can be freed quickly if necessary, but I have had guests who wanted to look salty wrap the coil up in a fancy, seamanlike-looking affair, with loops passed back over loops, that takes a lot longer to free for running. Also, a flaked coil in concentric circles on deck may look great for Captain's Inspection in the service, but it is bad for the line and the deck on a sailboat, and serves no useful purpose except decoration.

Robinson's "Rules"

When we first established operations with *Brunelle* in the Caribbean and had a lot of guests coming for the first time, I got up a set of rules and regulations that point out some practical things, with a touch of slightly heavy-handed humor calculated to keep the document from being too stuffy. It went something like this, in pseudo-Navy style.

FROM: Commanding Officer, S/Y *Brunelle*
TO: All Guests
SUBJECT: Robinson's rules for a Richer, Fuller Life on Board
REF: Bulletin No. 1 / 80, Caribbean sector
1. LIGHTS: Use lights freely as needed. Turn out all lights when not needed.
2. HEADS: (Toilets to some.) Do not deposit any items (except t.p. of authorized issue) that have not been processed by your personal life support systems. Make sure operation of head is explained by a competent authority. (Jane is the most competent I know.)

3. WATER: Use water as though it has been priced by OPEC.
4. STOWAGE: Everything is supposed to have its regular place and should be returned to it after use.
5. STOVE: Should always be under supervision of one person (Jane when present).
6. DINGHY: Do not board or debark from same without Boarding Officer's OK. Anyone falling in more than twice will need a letter from parent, guardian, or Red Cross instructor for future trips.
7. SMOKING: Ugh.
8. ALCOHOL: No drinking of alchoholic beverages between 0500 and 0600 unless awake.
9. DRUGS: Are you kidding?
10. LEWD
    BEHAVIOR: Subject to Captain's approval.

The subjects covered obviously should be. The dinghy note resulted from actual occurrences of female guests trying to get in before the dinghy was under control. Our inflatable Avon can be skittish if not approached properly, and there were occasions when someone would march down a pier and take a long step into the dink before anyone was steadying it, only to end up ass-over-teakettle in the water as the dink slid neatly out from under.

Smoking and Drinking

Smoking is a tough subject. I have never been a smoker, and Jane quit 15 years ago. On a boat, smoking can be a disruption, a cause for conflict, and even unsafe, depending on how tolerant the rest of the crew is. Since I lived with a smoker for many years, I was used to the problems, but I have never liked them. We have only had a handful of smokers as guests, and, as more and more people give it up or at least become aware of the problems it causes, it is less of a problem. Smoking below is particularly offensive to others, and on deck it is a great help if the smoker is aware enough to sit to leeward and to keep ashes and sparks from flying into the eyes of others. We have had a couple of cigar smokers aboard, and they were considerate enough to take off in the dink or to take a walk on shore when they wanted to light up, without anyone having to say anything to them.

The facetious item about alcohol was the only way to bring up the subject since habits and tastes vary so in this department. We have had guests who started each day with milk punches during their pre-breakfast swim. Because each guest's visit is a holiday for them, we let people set their own pace, and we have never had any trouble. (Pre-invitation screening on this situation helped along those lines.) Because we were aboard for months at a time, while our guests were on a party for a week, our own routine was confined to preprandial cocktails and an evening *chapeau*. Otherwise we could very well have become candidates for the dryout ward. We both enjoy social drinking, and this regimen worked out quite well. My only exception was an occasional "anchor cup" at the end of a stimulating sail.

As for overall compatability, I have a theory that couples only get along if the wives get along, and we have more or less operated on that principle. (I may be prejudiced, but I think almost everyone gets along with Jane.) If Jane has reservations about the wife of a couple, that is good grounds for not inviting. A couple of times, Jane did not particularly like the husband, but that was my department.

Luggage and Clothing

In making advance arrangements, we try to suggest to our guests a few practical details. Just about everyone understands that soft luggage— duffel bags that can be rolled up and tucked into a locker—is important. We have had friends who came direct from a resort hotel, or in the middle of an extended trip, so extra luggage, including hard cases, had to come along. We understood this and found places to stow the luggage under a bunk or at the bottom of a hanging locker, or something.

The clothing rule that "less is best" is very hard to follow in practice, and we are usually guilty ourselves of overdoing it on clothes for cruising. When we were living aboard *Brunelle* for several months at a time over a period of years, we had some clothing that stayed aboard. This was especially handy when arriving in travel clothes, hot and sweaty by the time the San Juan airport was negotiated, and we could get right into boat clothes before unpacking. Also, we could bring less.

Actually, these days it is silly to travel in formal, business-type clothes. Airline travel has become extremely informal, especially to resort areas, and there is no need to be encumbered with city clothes, overcoats and the like.

Cruising in Newfoundland one summer, we felt we had to bring heavy sweaters, gloves, wool hats, windbreakers, boots and foul weather gear, which add to the luggage load. For several days, it was warm and sunny, and then came a brisk northeaster, freighted with rain from the open North Atlantic, that called for the whole kit and caboodle, and we were actually glad to put it on as justification for bringing it.

Onboard Cooperation

In our rotation of guests on *Brunelle,* which often took place with no break in between, we usually asked guests to bring their own sheets and towels, since it was hard to get laundry done on that sort of schedule. Laundry facilities are not hard to come by in the BVI as there are excellent and inexpensive local services, as well as coin-operated machines in many marinas, but it is still a help not to have to keep providing fresh linen.

We would ask for foreknowledge of guests' transportation arrangements so we could be ready, and so that a rendezvous could be arranged without confusion. In the BVI, the Beef Island Airport is adjacent to the good anchorage at Trellis Bay, and we very often met guests right at the plane. Sometimes the row out in the Avon made an exciting start to the visit if it happened to be blowing fairly hard. This was one time when an outboard might have been helpful.

We usually came to a financial understanding ahead of time, and our usual arrangement was for guests to share food and liquor costs. This could be done by a cash settlement or by alternately handling shopping trips. Most of the time, we knew guests' liquor preferences, and we would be stocked up ahead of time. We also made it clear that liquor was so much cheaper in the Caribbean that bringing a hospitality present of liquor would be silly. The opposite is true in parts of Europe. When flying to join friends for cruising there, we would buy what was allowed at an airport duty-free shop on the way. Scandinavian prices are particularly outrageous, and gifts are most welcome.

In a normal guest week, we would probably eat ashore twice, and these would usually be split as a "captain's dinner" and a "crew's dinner." Jane and I have spent whole weeks cruising in an area strange to us, like the Fyn archipelago in Denmark, when we ate ashore every night as an adventure, and some guests prefer to do more of this than others.

On board, there is a division of chores in the galley. Jane likes to be in control at all times, except when our daughters are aboard, when she is perfectly willing to let them take over, as they know the galley's ins and outs as well as she does. With nonfamily guests, Jane likes to prepare breakfast solo, with help taking the form of buttering toast, pouring coffee and tea, and handing condiments up to the cockpit. Lunch can often be a cooperative job over a salad or sandwiches. Jane's usual salad is a concoction of chopped celery and tuna, chicken, shrimp, or salmon. Dinner, again, can afford some cooperation in the preparation, and on *Brunelle* there was room for two to work. On other boats, as mentioned before, where the galley was not well laid out, it was impossible for two people to find enough working space.

After meals, the cooperation consists in cleaning up, and most guests have been great about this. We have established a routine that works best and most efficiently in the available space, and extra hands can make short work of it. As for bartending, I usually take over for that, but not always, depending on how eager and enterprising my opposite number is.

Foul weather gear is a nuisance for guests to bring along. If they are terribly attached to their own brand, fine, but we do have extra stuff. In the Caribbean, it is seldom needed, but it is a more important item in colder climes like New England, the Pacific Northwest, and Canadian areas.

Hitchhikers and Hired Hands

I have mentioned that one hitchhiker was about the only guest we were happy to see leave. At the request of a friend, we carried the young man from Antigua to St. Martin after a session at Antigua Race Week, and it was a good lesson in not inviting strangers aboard. Without even trying, he was rude and uncooperative, knew nothing about cruising boats, and yet offered nautical opinions on every subject, and was generally insufferable.

In contrast, we did take a young Dutch woman on an interisland passage in the Caribbean without an introduction or previous acquaintance because we were impressed by her hard luck story of being bilked of her funds by a supposed "boyfriend" she had been traveling with. She could not have been nicer or a better shipmate, but in general it is not a good idea to carry strangers.

In Samana in the Dominican Republic, when we were on our way down from Florida to the Virgins in *Brunelle,* we were approached by a young woman with tears in her eyes asking us to take her to Puerto Rico, although she admittedly had no papers. Tears or no, that was not a situation to take on.

We have never had a paid hand, but we did have a crewmember for our ferrying passage down from the States, a young man who came to the *Yachting* Magazine office in New York to inquire about opportunities to go sailing just when we had had a cancellation of plans from friends who were to help us on this leg. I did not want to handle this passage with just the two of us, so I interviewed Jim Lillie, a recent college graduate not ready yet to settle into a job. He was personable and knowledgeable (his family owned a 35-foot sloop), and I made sure he had no interest in "controlled substances," and signed him on on the basis that we would pay for transportation and keep. He could not have been a better shipmate, handling himself well nautically and socially, and we signed him on for the next season too, when we were making passage down island in the Eastern Caribbean.

In general, a paid hand on a boat as small as 37 feet would have to be very compatible in such close quarters, and the setup did not call for professional help even if I could have afforded it, but this was an excellent solution for us that worked very well.

In taking on someone under similar circumstances, it is important to check background and references and not to take chances with a "pier head jump." Jim was a great reader, keeping himself well occupied that way on board, and he took a lively interest in the places we visited. I had been worried about his becoming bored, isolated with people old enough to be his grandparents, but there was no problem in keeping him entertained.

Entertainment aboard is a special subject that applies to all hands. Skipper and wife, adult guests, deck hands, and children all have special interests that vary greatly, and the question of entertainment and special activities will be covered in a later chapter, after we go into the subject of children aboard, since it applies to them, too.

VI

Cruising with Children

Special considerations and routines

~~~~~~

As I have said, cruising with children has been an important part of our cruising life, on into the second generation. We have enjoyed it, I think our children have, because they keep coming back for more, and it definitely has been a major factor in family relations. We have done it at all ages. We started all three of ours daysailing in their first summer (all three were born in winter), secure in a basket, and a little later ensconced in a carseat rigged to the cockpit coaming. We started them cruising when the youngest was three.

One very important thing about any such activity with children, whether it be sailing, camping, skiing, or other kinds of sports, is that the children should want to do it. If it is forced on them and made to seem a chore, which becomes a form of punishment, the result will be rebellion and disaffection, and it is a fine line to toe in arriving at a good arrangement. Jane had seen, in her family, how a demanding athletic coach father, strict in his discipline and severe about concentration and effort, had driven some of his offspring away from his sport, and she did not want me to come on too strong in my enthusiasm for sailing to our own kids. When they were little, and our activity was confined to daysailing at home, they were never told that they had to come with us. We had a young neighbor girl as a sitter, and the children were always given the choice of staying home and having a friend over, going to the beach, or some other plan of their own, or of coming sailing with us. They usually chose the sailing, but not always, and

Jane's psychology worked so well that sailing was always fun and a treat, chosen by them.

Fun and Safety

Then it became a question of making sailing fun and interesting and not putting heavy demands on them. We had certain rules for safety that had to be observed, and the one rule that was enforced was that the captain's word was law, with no argument. We then let their activities suit their whims. Attention spans are short at early ages. If someone said, "Can I steer, Daddy?" and only did it for a few minutes before losing interest, that was OK. We didn't have sailing lessons, as

Our son's family spent five summers cruising the Med when the children were little, making special onboard adaptations to their presence

such, at any time. If someone asked questions or wanted to do a certain chore, that was fine, and we tried to see that it was done the right way. Friends could be brought along if it was understood that they would obey the captain.

These first few years of daysailing got them familiar with boats and the water and with what "went" and what didn't with Daddy, the Captain. We had a rule that life jackets had to be worn until each could pass a 10-minute swimming test. This was OK in protected home waters, but it was understood that there were exceptions in rough water. We tried to get good, comfortable jackets that were their own and familiar.

The first time the whole family went cruising was a powerboat venture on Barnegat Bay on the Jersey coast, and I got an inkling of how it appeared to the kids when we put into the state marina in the not very exciting—to me—harbor of Forked River on the first night. In the evening twilight, as a full moon rose over the trees across the way from the marina, we walked up the pier to an ice cream stand on the main street of the little town, and headed back for the boat with the kids happily licking and slurping away. As we walked along, there was a nudge of an elbow against my knee from three-year-old Alice, who looked up at me with a face ringed in vanilla and said "Gee, Daddy. Isn't this an ADVENTURE!"

We had a few sailing cruises on Long Island Sound in those early years that were kept carefully on a tame basis, with emphasis on swimming stops, expeditions ashore like the ice cream junket, games, story reading, and playing with toy animals that had been allowed to come along. When an interest was shown in ship's routine, that was encouraged, and knowledge was gradually acquired through familiarity, with very little formal instruction.

Longer Voyages

All this was on a short-term basis of a week or less in confined waters, but many people have taken children on much longer cruises, sometimes on a permanent live-aboard basis, and certain provisions must be made for this kind of life. Babies born while their parents are cruising, who have never known shore life, adapt quite readily to the special nature of existence in a small sailboat, but others have to adapt to it as an unfamiliar business. First of all, special safety measures must be taken, such as netting on the lifelines for safety on deck, and special bunk space that can be comfortable and safe while the boat is heeling and in rough water, a nautical form of a playpen.

Our son Robby and his wife Carol spent five summers on teacher's vacation time moving about Europe in a Westerly Tiger 25-foot sloop. They had no children when they started, and by the time they finished they had Elizabeth, age four, and Will, two, and they had learned all the nuances of child care aboard, up to those ages, while cruising in strange waters and in countries with very different food systems and other customs. I cruised with them along the Dalmatian coast of the

Adriatic one summer, and it was a revelation to see how they had worked out their routines. At the time, Elizabeth was three and Will was a basket case. They were thoroughly used to the boat in their own way and were thoroughly adapted, more so than I was. I had forgotten how much children of those ages cried as a perfectly normal thing.

In moving the boat over the years, from England, across the channel, through the French canals, along the Riviera, down the Mediterranean islands of Corsica and Sardinia to Malta, over to Tunis, back across Sicily, up the Adriatic to Trieste, down it to Greece, and through the Aegean, they did not have to make too many long over-water passages. Though there were a few, most of their sailing was in short, port-to-port hops. It was cruising tuned to children in most ways, and a good bit of time was spent in port sightseeing, beaching, and relaxing. For sightseeing, Robby and Carol both had backpacks to carry the kids. Elizabeth could walk some and then would need a ride, while Will was strictly a papoose. When I cruised with them, I did some backpack duty, too.

Keeping Them Busy

They had a tiny inflatable boat, child size, that was not used as a dinghy but was mainly a toy for Elizabeth, and one of its major uses was to put her in it at the end of a painter for some peace and quiet during "happy hour." This worked well and was a version of the trick we used to employ on our early cruises of turning the kids loose in the dinghy and letting them row around the anchorage. When there were ducks to feed or a toy boat to sail this was a good ploy, and we have seen variations on it all over the world.

In Denmark, where evenings are usually spent in marinas and very few boats anchor out, almost every boat seems to have youngsters aboard, and diapers drying on the lifelines is a common sight. At the schnapps hour, the kids are all sent off in dinghies or little Optimist sailing prams, and the harbor is a katzenjammer kaleidoscope while the parents socialize in the cockpit.

66

A more sophisticated variation for slightly older youngsters is to let them take the dinghy—with outboard—for joyriding. We have done this ourselves, and we have seen it in many harbors. The latest gimmick is now windsurfing, which can keep restless teenagers busy for as long as there is wind. We have arranged the use of a sailboard on our last few cruises with grandchildren.

Food

For Robby and Carol in the Med, food was of major concern. They did not have mechanical refrigeration, and at the time they were cruising, it was impossible to find ice anywhere. (A trick we learned in Scandinavia was to go to fish-packing piers for ice.) They learned to live with warm drinks, and the way they managed fresh food was for Carol to head for local markets at the crack of dawn to buy milk, meat, bread, vegetables, and fruit. Fruit, bread, and vegetables could last a while, but meat and milk had to be used on the day of purchase. Sometimes it was quite an adventure for her in countries like Tunisia and Yugoslavia to negotiate *sans* interpreter with the baker or butcher. Buying meat this way was always a mysterious affair. When they were on passages away from markets, they had to depend on canned foods.

In recent years so many advances have been made in packaging foods that judicious shopping can help in the special problem of feeding children, but it is something that still takes a lot of thought and effort.

The In-Between Years

As the children grow older, things can be done differently from the tiny tot years, not only by way of peace and quiet at happy hour, but in most activities and the whole cruising picture. In the eight-to-twelve age group there is an eagerness to learn that can be catered to very nicely. It is a time for really learning nautical skills and for taking on more responsibility. Steering and sail handling gain in fascination, as well as knots, charts, rowing, terminology, and various aspects of boat-keeping. Kids can be challenged and rewarded, and every kind of new experience is especially fascinating. Again, all this must be done in relatively small doses, without putting on too much pressure, but progress can be visibly measured, and it is a time of great rewards on both sides, with personalities developing in the young, and relationships taking on a deeper meaning.

One of the best times I have ever had with a member of the younger generation was in taking grandson Sam, just before his eighth birthday, on a "cruise" in our 18-foot catboat, which is our home waters daysailer. It was just an overnight affair, with a day of sailing out in Sandy Hook Bay to start. This means a trip down river from our home pier, negotiating two drawbridges, one of which has to be blown for, always a thrill for a kid. Once out in the bay we had a fine sail, with the skyscrapers of New York on view to the north, big tankers going by in the Sandy Hook Channel, freighters in sight in Ambrose Channel farther out from us, and Navy ships at the long ammunition pier for Earle N.A.D. There was all sorts of traffic, mostly in sportfishing boats in and out of the river, other sailboats, and a few commercial fishermen. Sam took the tiller for longer than he ever had before, really excited by the feel of control. I think it was the first time he had ever had the real feel of steering a boat under sail, always a thrilling moment.

Late in the afternoon, we powered back up the river past our house and had a late sail on the way to an anchorage in one of the creeks at the very head of the Shrewsbury.

Sam also handled the outboard, which was another new experience for him, and I think he enjoyed steering under power almost as much as the sailing. We anchored in a quiet dead end of the creek, with sedge grass on the banks surrounding us and the sun lowering over marshes and trees inland. No other boats were near us, but some resident boats rode quietly to moorings further out the creek. After cocktails, a Seven Up for Sam and a martini for me, I cooked hamburgers and canned peas on a portable Sterno stove, and we settled in for the night with Sam playing with the shortwave bands on the portable radio,

Grandson Sam enjoys a wheel trick. Stints like this should be fun, and tailored to the appropriate attention span

excited at claiming to have Japan tuned in. After breakfast in the morning, we headed home after one of the best times, a proof of how that age reacts.

The Teens

Then come the acne years and a whole new set of problems. Often this is when a youngster can be lost for good to sailing, or any other project that seems forced on them by adults who have somehow suddenly lost all their brains. It is a time of adjustment in life in general and a critical time in parent-child relationships, and I truly believe that sailing, and particularly cruising, helped to get us through this

69

time with our own children in a very special way. We acquired our first cruising boat, *Mar Claro*, when they were in their early teens, and she was the means to a great amount of family fun and adventure, trailering her to the Great Lakes, Maine, and Florida, as well as a Bahamas season. We also did some Caribbean cruising in charter yachts while gathering material for books and magazine articles, and we included the whole family in many of these trips.

We tried to adapt and adjust to the special interest of teens, and on their part they made a conscious effort to fit in and to avoid conflicts. During their mid-teens, our daughters, three years apart in age, were in one of those stages when they did not get along very well, fighting about lots of little things. They were very different in personality and interests but they did enjoy our cruising junkets. At the end of one of them when things had gone especially well, we mentioned how much fun it had been and how well they seemed to have gotten on. "We made a vow," Martha said, "that we wouldn't fight in front of you." There was a pause, and Alice chimed in "but you should have heard us when you weren't around!" Actually, it was a maturing experience for both of them, and an eye-opener for us.

We learned to live with radio stations whose licenses I would cheerfully have had revoked, and, in our cruises in various parts of the states in *Mar Claro*, we tuned our schedule to ports where we could get ashore at night and where, preferably, there was a movie theater. If there was a place where the kids could mingle with other teenagers, as in the hotel and marina where we were based in the Florida Keys one Christmas vacation, it was a great success. Quiet isolation is not a teen priority.

Our first cruise in a crewed charter boat was in the Bahamas in a grand old vessel called *Alpha*, an 80-foot ketch captained by Lou Kenedy, one of the colorful pioneers of the charter field. The kids were between 10 and 15, and I think Lou was a bit aghast at taking them on, but he was committed to cooperating for the sake of the magazine article that would result, and he did a marvelous job of keeping them busy. He had them standing wheel tricks and handling sails, and he had them competing to see who could be the first one to get to the ship's bell to sound the appropriate bells for the time. They snorkeled and swam by the hour, and when things were quiet, Lou had a wonderful fund of sea stories to keep them spellbound. By bedtime, which came early, they were out cold. He had raised children of his own afloat, and he knew all the tricks. It was a memorable occasion for all of us.

One of the adjustments in cruising with the younger generation at almost any age is the basic one of simple housekeeping. Very few kids are neat by nature. When it is their own room at home it is not a community problem, but in the confines of a small cruising boat, it becomes everybody's concern. Indiscriminate clutter can't be tolerated, and it was a problem that Jane attacked with positive action to keep one step ahead of going nuts. *Mar Claro* was a very small container for a family of five, and the solution to keeping things in place was giving each kid a bunk net. They were supposed to keep everything in their own net and not leave things strewn around. Steady policing and reminders from parents kept the system working until a crisis stage would be reached, in which the net bulged so that its owner couldn't fit in the bunk any more. Jane would then supervise an inventory session, setting priorities on what stayed and what went.

The longest cruise all five of us had in *Mar Claro* was over Christmas in the Florida Keys for about 10 days, but we broke it up a couple of times with rooms ashore in a hotel or motel. Jane and I had the peace and quiet of a hotel room at Ocean Reef Club for a couple of days, though the traffic to the shower was pretty heavy. At Islamorada, we put the kids in a motel room, and in the space of less than an hour, it looked as though it had been lived in by a small army for several months. It did take the pressure off on board, however.

Live-Aboards

Quite different from adapting to a vacation cruise of a week or two with the younger generation is the situation in which the boat is a permanent home for long-distance voyagers. Handling kids in this setup takes a lot of planning and ingenious solutions. Over the years, we have seen many arrangements in the course of our cruising.

As in the experiences Robby and Carol had with their European cruising, very young ones can adapt without difficulty, and it actually takes more adapting for the parents. One thing they found in visiting strange countries was that small children are great "ambassadors." Local people who might be quite reserved with alien adults thaw quickly when kids are on the scene. This happened time and again in shops and markets, with local officials, and in sightseeing. Once, in a small port in Greece at a time when Greek-American relations had suddenly hit a low point, to the extent that there were "Yankee go home" demonstrations and other ugly manifestations of ill will, a hostile crowd gathered on the pier next to their boat, gesticulating at the American flag and Boston hailing port. Things were becoming quite unpleasant and even threatening when Elizabeth, unconscious of the situation, came out in the cockpit with a cooking pot on her head as a comic hat and started to do a little dance. In no time the crowd was laughing at her and making goo-goo noises and soon quietly dispersed.

For families on extended cruises, education of school-age kids can present a problem, although the experience is probably more educational than that of 95 percent of children in conventional shoreside existence. There are correspondence schools, like the Calvert School in Baltimore, that specialize in home study courses for all grades, and some parents set up their own curriculum. It is hard to stick to a routine amid the variables of a cruising life, with frequent temptations to put things off till *mañana*, and the parents must be dedicated to maintaining a regimen.

More problems arise when the children get into their teens and have a greater awareness of life over the horizon in the wide, wide world, and also a sense that their life is not their own in the close confines of the boat and constant association with parents. We have seen cases of this often enough to establish it as a pattern. When our girls were 11 and 14, we took them on a professional charter out of Antigua, and the skipper and his wife, perhaps in self-defense, brought along a 13-

year-old boy who was the son of live-aboard parents. This lad had sailed around the world via all sorts of exotic ports, with every kind of glamorous adventure, and he and the girls started exchanging stories of their experiences. They listened politely to his tales of those strange ports, and then they countered with accounts of visits to New York, Radio City Music Hall, Broadway shows, shopping malls, school activities, football games, and the usual goings on of suburban teenagers. At the end of the cruise, we met his parents, and his first words to them were, "When can we go to New York?" He knew what he was missing, and the girls had won the "Can you top this?" exchanges hands down. They did not ask me to take them sailing around the world, but they did like their vacation cruises.

On another occasion in Samana, an isolated port at the northeast tip of the Dominican Republic, when Jane and I were taking *Brunelle* from Florida to the Virgins, a boy in his early teens came alongside us in a dinghy while we were berthed at the town dock and asked if he could hold there while waiting to ferry his father back to their boat. It was a 38-foot yawl of uncertain vintage, anchored out in the harbor. We got talking to him and found that he had been aboard since he was six years old, mostly in Florida and the Bahamas, with his father and a succession of the old man's lady friends. We said that this must have been a pretty exciting life, and he sighed and gave a weak assent, but then started to expand. It came out that he was thoroughly bored with the existence, mainly because of a lack of friends his own age.

"I really wish I could go to a regular high school and do all the things that kids do there," he summed it up with a sigh.

In contrast, we have seen thoroughly well-adjusted kids living on cruising boats, reveling in their adventures and freedom from a humdrum life ashore. What it all boils down to is that cruising with children of all ages, and over any period of time from a short vacation to a live-aboard existence, depends on how the adults relate to them, understand their special problems, and make an effort to solve them.

VII

Entertainment

Activities after sailing

~~~~~~

Whether it be children or adult guests, the question of activities and entertainment is an important one in making a success out of a cruise. There are, of course, all sorts of variations depending on age, interests, inclinations, and the nature of the cruising area.

For children, when it must be an almost constant consideration, I have discussed some of the ways of keeping them happily occupied. The emphasis is usually on the most active pursuits like swimming, diving, exploring ashore, boardsailing and dinghy riding, along with the more sedentary games and story times.

Adult guests can be assumed to have a few more resources of their own, and they can be left alone for a while to read, listen to music or contemplate nature. They can, in certain cases, be very involved with the operation of the boat, and with galley activities. Some people are happy just to be sailing without worrying about anything else, and the older I get the more I tend that way myself. When we have guests for a week at a time they often want to seize each moment, following a sailing passage with a snorkel expedition or a trip to explore ashore, while I am happy to sit in the cockpit and relax.

Swimming

Swimming is naturally the first thing that comes to mind for most guests, at least in warmer climates. In Newfoundland and Scandinavia we wouldn't have thought of swimming, though some hardy shipmates did—briefly. The same was true in British Columbia, although there it was possible to hike a few hundred yards inland at many anchorages and find a relatively warm lake or pond. Maine is famous for its cold water, and swimming is not a treat there. I did it once in 1940, and I'm still a bit short of breath.

In the Caribbean and Bahamas and other tropical areas it is naturally a major adjunct to cruising pleasure, and the day often includes a noon stop for swimming and lunch as well as a post-anchoring dip in the evening. It is up to the skipper to be aware of any strong currents that might cause a problem, as this would certainly be detected during anchoring. It is surprising how tough even a slight amount of current can make it for the average adult swimmer who is not exactly an Olympic champion.

Snorkeling

Snorkeling naturally goes along with swimming, and almost everyone wants to take a shot at it to some extent. We keep snorkel gear on board, and the charter boats all provide it, but some people prefer to bring their own to make sure of a good fit.

A thoughtful skipper will be familiar with good snorkeling areas when he knows that guests will want to try it. We carry a waterproof fish identification book on board for use by the swimmers. We became quite familiar with BVI spots as well as some others on down the islands, and it was sad to note that hurricanes really do change the underwater picture, roiling shallow reefs with their heavy wave action, tumbling the coral, and killing it. We have seen this happen in several locations over the years.

Snorkelers should operate in company, not alone, unless they are very close to the yacht and someone on the yacht is aware of where they are. When divers want to go farther afield, operating from the dinghy, they should always have a buddy system.

A variation that we call "sissy snorkeling," which we've done quite

Snorkeling above these underwater sights is delightful

often, and which is especially appreciated by those not too confident of their swimming ability, is to take a glass-bottom bucket in the dinghy and drift slowly over good snorkeling areas. This gives an excellent view of the coral heads and myriad multicolored fish as long as the water is shallow enough.

Scuba

Scuba diving is something else again. We have never had equipment aboard, and few private boats do. Charter boats normally do not provide it unless they operate with diving as a specialty, but qualified divers can usually arrange a day's action with professionally operated dive boats that pick up their customers right from the yachts. It is naturally a major attraction for experienced divers, and instruction is available from the pros for those who want to become qualified. Just about every popular cruising harbor in the Caribbean has a dive shop and professionally operated boats.

Although the scuba operators offer night diving expeditions, we have a hard and fast rule of no swimming after dark in southern waters. Sharks are not as common as it might seem, and in fact I have never seen a shark in close to 30 years of operating in the Eastern Caribbean, but there are some, and it seems that they are more prone to attack in the dark. Once we were in Bimini in the Bahamas in *Mar Claro*, tied up at a marina that was heavily populated by professional sportfishing boats, when, about 10 P.M., we heard a splash of someone diving in from a nearby boat, followed almost immediately, by a frantic chorus of shouts to "Come out!" that erupted from just about every boat. A girl on one of the boats had jumped in, but she was soon back on the pier under the frantic urging of every boatman in the place. Sharks evidently made a habit of foraging in the marina after dark, especially when the catch from the boats had been cleaned and the guts thrown overboard. Not many areas have that kind of concentration, but it was an incident that made a vivid impression on me.

Another good rule for swimmers in tropical waters is to avoid wearing any shiny bracelets, dog tags, rings, or neck chains. Barracuda are not supposed to attack people (I always think, "I hope they know that," when I see one swimming near me) but they have been known to strike at shiny objects, probably mistaking them for small fish.

In some tropical areas it is important to keep an eye out for sea urchins, the purplish-black, spine-encrusted orbs that cluster near the shoreline in shallow areas. The spines have a painful poison, and a barb that makes them hard to remove if stepped on. They have disappeared from some areas of the Caribbean but are expected to make a comeback.

As mentioned, boardsailing has become a popular after-sailing activity, especially for the younger set, and most charter boats now provide a board or two. In many of the popular cruising ports there are schools that give instruction to anyone wanting to take it up.

Fishing

Another activity is fishing, and this depends a great deal on personal interest. We used to troll a line over the stern most of the time we were

If the cruising boat is big enough, a board-boat or a sailboard make good harbor entertainment

sailing in southern waters, but when too many barracuda took the lure we lost our enthusiasm. I have never been much of a fisherman, but some people only go on the water to fish and there are plenty of chances to cater to this no matter where the area. My personal opinion is that fishing from a cruising boat is an invitation to mess and disorder, but for those who do it properly and handle the gear with care, it can be a source of pleasure. One reason we never fished from *Brunelle* is the existence of that disease called ciguatera in many tropical areas. It is a debilitating affair that lasts for several days or more, with acute nausea, violent pain, and general disability, along with a strange reaction in which water on the flesh feels like fire. It comes from a reef fungus and can be transmitted up the food chain from the small reef-feeding fish to larger fish that eat the little ones. Commercial fishermen seem to know the safe spots locally, but it is unwise for visitors, fishing casually, to eat their own catch unless they have checked ahead of time on safe areas.

An allied pursuit to fishing is shellfish gathering that again should only be done when the condition of local waters is known, and with a license if that is a requirement. In Desolation Sound in British Columbia, oysters were everywhere for the taking from rocks along the shore, and there were mussels as well, both delicious and a great treat. Just gathering shells on a beach can be a lot of fun.

In many areas, it is the next best thing to catching your own fresh fish to deal with local fishermen. In Newfoundland it was easy to come by freshly caught cod this way, and cods' tongues, a delicacy for the locals, crab, squid, and salmon were also plentiful. In the Pacific Northwest, salmon is ubiquitously available, and just about every area has its local specialty. Try mahi mahi in the Pacific, crab and oysters in the Chesapeake, coho and whitefish in the Great Lakes, shrimp or snapper in Florida and the Gulf, lobsters in Maine, and another form of lobster, the clawless ones, in the Caribbean.

Eating Aboard

This leads to the subject of eating in general, which is a major form of entertainment for many. In a later chapter on equipment, I will discuss galley gear and methods of refrigerating and cooking food. Eating aboard is so much a matter of personal taste that it is impossible to cover it for everyone. Whole books have been published on seagoing recipes, and it is, in truth, a book-length subject in itself. My own theory is to keep it simple, probably stemming from my first summer of cruising as a collegian, when that favorite recipe of corned beef hash and canned peas (cooked on a Sterno stove) got me through just about every night of a month's cruise. I once spent a week on *Mar Claro* by myself in the Bahamas and never turned on the stove. I wrote this up in a tongue-in-cheek article in *Yachting*, promoting the managing editor, Bill Taylor, a hearty meat and potatoes type, to grumble, "Remind me never to cruise with Robinson!"

Actually, if you don't drink coffee, which I do not, it was not so much of a trick, especially in a warm climate. For breakfast I had fruit, fruit juice, cereal, and milk. A sandwich and a beer did very well for lunch, and at supper I had cold cuts or canned tuna, shrimp, or salmon, and raw vegetables like carrots, celery, and lettuce and tomatoes. I don't really recommend a complete lack of hot food as a steady thing. It was sort of a running gag, and I'm sure it was healthy.

With a good propane gas stove on *Brunelle*, we had normal breakfasts of bacon and eggs, toast, and tea or coffee, along with fruit and fruit juices, and those who wanted cereal had it. Milk was not always available, but we had a form of milk called Long Life, in cartons that could be kept unrefrigerated for weeks at a time unopened, and then kept cold after opening. In the tropics we never lit the stove for lunch, though soup was a favorite in colder climates. Dinner would of course depend on what meat or fish was available in local markets, with, again, whatever vegetables we could find. We did not try elaborate recipes, or special concoctions, as they would usually take up too much time in the preparation, but we have cruised as guests aboard boats where the menu was much fancier than ours. If fresh food was not to be had, we find canned meats such as ham, stew, and the good old corned beef hash to be perfectly OK, as well as canned vegetables and fruits. Unless the cook really wants to spend a long time slaving over a hot stove, I recommend simplicity as an easier way of life.

Once when daughter Alice flew down to cruise with us, she cooked four or five very special dishes at home and froze them in containers, packed them in dry ice in a plastic cooler, and brought that down as checked luggage. The ice survived, and we had a week of special treats without much time taken from onboard pleasures.

The preceding refers to cooking with overnight stops at anchor, as cooking underway is something else. Jane made it a challenge to have a hot dinner of at least a bowl of stew, if not something more elaborate, when underway at dinnertime. A gimballed stove is of course a great help in this, as is a galley where the cook can brace against a counter or bulkhead, or if need be wear a safety belt or harness. As mentioned, some layouts in which the galley is a counter along one bulkhead, with an open cabin and no chance for bracing oneself inboard, make cooking underway, or even making sandwiches, almost impossible. On very rare occasions, in really rough going, we have resorted to finger food such as celery and carrot sticks, hard-boiled eggs, and fruit to fill the bill.

Another form of cooking that is popular on bareboat charters and many private yachts is hibachi cooking on a charcoal grill over the transom. This has become so common that there are now propane grills to do away with the fuss of getting charcoal started. It is not one of my skills or pleasures, and I refuse to do any cooking this way, but we did have a grill on *Brunelle* as some guests enjoy the performance, and even beg for the opportunity to do it. I'll admit that a well-broiled

Some guests enjoy working the hibachi astern

steak from the hibachi can be a treat as long as I don't have to do it myself.

There can be hazards to hibachi cooking. First of all, it is absolutely taboo in marinas, and rightly so, though I have seen people lighting up before someone from another boat or the management set them wise. There are barbecue fanatics who will even take grills ashore in a marina to an isolated spot where they can be used safely. Another problem is back-drafting through the cockpit. In some harbors with good sized hills surrounding them, the wind swirls in eddies and back-drafts when it descends from the hills, and a happily blazing grill can suddenly shower the cockpit with flame and sparks, causing something of a panic party. When anchoring in a harbor like this, the wind behavior should make it apparent whether it would be a good night to forget the hibachi, but a lot of people fail to get the message. Also, it can be a bit inconsiderate of the boat anchored close astern in any harbor to send your smoke fumes and odors downwind to add aroma to their cocktail hour. As for lighting charcoal, it is important to have a starter fluid or to use the kind encased in cardboard to get the stuff burning without too many expletives.

We had a horrible mishap once with a grill that extended aft on an arm secured by a butterfly nut. The nut was not tight enough, and four beautiful filets mignons were delivered to the groupers in Bequia when the chef (not me) poked too hard at them with a fork, and the arm collapsed downward.

Eating Ashore

Since cruising is so often supposed to be a vacation, it is not exactly fair to saddle someone with continuous galley duty unless that happens to be a form of recreation for them, like the above-mentioned hibachi lovers. There are two solutions. Either charter a professionally crewed boat, which is a real vacation of pampered luxury (if all goes well), or plan to eat ashore fairly often. Actually, this is one of the real pleasures of cruising, whether it be for the regional cooking of Chesapeake Bay or Maine, or the fun of sampling the fare in foreign countries. There are very few cruising areas now in which it is not possible to eat ashore fairly often. If someone is slogging up the Red Sea or along the west coast of Central America to the Panama Canal there may not be many opportunities, but the popular areas worldwide abound in good eating places.

When we first cruised in the BVI in 1964 on a crewed charter, there was exactly one place there to eat ashore, Marina Cay. Now there are any number of delightful places, and one could cruise there for weeks without a repetition in meals ashore. Down the chain of islands there is a chance to sample different cuisines. There are some excellent French restaurants in St. Martin and of course Guadeloupe and Martinique. Some islands are proud of their native cuisine, usually well spiced and featuring seafood and chicken dishes, and St. Martin, for example, with its Dutch heritage on one side (Sint Maarten) and French on the other, not only has top French cuisine, but also offers Indonesian and Chinese cooking.

As mentioned, we have had interesting adventures eating ashore in the Danish islands of the Fyn archipelago, where we found that three magic words took care of ordering. They were *schnapps, fiske,* and *øl,* or aquavit, fish, and beer. Sometimes there were variations, but these words usually got us an interesting repast. Of course we once ended up with boiled chicken, but in general it worked well. Eating ashore in the Greek islands is always an interesting project, but we usually had Greeks with us to do the arranging and ordering. You do have to get used to having a raw fish brought out and shown to you, its eye glaring at you balefully, to show you what you are going to eat, and you also have to get used to octopus, black olives, and feta cheese for hors d'oeuvres during cocktail hour over ouzo, and retsina wine with dinner.

We have had great times eating ashore at out island resorts in the Barrier Reef area of Australia, where we were put at a big table of vacationing hotel guests and had a fine time comparing notes and exchanging information, and some really excellent meals at small restaurants in Les Iles sous le Vent, the Leeward Islands of French Polynesia. In Tonga, the shore meal adventure was a native feast where we sat cross-legged on the ground in front of a mammoth spread of unidentifiables neatly arranged on banana leaves, all finger-licking good (because there were no utensils).

In other words, eating ashore can be a big part of the fun of cruising in strange waters, or even on a weekend in the waters of home. It is not only a great relief for the cook to get out of the galley, but also a good part of the whole experience of cruising.

Shopping

There are some people for whom shopping is the breath of life, even while they are cruising, and we have had quite a few guests aboard, especially in the Caribbean, who really enjoy poking around in local shops for bargains and for interesting native items. Sometimes the native

Excursions for exploring or shopping make guests happy

items are native to Korea, but there are genuine local things in many cruising areas that are fun for the shopping enthusiast to search for. There are also good buys for bargain hunters in duty-free areas, such as Sint Maarten and St. Thomas, and I have to admit to finding them in binoculars and perfume, for example, in some of these places.

If a shopping buff is aboard, it is thoughtful for the skipper to arrange some time for such pursuits, and it can often be fitted in to a fuel stop or a provisioning expedition.

Bird Watching

We have had birders as guests, and this can actually add a lot of fun to a cruise. Once they get over the initial excitement at seeing pelicans and brown boobies in the Caribbean, there are real rewards in tracking down more exotic species. We have made special stops and allowed time for birding expeditions that turned out well. I am not a birder, but I can get caught up in the excitement when something special shows up. One woman who was with us in Sint Maarten and Anguilla was practically a professional, with her own boomed mike recorder, and it was great fun to make a special expedition to a cove on Anguilla that was a nesting area for tropic birds, delicate gull-like creatures with long, forked tails, and to have her record their cries on her machine. Through birding, she met kindred souls on shore and went back later on her own for more birding activities.

Sightseeing

Sightseeing is something else that should be allowed for in many areas. A lot of it can be done right from the boat while sailing, but there are also shore expeditions worth taking time for. When we were based in Tortola for so many years, we took guests for a ride, either in a rental car or taxi, on the extremely scenic Ridge Road, a winding drive along the top of the central ridge of Tortola, over 1,000 feet up, with gorgeous views.

Depending on the area, there are all sorts of attractions that can be visited, and it is a rewarding break from the steady routine of sailing to take in a local maritime or art museum, an historic building or some other landmark. Both New England and the Chesapeake, for example, afford all sorts of opportunities like this. One of the most successful cruises we ever had was in the Aegean. Jane is an archaeology buff, having studied Greek in college, and the combination of sailing and then visiting the Temple of Poseidon at Sounion, or the Aesculapion at Kos, the hospital of Hippocrates, made for a marvelous combination of interests. Somehow, there is an extra thrill to visiting a classic landmark in coming to it under sail instead of on a tour bus.

Fun and Games Aboard

As for entertainment on board, that is so much a matter of personal inclination and choice. Jane reads incessantly, losing herself in it. I, too, like to read, but I find it harder on a boat to settle into a "good read," as there is always something to take up my attention, or some chore that needs doing. When I do read, I try to find a long book that can be put down easily, rather than a page turner, since I'm often called away from turning the page. One winter in *Brunelle*, I took the entire season to read Michener's *Chesapeake*, and I felt quite bereft of friends by the time I finished it. Short story anthologies are another good answer for me, and the collection of John Cheever's got me through another winter. Two volumes we found ourselves using time and again were a dictionary and an atlas.

We are both crossword puzzle buffs, and I find that they are wonderful "time wasters" when there is a half hour or so of free time, too short to get into a book, but long enough to relax over a puzzle. I load up with crossword anthologies before taking off for a long session afloat. We also enjoy Scrabble and play that quite often when there is time for relaxing. It is a good all-generations game when the grandchildren are aboard and we split up into teams. We have tried Trivial Pursuit, but that usually goes on too long to be manageable on a boat. Once,

Raft-ups and rendezvous are a congenial part of cruising

in an especially rough inter-island passage, when there were a couple of seasickness victims, a guest suggested that we play Ghost to keep our minds occupied and our spirits up, and, as *Brunelle* heaved over great, foaming trade wind seas and various people heaved at the leeward rail, we passed words around and became two-thirds of a ghost, etc. It worked well for the group in hand, but I haven't played since.

Most charter boats now have all sorts of electronic goodies as an "entertainment center" with videos, tape cassettes, and even TV when available. On crewed boats it has become a standard thing to shoot guests' activities during the day and then show them on the video as evening entertainment. We had a portable radio-*cum*-tape player on *Brunelle*, and many an evening was spent in simply enjoying old favorites over our *chapeaux*.

But really, the best entertainment of all while cruising is just the joy of sailing. That's what it is all about.

Part II

Equipment

In 1938, between junior and senior years in college, a classmate and I chartered (for $105 for the month of August) a 26-foot gaff-rigged sloop in which we cruised from Long Island Sound to the Vineyard, Cape Cod, Nantucket, and back. She was a carvel-planked wooden boat, with wood spars, cotton sails, a gasoline engine, Sterno stove, kerosene lamps, no radio, no dinghy, an ice chest, a "yachtsman's" anchor, manila cordage, galvanized rigging, tiller steering, and a narrow, round-bilged hull with bowsprit. She was the first vessel I had ever "commanded" and the month was an experience that shaped a lifetime.

Today, I don't think anyone can have more fun that we did cruising that long ago August in New England, but the different boats we cruise in certainly make an interesting contrast in all their particulars. In the chapters in this section, those particulars will be investigated, and it should be quite an eye-opener to see just how much cruising has changed in the materials used and the equipment available to make it easier. This is a world of fiberglass, aluminum, Dacron (and allied materials), diesels, nylon, propane, freon, electronics in all their ramifications and 101 handy gadgets.

In looking over all the developments that have changed the accoutrements of cruising in the second half of the 20th century, there would be a danger of simply becoming a buyer's guide or catalog, listing items and their manufacturers, but that is not the intent here. Of course brand names will find their way in, but it would be impossible to list all of them in a given field. Omission does not mean criticism, and inclusion does not mean unqualified endorsement. Naturally, I have not been shipmates with everything mentioned, but the idea is to give a broad picture of the kinds of things that enhance cruising pleasure today.

The emphasis here is on equipment that is used while actually cruising, and to give an idea of what is generally available. Complete books have been written about many of the items touched on here, such as sails and sail handling, self-steering vanes, electronics, and nautical housekeeping. The idea here is to bring subjects up to date with newer developments, or improvements on older ones. Also, the subject of spring fitting out and seasonal maintenance is not part of the theme of making things easier afloat. It is a vast subject in itself, with so many different types of construction and materials, and each owner has his own approach to how much of the work he wants to do himself, or have done professionally. Once done it makes life afloat more rewarding, and there are people who are at their very happiest puttering around the boat in the yard, but here we are mainly concerned with afloat action.

VIII

Sails and Sail Handling

Rigs and materials

Basic to a sailboat are its sails (natch) and this is an element that saw remarkably little development from the days of the Phoenicians right up to our 1938 cruise in the gaff-rigged sloop. It is therefore rather astounding to look at the subject of sails today and see just how many developments have taken place in very recent years, and are still taking place.

In racing, the technology has become very advanced, and the computer has taken over. "Wonder materials" like Kevlar, Mylar, and other synthetics soon to be introduced now dominate the field. No longer is the making, fitting, and handling of sails an art like that of the violin-maker, where a special "feel," based on the trial and error of experience, produces the most successful results. Today it is a matter of numbers on the little greenly glowing screen, though someone with knowledge must provide the input that produces the numbers.

Cruising sails, too, can be computerized and some are, but there are different criteria for a cruising sail than those that are demanded of a winning racing sail. Durability and strength rank right up there with proper shape, and ease of handling is a major requirement. Will it resist sunlight's ravages well? Will it adapt properly to easy furling? Can it be reefed easily? Can it be raised, lowered, and stowed efficiently? These qualities are demanded of cruising sails, and a great deal of effort and innovation has gone into developing them in recent years, completely making over the trade of sailmaking and the way cruising sailors live with their sails.

Sail Inventory

In the sails department, the first consideration is inventory—which sails to have on board, based on the boat's sail plan. It is not necessary, or even a good idea, to have a big inventory of sails on a cruising boat. Aside from initial expense, which is considerable, there is the question of stowage, and of the nuisance of making sail changes in the course of a cruise. Serviceability and adaptability are the keys, and the smart cruising owner will figure out the minimum number of sails that will sensibly fulfill his needs. This, of course, depends on rig (refer to Chapter I), size of boat, intended use—daysailing vs. offshore passagemaking, for example—and adaptability to changing conditions.

A mainsail is basic, of course. It is an odd rig indeed that has no main. One main should suffice in almost all cases, as a spare one has to rate as a luxury in cruising, unless the cruising is to be far from civilization.

Brunelle's original main did yeoman service for five years, in use between 120 and 140 times a season in the Caribbean. It was damaged in an accident, and we ordered a new one, had the old main repaired, and kept it as a spare (which was never used in the next four years we had her). Incidentally, in that time, the type of Dacron cloth from the same sailmaker changed quite radically. The original main was rather soft and pliable, easy to furl and reef. The new one was of much stiffer Dacron, supposedly more resistant to sun damage and better able to hold shape, but it was much more difficult to work with.

There is no unanimity of thinking on headsails. Whether to have a double headsail rig, with its easy adaptability to changing conditions, or to opt for an overlapping genoa, with its slightly better driving force but greater difficulty in handling, is a question often decided by an owner's personality. A genoa usually means that there should also be smaller sails to switch to, an added expense as well as a nuisance in making changes. The prevailing winds in your sailing area should have some influence on this choice.

It is almost universal now to have roller-furling gear for jibs, and

a.) Roller furling main

this then comes down to the question: Is it roller furling or roller reefing? The cruising boat with hanked-on jibs is a rarity today, and more likely to be a boat that wants to be classed as a cruiser/racer. Furling and reefing gear will be discussed later in the chapter.

For many cruising boats, the extent of the inventory is no more than mainsail and choice of headsails. Increasingly popular is the cruising sail variously known as a Flasher, (see Chapter III p. 35) Multiple Purpose Sail, or Gennaker, among other trade names. This is a pole-less spinnaker, tacked down at the forestay, that is used as a drifter, a reacher or, in effect, a spinnaker, without the expense and bother of spinnaker paraphernalia—pole, lift, guys, etc. Used properly, it adds great zest to off-wind sailing, so often dull in cruising boats confined to main and jib. As explained, it can be used in winds up to about 15 knots, with the wind anywhere from just forward of the beam to 15 degrees on the quarter. It increases the fun of what would be rather lifeless off-wind sailing without putting too much strain on the crew. Although it can be handled by two in lighter airs, three make it a lot easier.

In divided-rig boats, aside from the proper sail for each mast, there is the option of light-air sails between the masts, such as mizzen staysails on ketches and yawls, and staysails or "fishermen" between the main and foremast on schooners. On boats with divided rigs, it would seem to be a mistake to miss taking advantage of these extra sails, and lightweight sails do not present a serious stowage problem.

In the increasingly popular category of cat-cruisers, whether single stickers, ketches, or schooners, the headsail problem disappears, although there is still the possibility of light staysails or multipurpose sails. Catboat mains are very often rigged with a wishbone instead of a conventional boom for ease of control. As the owner of an 18-foot catboat I am very partial to the rig for happy daysailing, but I have my personal doubts about single-stick cats beyond 30 feet in length. They have become quite popular, and they certainly are a simple rig, but depending on a single sail of that size somehow gives me pause.

Sailcloth Materials

The material for sails is something that has gone, and is still going, through tremendous changes and developments. The changes in the five years between *Brunelle*'s two mainsails was one example. Modern sailors raised in the synthetic era do not know what it was like to have to take care of the old cotton sails that were standard for so many years. They had to be broken in carefully, handled differently when wet, stretched and tweaked as wetness and tensions varied, and kept from rot and mildew as much as possible by careful handling. That was all part of the routine of sailing, happily forgotten now in the age of Dacron and its relatives.

The first synthetics tried as replacement for cotton were nylon and Orlon during the 1950s, but nylon had too much stretch for anything but spinnakers and drifters, and Orlon was taken from the sailing market to the clothing field (a slightly bigger market!). However, Dacron was introduced in the late '50s and has been the basic sailcloth for the past 30 years. Though giving way to higher-tech, higher cost Kevlar, Mylar, and variations for racing sails, Dacron has maintained dominance in the cruising field. I will never forget my first exposure to it in the 1960 Bermuda Race, when the full main of the 72-foot ketch *Barlovento* was carried through a night of winds gusting over hurricane strength, its leech vibrating like a machine gun gone mad, with absolutely no damage.

As mentioned, Dacron has been developed, and is now a stronger material, more resistant to the sun, but with an increase in stiffness that makes handling cruising sails harder. While the cloth does deteriorate under constant exposure to sunlight, it lasts a long time before losing strength, and the most likely failure point is in the threads of the seams. I have had catboat sails last for many as 10 seasons of New Jersey summer weather without benefit of sail cover (I use one now) before going soft. *Brunelle's* mainsail failure was in seam threads in a squall in Anegada Passage.

Just as Dacron itself has been changed to improve its durability, so have allied materials been brought along. Bainbridge, a sailcloth manufacturer for many years, has introduced a new product called SPF-UV to protect against ultraviolet rays. This is a lightweight, clear, pressure-sensitive film with an adhesive backing, which can be applied by a professional sailmaker to synthetic sailcloth fabrics as UV protection. Not only does it protect the whole sail, but it also does away with the need for acrylic "sacrificial" strips that have been used on roller-furling sails as UV protection.

As proof that Dacron's tenure is not unthreatened, a new material that is Tedlar-based is said to be stronger, lighter, and four times more tear resistant than Dacron. I say "said to be" since, as of this writing, I have only seen ads for it. It does not need a sacrificial cloth strip for protection and it is supposedly soft, and easy to handle and keep clean. Its initial use has been for roller-furling jibs.

Mainsails

It is now pretty old-fashioned to have a mainsail with short battens stiffening the leech that slides up and down the mast in the control of its halyard, and luffs and flaps and falls below the boom onto cabin top or deck when it is lowered. In racing boats, yes, but there have been all sorts of developments in the design and handling of cruising mainsails.

My concession to ease of handling the main on *Brunelle* was to mount a three-notch gallows frame atop the cabin so that the boom could be guided into one of them as the sail was being lowered. With this control of the boom, it is not a difficult matter to furl the sail onto it. Some people use plain old cloth stops to tie around the sail, but many boats now have a stopping line attached to the boom permanently. Ours was a shock cord that could quickly be passed over the sail and hooked on the other side of the boom, so securing the main was not a tough job, even in rough weather. There was a topping lift, of course, to control the drop of the outer end on the boom, but it was seldom needed because of the gallows frame. *Helios*, which has a permanent hardtop Bimini, has a single-notch frame on top of the Bimini into which the boom can be guided.

Helios, however, as mentioned in Chapter III, has a type of main that has become increasingly popular on cruising boats, a fully battened one with lazyjacks led from high on the mast to both sides of the boom. These contain the sail, already well controlled by the full battens, on its downward slide, so that it settles peacefully onto the boom in a pile of folds without flopping over onto the cabin top. This is a very handy arrangement, especially in shorthanded cruising, as the sail will stay there docilely without stops, and time need not be taken to do any more or neater furling until other chores are taken care of. Sometimes, we have come into a harbor and forgotten to secure the main until later. It might look a bit messy, but it is secure.

The other side of the picture with full battens and lazyjacks, as mentioned about *Helios*, is that raising the sail can be a tricky operation, requiring some care and teamwork. The sail must be absolutely eye-to-wind while being raised, or the battens will foul on the lazyjacks, blocking the hoisting action. The best way to manage this is for the helmsman to watch the sail and keep the boat heading correctly, making quick little adjustments before the batten ends can get tangled in the lazyjacks. If for some reason it is not possible to point the boat head-to-wind, the boom must be let out to the correct angle so that the sail is directly into the wind. This can be a bit more difficult. If there are enough hands on board, one person can help flip the sail away from the lazyjacks as it goes up.

In addition to the long battens and lazyjacks there are a couple of other new ways to control dousing the mainsail. One is a system called the Dutchman, a patented rig for controlling the descent. In it, two or more wires are installed vertically in the sail between the boom and the topping lift. They are woven through the sail to collect and flake the main is it drops, guiding it down to alternate sides of the boom, so that almost all the work of putting the sail to bed has been done by the time it lands on the boom. A variation on this concept is made by North Sails, a system called LazyMate that is applied to North's FullBatten mains. The sail is brought down to lie gently on the boom by a system of luff slides and leech control lines. Both LazyMate and the Dutchman can be retrofitted to existing sails. One difference between them is that LazyMate does not require extra holes in the sail cover. Ulmer Kolius also has a full-batten system called Batmain (what, no Robin?) that has a self-storing sail cover, called a BoomBag, attached to the boom that can be quickly flipped and fastened over the sail once it has settled on the boom. Its stowage is accomplished by a zipper that encloses it when not in use.

Reefing

One of the greatest boons to cruising sailors, and any other kind of sailor, is the system of jiffy reefing that is now virtually standard. When I think back to the old conventional method of having to tie down the

b.) Roller reefing jib

sail at each end and each reef point, and the hard-to-handle, roller-reefing boom that was in vogue for a while, it seems amazing that jiffy reefing was not thought of sooner. Roller reefing was a real sweat to crank in, and it usually distorted the sail badly. Jiffy reefing, which can be handled at the mast by one person, is simplicity itself. As the sail is eased down, a grommet on the luff is attached to a hook at the gooseneck, and a line leading aft through the boom and on up to a grommet in the leech of the sail can be tautened by winch from the same position at the mast. This brings the grommet down snugly to the boom, and the sail is reefed in a matter of a minute or two. The belly of the sail can eventually be tied in with conventional reef points, but there is no urgency about this, and it can be done at leisure (if there is such a thing in a reefing situation). With the proper cordage attached and grommets located in the proper places, this system can be set up for more than one reef.

The relatively modern concept of roller furling or roller reefing has also come to mainsails, with variations. This involves taking the mainsail into or against the mast, rather than to the boom, when dousing it. The sail must be battenless and loose-footed to be adapted to this system. There are systems, such as Hood's, which require a specially built, grooved mast, because the sail is taken into the mast itself. As a method of reefing, the sail can be partially rolled up. One minor annoyance with this system is that, in a marina slip, with the wind blowing across the groove in the mast, it sets up a hollow howling like the sound of a giant blowing across the neck of a bottle. This can be very annoying on board and to the neighbors, but "Whistling Willie" can be controlled by hoisting a specially fashioned strip of cloth, called a flute-stopper, up the groove to fill the gap and dampen the noise.

An alternative method of roller furling the main can be retrofitted, without the need for a specially built mast. Forespar's E-Z Furl, which has four models for boats from 23 to 60 feet and can be added to almost any existing mast, is an example of this. It fits on the after side of the mast and is said to be aerodynamically superior to other retrofitted systems, as it fits closely against the mast. There is no gap between mast and luff, as is the case in systems where the sail is merely rolled on a wire. Another method hoists a zippered cover around the sail after it has been rolled up behind the mast.

With this outside-the-mast system, as in the interior furling method, the sail can be reefed down to a desire size. One caveat with mast-furling systems is that, should anything get out of true, jams can occur, preventing proper furling.

Jibs

As with developments in mainsail handling from the conventional days of old, the handling of headsails has also seen many innovations. In fact roller furling started with jibs quite a few years ago, and sophisticated advances have been made with the concept. We had one on *Tanagra*, our OI 36, in the early '70s, when the idea was quite new to us, and we have not been without one since.

There are quite a few companies making this gear, and there are variations. The basic idea is to roll the jib up on its stay as the quickest way of dousing it, and different methods are used. On *Tanagra*, as mentioned, the roller furling was on its own stay, separate from the boat's headstay. This had several advantages, such as the fact another jib could be readied, hanked on the headstay, if there was a possibility of a need for a change. Also, as often happens with roller furlers, when the sail has not furled all the way because of very tight turns under tension in high winds and the furling line is completely off the drum, the sail can simply be dropped on deck by letting the halyard go, as I mentioned that we did.

When the sail furls on a rotating headstay and this happens, it cannot be solved so simply. The sail cannot be lowered in its luff groove, and the best way to try to handle it is to let it out again, blanket it behind the main by running off (if there is sea room), which should ease the tension enough to reduce the number of tight turns.

In general, the quick handling of the jib without the need to go to the foredeck is a real boon to the cruising sailor, and I class the roller-furling jib as one of the major advances in cruising convenience in the past 60 years. The type of sail to put on the roller should be carefully thought out. The bigger the sail, the harder it is to make a neat furl, and the greater the likelihood of difficulty in getting it furled properly under tension. As I have said, we were very partial to the high-cut Yankee in a double headsail rig with a staysail on a club. As a sailing rig it worked perfectly well if the sails were trimmed in proper relationship to set up a good double slot. We found out in an early shakedown that we did not have enough halyard tension on the Yankee, causing the upper leech to fall off and flutter. Once this was corrected, the jibs had good drive.

The double headsail rig had several real advantages for comfortable cruising. The roller-furler feature was of course a big one, especially as very few of us or our crews were young and agile foredeck types. It tacked easily, being high cut, without fouling on the staysail stay, and we could even balance the two headsails on a dead run to have them wing-and-wing, feeding air from the staysail to the jib. This could only be done under perfect circumstances, but it was fun. Adaptability to conditions was a major plus. If we began to be overpowered, it was a simple thing to reduce to main and staysail in a jiffy, and, as already pointed out, as a "cocktail rig" it made for comfortable lunch hours with a minimum of heeling. The varying combinations of full sail; main and Yankee; main and staysail; reefed main and both headsails; or reefed main with one or the other, provided a great number of choices for the right amount of sail to meet almost any conditions with a minimum of fuss. We used them all at one time or another.

One of the big questions with jibs that roll up is whether, as I have said, they are reefable, or merely for complete furling. I have only had limited experience with this, but I have the feeling that roller reefing of jibs has never been solved satisfactorily. We have only done it in such emergencies as making that controlled landing without power, when the jib was gradually reduced. Once when I was a guest on a 42-foot cruiser/racer with a 130-percent genoa, we tried reefing the jib as the breeze increased, and it did not work well. Perhaps the lead should have been played with, but the foot went very taut, the leech fell off and the center of effort moved up and aft. It was a sad looking hunk of sail, but, had we been in serious trouble, it might have gotten us through. Time and again in the Caribbean, when the trades are putting on a good show in the 20s, I have seen boats with large jibs trying to make do with semi-furled ones, and they have always been having a tough time of it. It also puts a heavy extra strain on the rig.

In researching this subject, I consulted with our local South Amboy, New Jersey, sailmaker. John Eggers has a very down-to-earth, no-nonsense approach to the subject of sails, and he allowed that certain things could be done to help a sail adjust to roller reefing, but that the end result was never that successful. A foam pad on the stay, in the shape of a cigar, and a sail cut to adapt to this, can make the fit better than an unadapted stay and sail. It helps the sail keep shape and the center of effort to stay fairly near the stay, and is about the only viable solution to the problem.

As for furling systems, in addition to the separate stay, with which sagging is a problem, there are quite a few available. Three brands, Furlex, Harken, and Streamstay II have two grooves for sails and easily removable drums and halyard swivels. Eggers points out that an owner can use a deck sweeper for racing and convert to cruising mode in a matter of minutes. Furlex and Hood Seafurl have furling systems specially adapted to cruising use, and there is a wide choice of manufacturers in the field. A key factor is to have the sail and the stay compatible, planned from the start.

Spinnakers

Spinnakers are not so important to cruising boats, though there are owners who would not be without them. I have already mentioned the Flasher types, poleless spinnakers which are a very good solution for the cruising skipper who still looks for a little excitement. We have had some fine sails under ours, particularly a daylong broad reach across the Great Bahama Bank in a fresh northwester. If nothing else, it allows the owner to show off a bit with a multiple choice of colors. I ordered every color available in the vertical stripes and then had my old college and school colors in the four horizontal bands across the bottom. How's that for personalized corn?

The only major variation in using this sail is whether to have a sleeve for setting and furling. Various manufacturers have different trade names for it, and it can be used with the poleless sails or a full-fledged spinnaker. The sail is encased in a long, cloth tube or sleeve and is hoisted in it. The tube is then pulled up by control lines, gradually breaking the sail free, until the sleeve is bunched at the head and the sail is drawing. When time comes to douse the sail, the sleeve is simply pulled down over it by downhauls, gradually encasing it. It is a handy gadget for shorthanded crews. If there are only two people aboard, the helmsman needs about four hands to do everything necessary, but a couple of knees against the wheel can help.

Instead of carrying a spinnaker, some cruising boats just carry a pole and wing out the genoa, which can certainly make downwind sailing

c.) The poleless spinnaker

more rewarding than wallowing along with only the main filling. We had one on *Tanagra* before the poleless spinnaker was introduced and used it fairly often.

If there is still the feeling that a regular spinnaker should be part of the sail inventory, there is a recently introduced system from Forespar called Gybe-o-Matic that looks like the cleverest thing since sliced bread, and I wonder why nobody thought of it sooner, as it looks and sounds so simple (I have not seen it in action). It allows jibing the spinnaker from the cockpit, with no need for anyone on the foredeck. In cruising, it can be handled easily with a shorthanded crew, and in racing it has a wonderful tactical advantage. Without the warning of a crew member poised on the bow to execute a conventional jibe, an opponent can really be caught by surprise by a jibe executed completely from the cockpit.

The key to the Gybe-o-Matic system is an internal track in the pole.

A sliding car running along this track is attached to a fitting on the mast, and the pole can slide along the mast in either direction, controlled by windward and leeward lines. Guys and sheets are attached to the sail normally. The pole can be made ready for using during tacking on a windward leg, with no need to set it up on a given side before rounding a mark. While this is a racing advantage, the cruiser who also wants to race should find this a fascinating gadget.

In the foregoing analysis of sails and their developments, one fact should be very obvious. New ideas and new materials are coming into the field all the time, and it would be worth one's while to continue to keep up with them.

IX

The Steering Station

Helm, vanes, autopilots, controls

~~~~~~

The absolute heart of a cruising boat, the "command post" and nerve center, is the steering station. Until an owner can take position at the wheel or tiller and feel the vessel in his hands, his is not a complete relationship. This is the essence of sailing, to be at the helm guiding the boat in reaction to the wind and waves. For this reason, the steering station and the equipment that goes with it deserve a great deal of thought and analysis. As I mentioned in Chapter II, I have been on several boats in which the steering station was not given sufficient thought, and it made quite a difference in my reaction to the boat as a whole. If the steering station is inefficient, the whole boat suffers, and it also might be an indication that not enough thought has been given to the rest of the boat.

There are several key elements. First of all, the helmsman must be comfortable. If there is strain involved in steering because the setup is awkward and uncomfortable, the pleasure of it soon turns to an irksome duty. He must also be able to see well while steering. Blocked visibility is not only a nuisance; it can be plain dangerous. Not only must the view ahead be as clear as possible, but it must also be easy to see the compass and the instruments and to work the controls. The whole steering station must be worked out as a unit, with all functions coordinated.

Despite the importance of the helmsman operating comfortably and efficiently, there is a paradox involved. Too long a wheel trick becomes fatiguing, wiping out the joy of the action, and, especially on long

passages, it becomes important to have an alternative to a human hand on the wheel. This brings up the subject of self-steering vanes and autopilots.

Steering Stations

First, to the station itself. There is no standard doctrine for setting one up, as boats and cockpits vary a great deal. As far as equipment goes, the Edson Corp. has been prominent in the marine industry for more than 100 years. Edson manufactures extensive lines of quality marine equipment, steering gear, and accessories, including wheels, pedestals, instruments, and the linkage between wheel and rudder. A study of what Edson provides is a good indication of what this field involves. In a typical installation, the steering pedestal serves as a binnacle and instrument column. A small, solid wheel on the side of the pedestal can be hand-operated to control tension on the steering column, and, when tightened completely, it acts as a lock of the steering gear. When leaving the wheel for some quick, temporary action, for longer periods if conditions are stable, and as a lock in port to prevent the steering wheel from flopping around, the helmsman can make quick use of this item.

It is important to have the compass easily visible while steering, and having it mounted on the pedestal takes care of this. For night operations, the binnacle light should be of low power and preferably red. I have been shipmates with binnacle lights that were so bright they took away the helmsman's night vision, a serious problem. To complete the compact, efficient steering station, instrument housing can be attached to the pedestal with suitable mounts that swivel if need be. The final item is the engine control, and I much prefer a single-lever gear-and-throttle. The fewer hand actions the better when making quick maneuvers in docking, anchoring, or picking up a mooring. As I have pointed out, it is a real drawback to have to reach through the wheel instead of around it to work the engine controls, especially if gear and throttle are separate handles. Even worse was the boat I described earlier that had the controls down at foot level. An important check in using a single-lever control is to make sure that the disengage button is in the desired position. This is simply a small button at the hub of the instrument that disengages the gears when it is pulled out, allowing the throttle to be set at any desired level for charging batteries or refrigerator while in port. Otherwise, the gears are disengaged only when the throttle is at idle. A booby trap here for the confused helmsman is forgetting that the disengage button is out and wondering why the boat is not responding to increased throttle. This has been the cause of a couple of serious groundings I have witnessed over the years.

Mentioning reaching through the wheel to get at the controls brings up the question of the size of wheel. There has been a vogue in recent years, fostered in the racing set, for super-large steering wheels. This is fine for the fingertip control of a racing helmsman, but I do not think it is a good feature on cruising boats. A conventional smaller wheel, no more than three feet in diameter, should work perfectly well for most cruising boats, and it has advantages. There is the aforementioned ability to reach around it rather than through it to work controls. A big wheel is a nuisance in the space it takes up in a cruising cockpit, awkward to get around and generally in the way. A comfortable cockpit is much more important than having the skipper think he looks like Dennis Conner.

The Helmsman's Seat

Key to a helmsman's happiness and efficiency is the place he has to operate, mainly the seat. If he enjoys standing at the wheel as lord of all he surveys, more power to him, but this can get tiring after a while. The treatment of the seat and the cockpit sole under the steering station is very important. *Brunelle*'s worked out very well. Right against the transom, the seat was a comfortably upholstered U-shape, which gave some support when the boat was heeling, and there were slanted sections of the cockpit sole to port and starboard of the wheel station to give foot support while heeling. This worked either standing or sitting. The side benches were close enough so that the helmsman could steer from the side, with the best view forward of the jibs along the leeward rail. An oversight on the seat was that it was at a height from the sole for an average male. It was a bit too high for Jane, as her feet could not reach down to the sole or the slanted panels, and it should have had a footrest at a proper distance to give her feet support. I kept promising to do something about it but somehow never did get around to it.

Since there was no after deck and therefore no lazarette, the seat was right at the transom. On an offshore run in a good following sea it was a thrill of a sort to look back from the seat and realize that there was a very close relationship between the helmsman and the wave looming up behind him. Since *Brunelle*'s afterbody was shaped nicely, she was never pooped in all the passages we made, but the possibility was sometimes an exciting feature of steering. Another was that the body of the seat was also the vented compartment (through the tran-

som) of the propane tanks. With a weak attempt at humor, the seat was known as the "ejection seat" (but thankfully never was).

Tillers

All this discussion has been with the assumption that steering is by wheel, which is certainly the case in a high percentage of cruising boats, but there are those which are still steered by tiller. Tillers are usually found in the smaller size ranges, although some sailors insist on having tillers in larger boats, and some racing skippers think that this gives the best control of all. Of course there is no gearing, and the helmsman is one-to-one with the rudder, so the boat should be fairly well balanced. This is not the case with many catboats, and the helm of our 18-foot cat can give quite a tussle, a real workout, in a breezy broad reach or run. Even with wheel steering, which can of course be arranged, cats can give a real fight. *Mar Claro*, our 24-foot Amphibi-Ette of long ago, had a tiller. She was a joy to sail, and a tiller seemed right, but it did take up extra room in the cockpit.

This space-sweeping characteristic is a problem, as is where to put the compass, etc. With a binnacle forward of the tiller, the cockpit is even more encumbered. On *Mar Claro*, I had a special board that fit in the grooves for the companionway hatchboard. The compass was mounted on it. Nowadays, without glasses, it would probably be too far away to read. In most cases, it is difficult to stand and steer by tiller, and forward visibility can be a problem.

Forward visibility was a problem on *Brunelle* because of her raised deck. If close visibility forward was required, I would have to remain standing, and for Jane it was even more difficult from six inches lower than my point of view. This was one of those compromises I have cited.

When there is no self-steering device during passage-making, scheduling wheel tricks for most efficient results is important. When Jim Lillie was with us for our voyage through the Caribbean, including some overnights, he and I would stand two-hour watches, and Jane would take 1000 to 1200 and 2200 to 2400. This way, Jim and I had two "rest periods" in 24 hours, and this worked out quite well for relatively short trips—our longest was 45 hours. We found that a two-hour trick was about the limit for decent concentration on the job at hand.

Hydraulic Steering

All of this discussion has been about mechanical steering, but some boats are equipped with hydraulic steering. This is fairly standard in powerboats, but it is not a good idea in sailboats. Hydraulic steering can actually be installed less expensively than a good mechanical steering system, and it was used as a gimmick in the days when sailboat manufacturers were trying to lure powerboaters during a period of fuel

The strange rock formations at The Baths, Virgin Gorda

Brunelle

Road Town provides all maintenance and repair service,
easy shopping for food and supplies and good communications

Snorkeling is a favorite activity

Brightly colored fish and coral formations abound

Nantucket Harbor

Rhode River, a quiet Chesapeake anchorage

English Harbour, Antigua

The Cochinos, Bay Islands of Honduras

Fort de France, Martinique

Desbarats, North Channel, Lake Huron

The lagoon, Bora Bora

Cave exploring, Tonga

Kornati Archipelago, Dalmatian Coast

Mullerup, Denmark

Smogen, west coast of Sweden

shortages. We had hydraulic steering in *Tanagra*, and I did not like it. There was not the real "feel" of the boat as she was sailing, the direct relationship between helmsman and rudder. There was a less sensitive reaction, and it was not as much fun to sail this way.

Self-Steering

Then there are those times when it is good to have steering assistance, and there are a great many ways to make this possible in sailboats. The simplest form, a makeshift solution, is to use the wheel lock, or to lash the wheel or tiller. This can be effective long enough to do some quick chore on deck on most points of sail, but not on a run or quartering reach. Ingenious skippers have sometimes been able to work out a lash-up between the mainsheet and the wheel or tiller in which the pressure of the sheet will correct changes in steering, but this is a temporary sort of thing that cannot be relied on for long.

Wind Vanes

Of the self-steering devices now in use, there are two main types: wind vanes and automatic pilots. The vane system does not need any power except that of the wind, while the autopilot must be provided with electricity. Wind vanes are naturally the choice of long-distance voyagers, with whom constant use of electricity would not be possible, and autopilot systems are popular for normal short-haul cruising. In more sophisticated forms, it may be adapted to long voyages if the boat is equipped to provide the power output (or, in a field that has only begun to be explored, has a means of harnessing substantial solar power).

International Marine Manufacturing Corp. of Miami, makers of the RVG wind vane self-steering system, put out an amusing advertising flyer that listed reasons why anyone should have a windvane. The spiel claimed that the RVG will—

provide you with an emergency rudder;

steer a more accurate course than a human in all weather and sea
conditions;

allow almost total freedom from the tiller or wheel to do other
things that always need doing on a boat;

teach you to be a better sail trimmer;

teach you to balance your boat better;

give you greater safety factor in rough going;

allow you to travel greater distances in a given time;

expand the physical and mental limitations of captain and crew;

afford more precise navigation and course accuracy than a human;

add to the pleasure of any cruise;

add to the value of the boat;

afford that extra confidence to attempt and make a certain passage
that was heretofore a dreaded experience;
be a hell of a status symbol and conversation piece;
never eat;
never complain or talk back.

These are all quite true, and it is folly to set out on long transoceanic
passages without a vane. I have known solo circumnavigators who made
the whole voyage and hardly touched the wheel from harbor to harbor.
Actually, as a side issue, I have been shipmates with a singlehandler
who would have to be classed as an inexperienced helmsman. He had
done so little wheel time that he was not very good at actually steering,
and he was soon bored by it.

The important thing about vanes is that they must stand up to continuous, rugged duty. There is no rest, and the components must be
very strong and well engineered. It is doubly galling when the crew

has come to be thoroughly dependent on a vane only to have it break down and put them back on regular wheel tricks. With a shorthanded crew on a long passage, this can be a serious problem.

Autopilots

Electrically operated autopilots, of which there are quite a number on the market, are a real luxury for relaxed cruising. They have been available for powerboats for many years, but it is only fairly recently that they have become popular for sailboats. Naturally they are dependent on electrical power, and they cannot be operated indefinitely without some means of keeping the power supply up. This means charging via generator or main engine, or possibly through solar panels or wind generators.

Autopilots can be adapted to wheel or tiller steering. Units that are mounted in exposed areas must be waterproofed. The bottom size limit for an autopilot-powered boat is about 26 feet.

I have never owned an autopilot, but I was shipmates with one in a borrowed boat, and I must say that it was a distinct advantage on a day of cold wind and rain to handle the boat by the autopilot control keypad, as the modern terminology would have it, from a dry, protected spot under the cockpit dodger, instead of standing out in the elements. If I decided that an adjustment in course was necessary, I simply pushed a small button on the keypad, and the boat responded. I felt a bit guilty doing this, but I must say it was comfortable.

Modern microchip sophistication has been introduced into this field. Features that can now be expected of an autopilot include microprocessor control that makes them capable of making small course-keeping adjustments. They use electronic flux-gate compasses, eliminating errors inherent in conventional compasses by taking thousands of readings every second that are assimilated, averaged, and transmitted to the autopilot. As was the case with the one I used, remote control from many different stations on the boat is possible. If there is no need for human checking via this remote control, the boat can be locked into the autopilot on a given course, and it will react to changing loads on the helm, varying sea conditions, and small changes in wind direction. Some types have an optional digital windvane attachment that allows a constant course to be sailed relative to the wind. This can be alternated with compass or radio-navigation inputs if desired. A helpful feature is to have an alarm that signals if there is too much of a variation from the programmed course. It is important, always, for the system to be quickly and easily disengaged if there is a need to revert to manual steering. Most of the units available are easily adapted to many sizes of boats and types of steering systems. Manufacturers boast of such features as a pulse width modulation drive circuit (which translates to very precise motor speed control). This sort of technology, and the availability of these autopilot systems, is just one more example of the many advances that have become available in recent years to make cruising easier.

X

Special Gear and Gadgets

Anchors, windlasses, winches, Biminis,
safety gear, dinghies, swimming ladders

~~~~~~

Once a new boat has been delivered, the owner looks her over with excitement and pride, and then reality sets in. As the list in Chapter XI will show, equipping a cruising boat is like setting up a whole new household, with nautical embellishments that no house or apartment ever needed. As I pointed out in Chapter I, part of the basic cost of a boat is outfitting her with the 101, or maybe it's 1,001, items that make her comfortable, safe, and truly usable. Flowers on the table and a stereo are not enough.

Just a glimpse through the catalogs of marine mail order houses like Goldberg or E & B, or manufacturers like Schaefer, Hood, A & B, Bomar, Haft, or Forespar, to name just a few, gives a quick and eye-opening idea of all the possibilities there are for outfitting a boat. This tends to create a mental image of a vessel so laden down and bulging with equipment that she can hardly float, much less get underway, but it is amazing what a boat will absorb in the way of incidental gear. Years ago, when we had *Mar Claro* in Florida waters for a winter of family cruising, we entered her in a regatta near the end of the season. To cut down on weight, always important but especially so in a light-displacement boat, which she was, we took off all nonessentials for racing, and the accumulation was staggering, filling two trunk-size pier lockers at the marina, and this from just a 24-foot boat.

When we sold *Brunelle* after nine live-aboard sessions in the Caribbean, I couldn't believe all the gear that had collected in her. Most of it went with her as part of her basic equipment, but our own personal stuff was still an amazing pile. A boat that is only used for weekending and relatively short vacation cruises may not become quite so loaded, but there are still many essentials.

As a nonmechanical gadget-free sailor, I have perhaps deprived myself of some helpful gear under the "keep it simple" theory I have always maintained, but I recognize the fascination of this sort of thing for a great many sailors. The basic necessities are worth some discussion in detail, and I will also try to give an idea of some of the myriad gadgets that are being introduced all the time.

Anchors and Windlasses

The only time I have ever cruised without once using an anchor was in Denmark (see Chapter XXII), and it is certainly basic to good cruising to have the right anchor for the boat. There is nothing startlingly new in anchors, and the only thing that has made anchoring easier in recent years is the increased use of windlasses. The basics for cruising boats are the Danforth, the plow (CQR), and, to some extent, the old-fashioned yachtsman's anchor. The Bruce anchor has come onto the scene in recent years and has its devotees. I don't happen to have ever used one, so I cannot give a personal report, but they are seen increasingly, and one of the obvious advantages is ease and neatness of stowing at a bow chock.

This same factor, which also includes the ability to drop it quickly, is a major reason I have had plow anchors on *Tanagra* and *Brunelle* and have been quite pleased with them. *Brunelle* came from the builder's yard with a 25-lb. plow and I upped the size by 10 pounds, based on experience with *Tanagra's* 25-pounder. *Brunelle* was heavier, and we were headed for the Caribbean, where I wanted to be sure of enough anchor power. As explained, the only time I have had trouble with a plow dragging is on hard, grassy sand.

Over the years I have also had good luck with Danforths, and they are a marvelous combination of light weight and holding power. We had one in my Navy days aboard a 110-foot subchaser that worked well in a lot of odd anchorages in the Caribbean, South Pacific and New Guinea, and I use a small one for day anchoring in our catboat. Danforth has improved the strength and construction over the years and its latest products are high-tensile, which means more strength for weight. On *Tanagra* and *Brunelle*, I had a 15-lb. Danforth as a lunch hook or for doing a Bahamian moor or a fore-and-aft one. Given the proper scope, which means double what a heavier anchor might require, and proper set, a Danforth will hold like a bulldog. My only reservations about it are the possibility of its fouling by impaling a foreign object like a beer can on its sharp flukes, rendering it useless, or of emergency resetting if it is pulled out by a violent change of wind direction.

On *Mar Claro*, back in the '50s, I used a Northill anchor, a folding one that had been developed for seaplanes because of its weight-to-power advantage, and it was a good one despite the nuisance of having to fold it for stowage and unfold it for use. Somehow, I have not seen Northills around in recent use.

The old-fashioned yachtsman's anchor, or fisherman's, or Herreshoff, as it has variously been called, has never died out completely. It is a good holding anchor, but does depend on weight, and it has always been awkward to handle and stow. If a boat circles around it too much, it is possible to foul the anchor line on the half of the flukes that stick up above the bottom perpendicular to the stock, and this can result in pulling the anchor out and rendering it ineffective. Paul Luke, the East Boothbay, Maine, boatbuilder, has revived the type, calling it a storm anchor. His version disassembles into three pieces for stowing, and his recommendation is two pounds of anchor per foot of waterline for holding power in a blow. One advantage of this type is that it adapts to just about any kind of bottom. And a good hefty storm anchor can certainly be called "an anchor to windward" if the need arises.

Oddball types like grapnels, folding anchors and mushrooms are seldom seen on modern cruising boats, where the big emphasis and advantage is on being able to chock the anchor at the bow roller without having the awkward mess of bringing it aboard and having to get rid of mud, weeds, and what have you.

Nylon is the preferred cordage for anchor rodes, and such a welcome advance on the old manila stuff we used to use. Its elasticity adds greatly to its effectiveness, and it is resistant to rot and to chafe, although it is still a good idea to protect it with chafing gear where it goes through a chock. It can also be chafed through by coral or sharp rock, and in areas where this is a problem all-chain rodes are recommended despite the added weight. This is where windlasses become very important.

As a side comment, in all my years of cruising, I have never put out two anchors for security. I have used them, as mentioned, for Bahamian moors and fore-and-aft, and I have, fortunately, never been caught at anchor in a bad storm situation, when something like the Luke anchor would obviously be a help. From this experience, it has been interesting for me to note how often boats are seen with two anchors out in normal weather in well protected harbors. To me this is a waste of time and effort, and it can sometimes lead to a tangled mess. The important thing is to trust the anchor you have out and to make sure it is set properly.

As an aid to an anchor's holding power, it is a good idea to run a weight down the line to give it a better angle at the anchor, and also to hold the rode deeper, which helps to avoid having passing boats foul it. This is an age-old idea, but a company called Ada Leisure Products of Ada, Michigan, has made it easier to do this with its Rode Roller and Rode Rider weights with built-in blocks for ease of sliding down the rode. We once used a makeshift of this idea, sliding a diving belt down the line to free it from under the rudder of a boat that had dragged across our rode.

In recent years, windlasses have come increasingly into use, and it is now a rare cruising boat larger than 35 feet that does not have one. There is a wide choice on the market, and the builder of a new boat will naturally fit the correct model to the boat in accordance with an owner's requirements. Older boats can be retrofitted. A power windlass puts quite a load on the electrical system, and it is mandatory to have the engine running when using a power windlass. If not, it will soon flip its breaker or run the batteries down to nothing. Although I never bothered to keep *Brunelle's* in commission and was used to weighing anchor manually (or would "dorsally" better fit the phrase?), a windlass was absolutely necessary in such an area as Les Iles souls le Vent in French Polynesia. The shallowest anchorages at islands like Bora Bora, Tahaa and Raiatea are at least 80 feet, and all-chain rodes are required because of the possibility of chafing on coral. The time and effort to get an anchor up under these conditions without the use of a windlass would be considerable, and almost impossible without a lot of manpower on board.

A windlass should be well protected in its construction against water in its exposed position on the foredeck, and it must be kept lubricated as well for protection. Manual windlasses are available for those who prefer not to tax the electrical system or to have to depend on it, perhaps conjuring up images of sailors of old marching around the capstan singing chanteys ("Hooray, and UP she rises"). A & B Industries of Corte Madera, California, which has several models of power windlasses, has two manual ones as well. There is a two-speed double-action model with double chain pipes, and a removable handle that engages the clutch, controlling the brake and allowing full control while anchoring. A wildcat pawl allows independent operation of the rope capstan while the anchor chain remains under full load on the wildcat. Power windlasses have horizontal or vertical motors, above or below deck, and can be fitted with chain or rope wildcats. Maxwell Marine of Costa Mesa, California, has a vertical dual direction windlass for all chain systems. An overload control and a chainstopper are recommended as necessary equipment. Power windlasses should have a step-on switch, freeing the hands for working the windlass itself. Lighthouse Mfg. Co. of Riverside, California, has four models that provide a choice of all chain, all rope, or combination of rope and chain. So-Pac of Seattle imports Muir windlasses from Australia with a choice of functions, and also offers accessories that provide for remote control. Windlasses definitely make cruising easier, and an owner would do well to investigate the best type for this boat.

Winches

Just as windlasses have become more available and more sophisticated, winches are now available with refinements that were not heard of several years ago. Of course, one of the major advances was the self-tailing winch, which makes trimming so much simpler, especially for a shorthanded, low-muscled cruising crew. Guests aboard our boats, trying to be helpful, would leap forward to help tail off a winch and would end up with a silly grin when they saw the line tailing off by itself. There are winches of every size and function imaginable; the important thing is planning their proper placement so that they can be used most efficiently. A look through one of Barient or Lewmar's catalogs can give a good idea of the variety and choice there is in the winch field. For those who want the utmost in comfort and ease of control, electric and hydraulic winches are available. A boat with roller furling gear on main and jib, worked by electric winches, can be operated with ease from the cockpit.

One type of winch that has fortunately gone out of favor but is still seen occasionally, especially on European and Australian boats, is the reel winch for halyards. These are dangerous contraptions that should be avoided if at all possible.

Biminis and Awnings

Moving from working gear to amenities, the subject of awnings, tops, Biminis and the like is one that has been given added attention in recent years. With the increased awareness of what the sun can do to human skin, which becomes increasingly evident as one grows older, there is new concern about protection from the sun in one of the most sun-exposed activities of all—sailing. Racing boats cannot afford to have impedimenta in the way of racing efficiency, but an awning is an important adjunct to sensible cruising comfort. In the nine years we used *Brunelle* in the Caribbean, we never once took the Bimini down when she was in commission, and we became quite used to this under-cover sailing. When sailing in New Zealand after that, where the sun is extremely bright and clear, though not tropical, we felt naked and exposed when there was no top over us. It was not only tough on the skin, it was particularly hard on the eyes. I normally get along without dark glasses, but I had to use them there. The business of not being able to look directly up at the sails soon stops being a problem. It is not a great chore to take an occasional gander around the side or back of the Bimini to make sure the main is OK., and many boats do have a window in the Bimini. *Helios* has one, but I seldom find myself look-ing through it. She has a permanent hardtop roof, with a cloth exten-sion that rolls out aft when desired.

If a Bimini is to be used, it is worth it to get a good, sturdy one specially fitted for the boat rather than a flimsy, flat canopy that some boats have. It should be collapsible without a wrestling match, and a helpful accessory can be to have a dodger curtain with see-throughs that snaps on the forward end of the main cloth. Side curtains for late afternoon sun slants are another pleasant addition. A lot of this depends, of course, on the cruising area. In northern climes, where the sun does not have the authority of tropical intensity, a Bimini is nowhere near as important, but it still can be very helpful on days of full sun. We were once very grateful for an awning over us during a heat wave on Lake Champlain in late August.

Having a permanent Bimini for use while sailing means that the rig has to be designed to accommodate to its presence. Many boats designed before Biminis became prevalent did not have space below the boom to rig one while sailing. This meant the fuss and feathers of rigging an awning over the boom, with all the attendant tying of lashings, if shade was desired in port.

A Bimini can come in handy in cool-weather cruising, when side panels can be rigged, making an enclosed "doghouse" out of the whole setup. This sort of arrangement can be very pleasant in colder cli-mates, and I have seen it quite often on boats negotiating the Intra-coastal Waterway in cool autumn and spring weather. Of course a permanent doghouse can be considered if there is going to be much operating in cold weather or in rough offshore conditions. When I used the remote autopilot mentioned in Chapter IX, it was very helpful to be hunched under a dodger instead of out in the face of a cold, rainy northeaster.

On some live-aboards I have seen in southern waters, practically the whole boat is enclosed in bow-to-stern awnings with side drops to ward off the effects of the sun. With a rig like this it probably takes about two days' notice to get underway. A boat I was a guest on once dragged anchor out into open water while no one was on board (I did NOT do the anchoring). She had a large awning with side curtains rigged from mast to stern, and instead of drifting off dead to leeward, when found some 20 hours later by helicopter, she had forereached quite a bit at an angle to the wind with the mammoth awning acting somewhat as a sail.

Swimming Arrangements and Deck Showers

One of the joys of cruising in most places (but not the Gulf of Maine or Scandinavian waters) is a swim over the side at a lunch stop or after a pleasant day's sail. This is especially true of tropical waters, where snorkeling is a big attraction, too, but it is an important adjunct to cruising in almost all areas. This means a swimming ladder of some sort, and there have been helpful advances in this department in recent years. For years on my own boats, we put up with portable ladders lashed to the lifelines and wrestled into position for each swim. We found that rope ladders were a snare and a delusion, and a ladder should be rigid to work best. Finding the right spot for it, working out its ties, putting nuts and bolts into small deck fittings to hold it in place (and dropping them overboard every so often) got to be quite a nuisance. We really began to live when a bunch of our repeater guests on *Brunelle* got together and gave us a permanently installed ladder for the transom. What a difference! Of course, this can only be done on a boat with a flat transom. *Helios* has a sloped transom, and we still have to rig a portable ladder.

Another one of those items that make you wonder why it took so long for someone to come up with it is the built-in swimming ladder in the transom, a permanent set of steps and a small platform, reached by a hinged gate. This is a real amenity for a cruising boat, and very popular with those who have used them. Along with this, many boats with this arrangement have an outlet for a portable shower hose right at the transom, so the emerging swimmer can sluice off right there, followed by towel work, without slurping water all over the cockpit and the cabin. The built-in ladder is also a real safety factor in recovering a man overboard.

We did not have this shower rig, but we did acquire one of those black plastic shower bags with a gravity-fed hose controlled by a clamp. Left on deck in the sun for a remarkably short time before being hung in the rigging, it would absorb enough warmth to provide a hot shower, again much better than tracking down below. Another arrangement for having a shower on deck is to have a hose long enough on the shower in the head so that it can be passed on deck through a port or hatch.

We kept snorkeling gear aboard for guest use, and we also had a glass-bottom bucket for those who wanted to see underwater sights without the rigmarole of snorkel breathing. Using it in the dinghy while drifting over coral heads gave almost as good a view as in swimming. As I said, we called it "sissy snorkeling," and it was very popular.

The Dinghy

This is a vital adjunct to any cruising boat, and always something of a problem. Unless the "mother ship" is big enough to carry a dinghy easily and comfortably on deck without preempting importance space, the question of what to do about a dink is a tough one. Of course, if most of your sailing is to be in relatively protected waters, with no long, open-water passages, the best thing is to have a sturdy dinghy that tows easily. Charter boats in southern waters are all equipped this way, and the more or less standard type of rigid dinghy in use for this

is one of 10 to 12 feet, with good beam, a hard-chine model with flared bow and a broad run aft for good towing and load carrying. There are still problems with this arrangement. The charter boat companies clamp the outboard motor on the dinghy's transom to be left there all the time, but many private owners prefer to go through the nuisance of bringing it on board and clamping it on a bracket somewhere back on the fantail. Another problem is stowage of gas tanks or jerry cans on board, best done out on the transom or lashed down in the dink. It helps to figure out the right distance astern for towing, often at the third wave of the wake.

Most rigid dinghies are too big to bring aboard a boat under, say, 50 feet, as there is seldom that kind of deck space available. Even a smaller dinghy for private use must have a bridle for lifting by halyard, and it amounts to a two-man job. Some owners use davits over the transom, which presents a problem of weight balance, visiblity aft, and, in an extreme following sea, the danger of having the dinghy filled by a pooping wave. Edson, the steering gear equipment company, has dinghy handling systems for both hard and inflatable dinks. The Sattler Co., of Copley, Ohio, has davits called Easy Hold that keep an inflatable dinghy flat against the transom and pushpit. Boats with a stern swimming platform can carry the dink on its side on the platform secured to the pushpit stanchions.

On both *Tanagra* and *Brunelle* we had the same nine-foot Avon inflatable that did the job for us for 13 years, given that she was not a very good rowboat. We did not have an outboard, mainly for the aforementioned reason of stowage of the engine and gas on board. Now there are 12-lb., 1.5-h.p. outboards (Cruise n' Carry), so at least some of that inconvenience can be mitigated. Our big plus was that flat section of cabin top, afforded by the raised-deck construction, was perfect for stowing the Avon, and also the fact that I could launch and retrieve her by myself with no sweat.

Safety Gear

Life jackets are legally required, and, if children are aboard, might be required for wearing, depending on their swimming ability and the conditions of the moment. In any event, jackets should be comfortable to wear and resistant to mildew and dampness, as they will inevitably be stowed without use or airing for long periods of time. Where they are stowed is a matter of each boat's layout and locker arrangement, but everyone on board should know where they are.

A man-overboard horseshoe or ring, with marker pole and strobe light, is vital equipment on all cruising boats, properly mounted near the stern and easy to be freed and thrown. Everyone on board should know the essentials, as it just might be the skipper who has to have it thrown to him. Port Supply of Watsonville, California, has a special overboard rescue system called Lifesling that delivers 20 pounds of flotation to the person, plus a retrieval line and assists for getting the person back on board, which is difficult on boats without permanently built-in ladders.

For offshore work, or for night work even in confined waters, safety harnesses should be available for any crew having to leave the cockpit. For example, Lirakis Safety Harnesses of Newport, Rhode Island, has a safety line that automatically keeps the head up for towing and a positive locking hook rated at 4,850 pounds.

Unless offshore work is intended, a life raft is not needed on a cruising boat, especially if the dinghy is an inflatable. For offshore voyaging, this special subject should be carefully investigated.

Flotation cushions, while not official safety gear, are good to have around, as they are the easiest thing to throw quickly, and help serve as markers in a man-overboard situation. In the meantime, they are handy backrests in the cockpit, especially on boats that do not have a high enough backrest. An all-day sail in a cockpit without proper back support can be unpleasantly tiring, and I have had it bring on back trouble. The seat cushions should also be comfortable, and it is false economy to get anything but the best, as they take a tremendous beating.

Which more or less gets us into the boat housekeeping department, the next thing to look at.

XI

Boat Housekeeping

*Bunks, refrigeration, air conditioning,
heating, hot water, solar and wind energy,
odds and ends*

~~~~~~

The subject of layout and accommodations has already been discussed in the first few chapters, but there are many more details to do with living in those accommodations and making the best of them. This is what is addressed in the long list at the end of this chapter. I remember going to a department store in Tampa to equip *Brunelle* before her commissioning and thinking how unromantic it was to be buying dish-cloths, pot scrubbers and can openers for our glamorous new boat. Cruising should not be roughing it, and the more attention that is paid to the details and arrangements of housekeeping, the more at home everyone will feel while on board.

In Chapter II, one of the items I listed in the instructions to guests was that everything belonged in a specific place and should always be returned there. It is amazing on something as compact as a 37-foot sailboat how easily things could be mislaid if they were not put back in their proper place, and this simple rule is one of the important ones for harmonious living aboard. Of course, I have reached the age where I can lose my glasses case every two minutes, but that's a bit different. Incidentally, I always have two pairs of reading glasses on board on the theory that I can usually find at least one of them.

Bunks

I have already pointed out how important good bunks are, both in size and accessibility. *Mar Claro*, for example, at only 24 feet, had good 6'4" bunks that were full-size in every way. We had large male friends aboard, football coaches and other husky types, but they were not cramped. Also, as stated, awkward access can be very annoying, with the "pigeonhole" type berth the worst offender. We had fitted sheets for the bunks on *Brunelle*, which Jane tailored herself. These made making up the bunks easy. We had Dacron blankets, but they were hardly ever used in the Caribbean. In northern cruising, sleeping bags can be a good idea.

Bunk mattress covers take a beating, and the right material is important. On *Tanagra*, the material was a rather loose weave of non-synthetic cloth and it wore out quickly, in less than two years. *Brunelle's* material was a tightly woven synthetic with a nubbly surface that showed no signs of wear after nine seasons, and it is certainly worth getting the right stuff for this job. Foam pillows are best to limit moisture absorption.

For those who would like some style with their bunk bedding, there are "designer" sleeping bags. Marine bedding is now made a choice of shapes and models that can be arranged as a double sleeping bag, single sleeping bags, or separated at the shoulders and joined at the legs to be opened from underneath, jointly or individually. There are many designs and patterns, fitted sheets for triangular and tapered bunk mattresses, and pack-bags for coming aboard with soft luggage.

It always annoys me to come aboard a boat in which there has been very little thought given to bunk placement, or, if any time at all is to be spent aboard, to a good setup for reading. Lights should be carefully placed for this, one for each bunk, well-directed to the individual bunk and shaded from the neighboring one.

The Galley

Whole books have been written on this subject, and it deserves that kind of attention. I don't propose to offer recipes here, and I have already talked about my ideas about keeping galley operations as simple as possible. On the average, women do not come cruising to spend all their time over a stove. Some men like to put on a big chef show, but, barring the exceptions who love to show off their cooking and spend time at it, the galley should be an efficient, easy place to operate. I have owned up in previous chapters to my "expertise" with Sterno stoves (as long as the meal is corned beef hash and canned peas), and that is certainly starting at the bottom with the simplest kind of cooking. One thing I learned early about Sterno is that it does not have a flame hot enough to cook frozen foods in any reasonable time. We used it on *Mar Claro* because the kids sometimes used the boat on

their own when they were in their teens, and I figured it was the safest and simplest for them. Somehow, Robby still managed to scorch the overhead with it, but there were no real disasters. It is a very limited form of cooking.

The old alcohol pressure stove that was virtually standard for so many years, and was the bane of Jane's existence on *Tanagra*, is not seen as much any more. It was certainly a frustrating, nerve-wracking way to cook, having to pump the pressure up and try to make the recalcitrant thing behave.

Propane has moved in as the preferred fuel, and well-engineered systems, with double safety switches, are important because of its volatility if it leaks. Propane settles in the lowest area and remains highly explosive, so the system must be virtually foolproof. It is an excellent cooking method, and propane refills are generally available in most cruising areas. Sometimes there is a problem with finding a depot to refill aluminum tanks. Location of the tanks is important, and governed by law. A vented compartment on deck or at the stern is the usual installation. Recently a lighter-than-air gas (CNG) has been introduced that does not gather in the lowest area if it leaks, and this may very well be the gas of the future.

Some boats are equipped with electric stoves, but the drawback here is that the engine or a generator must be running while the stove is on, since the load is too much for batteries. To keep the cook happy, stoves should always be gimballed for ease of cooking underway. A one-burner gimballed stove, bulkhead mounted, is a good way to provide one hot dish, soup or stew, while underway.

The other form of cooking that is popular on cruising boats is the hibachi or grill, rigged at the stern. This is the nautical version of patio cooking in suburbia and some people love it (I'm not one of them) because the old struggle to get the charcoal lit is no longer necessary. There are now grills that are hooded to cut down the effect of the wind, and charcoal comes in cardboard packages that are easy to light. Propane is also now available for hibachis, doing away altogether with the fuss over charcoal.

It is important to have good, manageable pots and pans that are

sturdy, easy to clean, durable, and of the right size for the burners on
the stove. The rest of the gear that goes with eating is important, too.
It is not a good idea to have china plates and cups, real glass glasses,
or silver cutlery. China and glass break, and silver is hard to keep
clean. Attractive plates, bowls, mugs, and cups are available in plastic,
and plastic thermal glasses make a lot of sense. Some people use mostly
paper plates and cups, which simplifies dishwashing but complicates
garbage disposal. Stainless steel knives, forks, and spoons make a lot of
sense. So do dish drainers made especially for boats, and nonskid gal-
leyware.

Garbage is always a problem, and control of it is more important
than ever in these environmentally conscious days. Cruising in the
Med, I have been horrified to see the amount of garbage, including
plastic, that is thrown overboard as a routine matter by otherwise
knowledgeable yachtsmen. Fortunately, there is more awareness of this
problem in the Western Hemisphere, and provisions for garbage disposal are available in most popular cruising areas. Marion, Massachusetts, for example, has a garbage float in the middle of the harbor, and
many other harbors have garbage collection service. Plastic bags are
the answer to handling it on board, and it usually helps to separate wet
and dry garbage. As noted, we used a product called Rack Sack that is
very handy. It is an open-bottom wire basket that can be hung up
under the sink, and it is supplied by a roll of plastic bags. When the
one in use is full, it is taken out and torn off the roll and the next bag,
which is underneath on the roll's continuous string of bags separated
by perforated tear strips, is pulled up and placed in the basket, a neat
method that saves stowage space.

Food storage should be done carefully. Some people put cans in the
bilge, but this is not a good ideal unless they are indelibly marked with
a code, as the labels will inevitably come off. With a three-compart-
ment refrigerator in *Brunelle*, we put meats and other perishables in
the freezer compartment, along with frozen foods, and then had a
definite system for what went into the other two compartments so we
always knew where to look for eggs, vegetables, fruit, cheese, or whatever. Since the compartments were deep, we had dishwashing trays

wedged into each compartment, overlapping slightly so that more than one could be used, to keep the food organized and to make getting at it easier. As for the crockery, cutlery, etc., everything had a specific place, but sometimes helpful guests would put things away differently, leading to some confusion the next time around.

Refrigeration

As a part of the galley area, refrigeration is naturally an important subject, and wonderful advances have been made in relatively recent times. *Tanagra*, for example, did not have mechanical refrigeration, but she did have a huge, well-insulated icebox. When we cruised in the Bahamas we would buy the largest bag of ice available and it would last quite a few days, even in the warm climate. In small boats like *Mar Claro* and our catboat, portable ice chests are the answer because they do not take up permanent space and can be stowed under a cockpit seat, for example.

However, mechanical refrigeration is readily available now and is not a complicated problem. From what I have seen, the most practical solution seems to be to have a 12-volt system that works off the main engine, rather than a separate generator. In *Brunelle* this meant running the engine an hour a day to activate the compressor, and we tried to organize this so that it would coincide with our time for getting underway in the morning. We would start the main engine so that the business of getting the anchor up or leaving a marina slip and making sail would be going on while the refrigerator was charging. Some refrigerators require two hours a day, which means another hour in the evening, not a good adjunct to happy hour.

Air Conditioning and Heating

Although it is available, air conditioning on a cruising sailboat is more trouble than it is worth in my book. Even in the hottest tropical areas, it is better to use wind scoops and fans and to have natural air than to be cooped up in an artificial atmosphere. Also, to work properly, air conditioning is a tremendous drain on a boat's electrical system, and a generator is almost a must. One situation in which air conditioning might be justified is in marina living in a hot climate, where air circulation in the marina is poor, and the system can be hooked up to shore power.

More important in many areas is some form of cabin heating. For spring and fall in northern areas of the United States, for ICW passages in those seasons, and for that cold, clammy, foggy evening almost anywhere, a cabin heater is a very welcome addition. The traditional Shipmate miniature potbelly stove for coal, wood, or oil, has been a favorite for years of yachtsmen in cool climates and commercial fisherman who operate in all seasons. It is now joined by more modern cabin heaters for kerosene or diesel, and wood, charcoal, or coal, and Shipmate now makes an open fireplace for coal, wood, or charcoal. We used a kerosene heater in *Tanagra* and were very happy to have it on some ICW trips, and we even used it in Florida in a cold spell. Ocean Options, Inc. of Fairhaven, Massachusetts, has an Espar diesel-fired cabin heating system. Balmar Products of Seattle, a stove manufacturer, also offers diesel or kerosene cabin heaters that use outside combustion air, avoiding depletion of interior cabin air.

Hot Water

Wolter Systems of Cincinnati has a forced-air cabin heater that utilizes heat from a hot water heater, which brings us to the allied subject of heating water, an important amenity. Most boats only have hot water available after the engine has been running or when on shore power, but it is possible to have a continuous supply. Wolter's Model 300 gas heater provides a continuous flow of hot water in a fully automatic system. There is no pilot light and water is heated only when the faucet is turned on. Allcraft Corp., West Newton, Massachusetts, has a stainless 12-gallon heater that provides hot water from the engine in 15 minutes through a copper/bronze heat exchanger and, with two-inch insulation, can hold heat overnight for morning use.

Another method of obtaining hot water is from solar panels built into a deck hatch. We cruised in a Freedom 40 that had this system (since it had no engine) and it worked very well, depending, of course, on the amount of sunshine.

Natural Energy Sources

There is a growing use of solar panels for battery charging, and it is also a common sight to see boats equipped with wind generators for the same purpose, using what nature provides free. A Hylas 47 we sailed in in Thailand had good results from solar panels mounted on each side of the pushpit, maintaining a continuous recharge. Golden Glow Solar Electricity of San Carlos, California, has flexible, shatter-proof portable panels that can be put on deck when needed and stowed under a bunk when not in use. Offshore Marine Systems in Severna Park, Maryland, makes a 30-watt Solar Electric Generator whose panels can be mounted anywhere on deck. It uses semicrystalline silicon cells like those used in the space industry.

Offshore Systems also has a Rutland wind generator that starts charging at 3½ knots of wind and has a special anti-vibration mounting that prevents transmission of noise to the hull. The noise of wind generators is one of their problems, as they can be heard around the anchorage as well as on board, but they can be braked if need be. Another model is Windbugger, of Key Largo, Florida, that rotates 360 degrees and produces one amp at five to six knots and seven-plus at 15.

Jack Rabbit Marine in New Rochelle, New York, has a hybrid electric system that incorporates wind, water, or solar generators plus a high-capacity engine alternator, taking advantage of all the methods in one system.

Water Making

Along with heating water comes the question of making it, and boats that are away from easy shore water supply can be equipped with their own water-making system via several different methods. Sea Recovery of Gardena, California, uses the reverse osmosis process for converting sea water to potable water by using pressure to force it through a sem-ipermeable membrane and then through a charcoal filter and an ultra-violet sterilizer, to put a complicated process into a few words. Pilot's Point Special Products in Westbrook, Connecticut, makes the Village Marine systems starting with a capacity as low as eight gallons an hour using the reverse osmosis method. ASC Marine Systems of Compton, California, has an engine-driven desalinator and an AC-powered Atlantis model. All these systems of desalinization are intended for good-sized, sophisticated boats.

To purify existing water on board, H_2O Purification, Inc., in Fair-field, Connecticut, has a Sea Gull IV system that removes impurities. It is six inches high and weighs five pounds. The filter normally needs replacing about once a year.

Odds and Ends

All the above only begins to cover the items that can be used on a boat according to individual tastes and needs. Just look at the catalog of one of the big suppliers to get an idea of the multitude of material that is available in every department from masthead to bilge and all through the cockpit, deck, and cabin.

A small vacuum cleaner is a handy thing to have on a boat, espe-cially if the boat is lived in for long periods of time. It is amazing how much dust, dirt, and sand can accumulate even in the clean marine atmosphere. We had a midget vacuum that only worked on 110-volt so we had to be plugged in to shore power to use it, but there is a 12-volt model called Wet-Dry Vac from National Marketing & Sales in Davie, Florida, that works from a 12-volt outlet with a 16-ft. cord. It works for both wet and dry jobs and can suck water out of the bilge as well as clean upholstery.

Speaking of shore power, it is certainly worth it to have a shore connection hookup for using 110-volt equipment (although the inverter on *Helios* fills this function), doing away with battery worries for the time being. A helpful accessory is a Constavolt battery charger, which trickle-charges the boat's 12-volt system while the boat is on shore power. A portable radio-tape player that can work on its own batteries or on a 110 plug-in makes a simple "entertainment center" wherever the boat is.

A cockpit table is an important adjunct to living aboard. It must be collapsible or portable so that it does not interfere with sailing action. As I mentioned, in nine seasons in *Brunelle* in the Caribbean, we almost never ate below, and the cockpit table, a portable one that stowed in our cabin when we were sailing, was the center of our activities in port. *Helios* has a folding one that rests against the binnacle when in the down position.

A cockpit light is a necessity, and there are many ways of having one. We used to use a portable battery-powered lantern suspended from the Bimini, while some people rig one on an extension cord from below. With her hard top, *Helios* has a built-in light.

In many areas, screens are necessary, if a nuisance. Some boats have them fitted for hatches and ports, which presents a maintenance problem after a while, and a general bother when moving in and out of companionways. An alternative is to have soft screens that can be rolled up, with Velcro attachments, so that they can be in place when needed and easy to stow when not. No boat should be without insect repellent, and, in tropical areas, cockroaches are an ever-present problem. Never bringing grocery cartons and boxes aboard can help keep them off, but any time a boat is at a pier for any length of time, it is very likely that the unwelcome visitors will somehow find their way aboard. We always ordered a fumigation before starting a season.

Hatches and ports and the hardware to operate them must be given some thought. The strength and contour of hatches is an important consideration. They are stomped on fairly often when the crew is bouncing around the deck handling sails, and unless they fit snugly to the deck, their corners can catch sheets or trip toes. A very handy development is the kind of hatch support that simply works by friction, without any tightening of knobs. The hatch is just pushed up and it stays there, and it can be pulled down quickly when that sudden rain squall calls for a fast closing. The old standby, Dorade vents, are a welcome aid to ventilation when the hatches have to be shut in wet weather. A new wrinkle in vents is the Water Trap from Nicro Corp. of San Francisco. This is a vent with a spring-loaded damper that seals off the opening if green water makes its way into the cowl. Once the water drains off, the damper opens automatically, resuming air circulation. The cowl can be rotated 360 degrees.

In many modern boats, the ports are set in a contoured area, putting them on a slant instead of vertical and making them excellent water catchers. Opening them then produces a small shower bath, but this can be partially prevented by the use of a port hood from Sailing Specialties in Hollywood, Maryland. The hood's flexible, molded rubber fits on the porthole trim ring and allows ports to be left open for ventilation when rain is coming straight down (not blowing on a slant). The old method of dogging ports, time consuming when action must be quick, can be avoided by using a Cam Latch from Beckson Marine of Bridgeport, Connecticut, which works with one 180-degree twist.

And finally, although the gadget list could go on for pages more, a word about interior decoration. There has been a trend, especially on boats set up for exhibiting at boat shows, to do some fancy decorating down below. The Pearson 37 was an unabashed example of this, with an open layout designed for partying, soft pastel colors, indirect lighting, contoured "furniture," and designer fabrics. Not to knock it for those who delight in a lifestyle that goes with this kind of thinking, I would say that only a minority of owners would want this, and most prefer a simple, efficient cabin that is pleasant to be in without being intrusive. I have been in boats that had very dark woodwork and fabrics, which to me breeds a claustrophobic atmosphere. A sailboat cabin is confined enough, and everything possible should be done to give a feeling of lightness and space, with white or light colored bulkheads, blond wood trim and neutral fabrics that are easy to live with for a length of time. This is admittedly in the realm of personal taste. I'll never forget going aboard a replica of Joshua Slocum's *Spray*, newly built but faithful to the old-fashioned rig and deck gear, and then going below to find a chintzy cabin with ruffles and lace as the main decorating features. The skipper's wife, pointing with pride to her decorating, said, "This is all mine. This is my apartment. Daddy can have his boat things upstairs, but downstairs is mine." So be it, to each his own.

As for the knottily unpleasant subject of heads, about the only advice I can give, considering the current state of the laws governing them, is to comply with regulations but provide for bypassing capacity for operation in areas where the laws do not apply, or where there are no pump-out facilities.

A & B Industries of Corte Madera, California, which provides all sorts of gadgets to the marine trade (deck plate keys, a wide range of blocks, bronze ports, latches, catches, and hooks), and whose windlasses were mentioned in Chapter X, comes up with new ideas every so often of the "why didn't anyone think of this?" variety. Among these are an anchor chain controller; a flush-mounted deck water pressure fitting used for deck wash down or shoreside water pressure hookup; and an engine water intake strainer with an easily removed cast bronze cap that can be lifted out for inspection and cleaning. Another recent item is a cast bronze cockpit scupper with a removable grate for easy cleaning. A rectangular deck prism of polished bronze, chrome, or stainless, with heavy glass, lights up dark cabin interiors, and three models of an anchor chute with roller have quick release, removable anchor lock pins. There is even an anchor roller lead for the stern, for ease of fore-and-aft anchoring or anchoring by the stern.

The A & B list goes on to things like coat hooks, toilet paper holders and soap dishes, compass guards, fog bells, boat hooks, oarlocks, locker vents, drawer pulls, and switch panels, to name just a few. It does bring home the conviction that a tremendous number of items are needed for the well-equipped cruising yacht. Just make sure there is room for them.

A Sample Equipment List for Cruising

Anchor rodes (two)
Anchors (two)
Ammeter
Anemometer, handheld
Ashtrays, beanbag
Awning or Bimini for cockpit
Batteries, two sets of 12-volt
Bilge pump, manual
Binoculars
Blankets, all bunks
Boat hook
Brushes
   longhandled scrub
   whisk broom
   dust pan
Chafing gear on lines
Clothes hangers, nonmetal
Clothespins
Compass, binnacle and hand
   held
Courtesy flags
Cushions
   cockpit seats
   flotation
Dinghy
   towrope
   oars and oarlocks
   outboard and gas can
Dishcloths and towels
Dish rack
Dock lines
Electronics, as desired

Fenders
Fire extinguishers
First aid kit, sunburn creams
Fishing gear
Flares
Flashlights
Flippers, mask and snorkel
Flyswatter
Fog bell
Foghorn
Fuel measuring stick
Funnels, water and fuel
Galley gear
   butter box
   coffee pot
   can opener
   bottle opener
   corkscrew
   double boiler
   frying pan
   funnel
   glasses
   ice pick
   cups
   juice squeezer
   juice containers
   knives, carving and paring
   plates and saucers
   soup bowls or mugs
   mixing bowls
   peeler
   pot holders

pressure cooker
sponges
sugar bowl
spoons, knives, forks
toaster, burner-top type
spatula
Insect spray and repellent
Lead line
Life preservers
Light bulbs, extra
Mattresses
Mirrors
Navigation gear
   charts
   guides
   dividers
   parallel rulers
   pencils
Pillowcases
Pillows

Screens
Sheets for bunks
Swimming ladder
Tool kit
   basic tools
   nuts and bolts
   tape
   cord
   cotter pins
   glue and cement
   WD-40
   sandpaper
   fuses
   engine spares
   gaskets, filters
Totebag for ice, groceries
Towels, hand and bath
Washcloths
Water jugs
Wind scoop for hatches

XII

Clothing

Fair weather and foul; footwear

Once, while meeting arriving guests at Beef Island Airport in the British Virgins, I happened to stand at the fence, waiting for the plane to arrive, next to a charter boat captain, and I asked him if he was meeting new guests.

"No," he said. "They're already here, but their luggage didn't make it, and it's supposed to be on this plane. They're all upset, but I keep telling them not to worry; all they really need is a T-shirt and a bathing suit."

Southern Sailing Clothes

This is so very true of Caribbean sailing, and if that were the only place people sailed, there would not be much material for this chapter. In the Caribbean, that is a sensible costume, although there is of course the necessity for protective clothing like sun hats, long-sleeved shirts, and long pants for those who have not yet developed a suntan. For going ashore, men can get along with sport shirts and light slacks, women with blouses and skirts (in some areas, women in shorts offend the natives), and only the lightest sweater or windbreaker might be needed for the occasional cool evening.

One feature of the weather that often fools newcomers is the sudden quick drop in temperature at sunset, when the sun's heat goes out of the air and the breeze is still blowing. This can have the same effect as walking into an air conditioned building from a warm street. The first shock seems colder than it is, but it is really only a drop from the 80s into perhaps the mid-70s. People grab sweaters and feel cold, but the body soon adapts to the new temperature, which really is in fact quite comfortable.

In the many years we have spent in the Caribbean and in other warm sailing areas, we've gotten along with "a T-shirt and a bathing suit" almost completely. I wear polo shirts, always white during the daytime when there is sun, as dark ones really absorb the heat, and for shorts I am partial to something called jams. These originated in Antigua, I believe, and they are simply Bermuda-length shorts of bathing suit material with a lining, held up by a drawstring (and with no fly). They are comfortable with good freedom of motion as shorts, and they double easily as a bathing suit. If a shower comes over, there is no problem about getting them wet. Daughter Martha has become adept at making them, and she has been my "tailor" for many seasons now. I also wear the same costume almost daily at home in New Jersey in the summer. It makes getting up in the morning a simple act. Combined with flip-flops for footwear, getting dressed does not take very long.

I wear regular pocketed shorts or khaki pants for Caribbean food-shopping excursions, as jams are not very good for carrying wallets and glasses, and I always switch from flip-flops to regular deck shoes when we are underway. Maybe I am extra clumsy, but I think bare feet or sandals are a danger in moving around the deck, where cleats lie in wait to jam between toes. My flip-flops have boating soles, so they are OK for moving around the deck in port.

You do need a good supply of clean shirts or frequent access to laundry, as the perspiration quotient is high in a tropical climate, and it soon becomes a bit tough to stand yourself in a well lived-in shirt, not to mention the effect on other people. Actually, laundry is not a problem in most Caribbean areas, as there are laundromats in most places, machines in marinas, and local services.

We sail in other areas, however, including some rather cold climates, and the proper clothing makes a tremendous difference in making cruising pleasant. The old image of a "yachtsman" in blue blazer, white pants, and peaked cap is only carried on by race committees and club flag officers at formal occasions, and perhaps by owners of 200-foot power yachts, and in ads for expensive Scotch. This is not the kind of clothing I mean.

Sensible Wear

There are specialty stores for "nautical wear," and it is possible to get togged out in all sorts of colorful items that would probably do better on a golf course or at a gambling casino. In reality, an Army-Navy store, now something of a vanishing breed, would be a far better place. Boating clothes should be tough, comfortable, and easy to wash, whether khaki pants and denims, polo shirts, T-shirts, sweaters, or windbreakers.

Almost anything goes that is comfortable when the weather is warm. It is when the breeze begins to blow with a nip in it that some thought should be given to proper wear. While a sweater is usually the first item put on when this happens, it often is not the best idea. Because of its relatively open weave, a sweater can be penetrated by the wind. There are, of course, fisherman's sweaters of heavy weave and moisture-resistant wool that do well as windbreakers, but these are usually heavier than is needed in the first onset of a bit of wind. A good move is to put on a light sweater and a light windbreaker, or just the windbreaker, at the first need for warmth. By light windbreaker, I mean just an unlined cloth jacket that lives up to its name.

When there is more of a nip, a good, lined windbreaker or parka can make all the difference, and, combined with a sweater with a high neck, can handle quite low temperatures. A windbreaker I acquired in Sweden when cruising there, where they are very familiar with cold weather cruising, has been ideal for this. It is light in actual weight, but it is well lined, very wind-resistant and extremely comfortable. There is an almost automatic impulse to snuggle down in it.

Just as important to avoid is heat loss through the head and hands. If a warm cap and gloves are worn, it is much easier to maintain body warmth and stay comfortable, as these are areas where the body's heat loss is most pronounced. Very often, clothing for other sports, such as skiing, can be adapted to sailing in these off-season conditions.

The question of clothing also involves luggage, and, as I have already pointed out before, soft luggage that can be easily stowed is important on a boat, and it is a cardinal sin to arrive with heavy, stiff suitcases. In flying to join a cruising boat, it is often possible to fit a piece of soft luggage capable of carrying a lot of clothes under the seat or in an overhead bin. It is great to be able to have all gear as hand luggage, avoiding worries about checked baggage.

Foul Weather Gear

Of paramount importance in cruising, especially in climates where cold, rainy weather can be expected, is good foul weather gear. As I have already pointed out, it is not terribly important in southern waters. We seldom bothered with it in the Caribbean except in really heavy rain periods, and in the whole nine seasons, Jane and I never broke out our sea boots. The opposite is true in northern waters and in off-shore passages, where foul weather gear is vital. There is a great measure of self-satisfaction in being out in nasty conditions and still being comfortable and warm.

The problem here is the basic question of what is good foul weather gear. Even experts in the field admit that the problem has yet to be licked to anyone's complete satisfaction. All sorts of experiments have been carried out with modern synthetic materials, and although questions remain, there certainly have been advances. No one wears "oil-skins" any more, the original foul weather gear of commercial fishermen, and pure rubber is not used much. It is great at shedding water, but it is also very effective at keeping moisture in.

This is where the real problem lies. There are many materials that can repel a downpour, but when they have to be lived in for hours at a time, with the human body exuding its own moisture, there is another side to the situation. The question is how to let the moisture escape before the inside of the foul weather gear becomes just as wet as the rain-soaked outside.

Materials that breathe, like Gore-tex, have worked for people who, like joggers or farm workers, remain upright and the material also adapts quite well to a freshwater environment, but salt water has a different effect during any sedentary period, such as taking a wheel watch or simply sitting in the cockpit. The extra clogging effect of salt in the water, and a lack of motion in the person wearing the gear, takes away the "breathing" ability of such material, and the old problem of interior condensation is still there. Great Lakes sailors have had more success with breathable gear, but saltwater sailors still have a problem.

The idea of these new materials is to repel outer moisture, like rain or spray, while an inner lining that absorbs body moisture passes it through and out the outer layer. The system works to some extent. There are also ways to combat the problem by adapting to the immediate situation. It helps to have a "chimney effect," an opening at the neck to let body moisture escape that way. When it is not raining hard enough to pour water down the neck, or when spray is the major source of outer moisture, this idea can help. Also, if there is water on deck but not a heavy amount in the air, it can be helpful just to wear foul weather pants, with a windbreaker top (perhaps at least a water repellent one if not an impervious one) and the body moisture will again escape through the neck opening. Of course when it is really pouring, and full gear is worn, it is more important to wear a towel around the neck to keep driving water from making its way down. No one has ever really solved the problem of water down the neck in heavy rain by any better method than wearing a towel.

A great deal was learned about foul weather gear at the 1987 America's Cup in the continuously wet sailing off Fremantle, Australia, where crews were almost constantly subjected to heavy spray and were almost always in foul weather gear of some sort. Since the weather was not very cold, the main question was protection, not warmth. Some of the sailors wore a light repellent garment called a dry top, with a rubber seal at neck and wrists, over just a T-shirt and shorts, and most of them found that heavily publicized and touted gear just did not

stand up under the extreme conditions of heavy action and constant dousings in spray. Although some syndicates had foul weather gear manufacturers as sponsors and were supposedly committed to wear that brand, I understand that many of the crewmen switched to Henri-Lloyd products out of preference. Henri-Lloyd has a reputation, as do Musto and Line 7, a New Zealand brand that I own. I find it a bit heavy in the tropics and only wear it at night, when there is a chill in the air, or in very heavy downpours.

Footwear

Boots are of course a part of foul weather gear, and it is important to have boots with nonskid boating soles. They should be knee-high boots of light weight, easily kicked off in case of man overboard. If possible, they should only be worn on board so that the nonskid patterns in the soles do not pick up dirt, pebbles, etc., from walking on shore.

The same applies to boating shoes, although it is sometimes quite a nuisance to shift shoes before going ashore. I have found that wearing boat shoes ashore also wears them down more quickly, ruining the nonskid pattern and making them dangerously slippery. For years, Top Siders were practically the only boating shoe, with a patented nonskid sole. Supposedly this was developed when Mr. Sperry, the inventor of the shoe, watched his cocker spaniel walking across ice without skidding and realized that the fine grooves in a symmetrical pattern on the pads of his feet were what kept him from slipping. He adapted the idea to rubber soles for boat shoes with great success.

Now the Sperry patent has run out, and other manufacturers have been able to use the same kind of sole, with minor variations, and the field is wide open to competition. Timberland, Sebago, and Red Wing are all very much in the field, and the major development in recent years has not been in sole design, but in the type of leather used in the shoes.

After a great deal of experimentation, with the Norwegian army as a testing ground, and cross-country skiers in the act as well, Norwegian leather importers have developed a waterproof leather that, like good foul weather gear, breathes. This leather should not be oiled. It works well in warm or cold weather, the idea being that there are very small pores that allow inner vapor and moisture to escape, but the pores are too small for outside water to work its way in. This experimentation in leather treatment was carried on over a period of 10 years before the results were satisfactory. The secret is that surface tension on the exterior prevents the water from penetrating. If water splashes in over the top of the shoes, it will soon evaporate its way out, and the shoes do not remain wet for very long.

To complete the picture, shoes must have thick soles, and the seams must be sealed. The soles, of course, should have the nonskid pattern that is now virtually standard. As I have said, I think it is very important to wear shoes at all times when working around the deck while underway. I cringe when I see people running about in bare feet or sandals, because I know what it feels like to have a cleat jammed between the toes.

A comfortable sailor is a happy cruising sailor, and clothing and shoes play an important part in this.

XIII

Electronics

Charts, Loran, GPS,
radar, instruments, radio

~~~~~~

The subject of electronics presents a few problems. First of all, as a "keep it simple" devotee who got along well for nine seasons in my own boat with a direct-reading depth finder and a VHF as the sum total of the electronics (a single sideband radio was improperly installed and never used), it is like a tone deaf musical ignoramus writing a review of a Beethoven concert for me to pose as an electronics expert. I did have radar on my subchaser in 1944, and sonar, which is not exactly an up-to-date experience. My last non-dead reckoning navigation was also in 1944. I had a sextant and a computerized navigation program all set to take to the Caribbean in 1979, but Bahamas Airways lost the bag with the program in it, and there went that exercise.

Also, the electronics field is so fluid, with so many developments and refinements coming out almost daily, that this chapter should probably be printed in a loose-leaf binder so that updates can be added as they occur. By the time this book is printed, all sorts of new improvements and developments will no doubt be available.

However, I have done my best to research the subject, and what I can try to do is give a layman's picture of the field, the many elements in it, and what some expectations might be. The subject of navigation rightfully belongs here nowadays, as almost all navigation depends on electronics. Even piloting can now be done by radar, computers, and electronic charts. (But I still like to look over the side and make a guesstimate of what our speed is. Over the years, this method has served quite well, as have yarn telltales on shrouds as wind indicators.)

I have learned a key word in the field: miniaturization. This is the wave of the future in electronics. Items that used to be bulky, taking up a lot of space, have been scaled down to compact size, making them a practical possibility for boats that formerly could not spare the space. Another welcome trend for the owner is that prices have been coming down under the press of competition and that same miniaturization process. This does not mean that the latest hot items in the electronic field are cheap yet, just less expensive. Something that might have been about $10,000 a couple of years ago can now be had for less than half that, and usually in a more compact format.

There are three main divisions in electronics, although they sometimes overlap now as functions are streamlined into one installation. Navigation, communications, and instrumentation are the basics, and there is a constantly proliferating choice of items in all three categories. It is up to an owner to decide just how much he wants to become involved in what can be a very sophisticated field. First of all, there is the cost, which is still considerable. Then there is the involvement. Is the object to relax and go sailing, or is to sit in front of glowing panels and digital displays and act like a space cadet? Where one plans to sail is an important consideration. For world voyagers, the latest models affordable in satellite navigation and other aids to piloting and navigation are a marvelous help. In areas of frequently poor visibility, radar and Loran are an important safety consideration. If cruising is to be done by choosing fair weather and making relaxed passages between close ports, why go to all the expense and bother?

Whatever the decision, it is a fact that the electronic side of cruising has seen tremendous advances and is bound to see more, and it must be considered by each owner according to his own situation. Whatever level of sophistication is sought, consultation with experts and specialists is mandatory, starting with the question of just how much electronic load an individual boat's electrical system can handle. Power source for the equipment is important, and the careful owner will be ready with nonelectronic backups in case of power failure. Also, a separate starting battery, independent of all other loads, is a very good idea.

Instruments

When I was commissioning *Brunelle* in the late '70s, I had a profound lack of respect for digital instruments, based on experience with some very unreliable ones. Since then, advances have been made in reliability and accuracy of performance of such items as depth sounders, speed and distance recorders, and wind indicators. I was perfectly content with a direct-reading depth sounder and yarn telltales. In addition to distrust, I figured that electronics service would be hard to come by in some of the areas we would be cruising. My other objection to digital items is the difficulty in reading them without glasses. When the instruments must be read across a fairly good-sized cockpit, they are at just the wrong distance for my eyes, and I certainly don't want to be tied down to wearing glasses while sailing. Once familiarity is established with a direct-reading dial, there is no need to see the numbers. Again, this is a personal reaction, but it is something to think about.

Here are some items to consider.

Brookes & Gatehouse, long a pioneer in instrumentation, has, in the $1,000 range, a multipurpose instrument called Focus that displays boat speed and depth constantly at the top and bottom of a round screen. By simply twisting the dial, other functions come into view in the center of the screen, such as trip log, average speed, water temperature, shallow water alarm, and anchor alarm. It has a memory function that records log and depths even when the display is turned off.

Depth-speed packages from Navico and other companies are in the $500 range. Plastimo USA has "budget" items like the Digipak Range that provide total-mile log, trip log, and speed for under $400, and a more versatile Digipak CW that combines log, speed, and depth info with wind speed in both Beaufort and meters per second for a bit over $500. Portable depth finders powered by transistor radio batteries are available for as little as $89.95 from Fish Hawk Electronics, and Honde Marine Electronics has one for about $400 that can be used from the bow or in the spreaders when venturing into iffy waters as an assist to piloting by eyeball.

Magnaphase Industries has a miniature weather station with a hand-held computer, working from a wind vane and speed sensor, that tells wind speed and direction, chill factor, gust record, current and high-low temperature, rainfall, time, auto scan, and metric/standard readings for a bit over $200. These are just a few examples of what is available from many companies and in many variations.

Navigation

Although there are all sorts of electronic developments in this field, don't throw the old sextant away. Celestial navigation should still be considered basic, since power failures can occur. And with the use of preprogrammed data and hand calculators and computers to do the mathematics, modern methods have simplified the process of navigating by sun and stars.

Electronic navigation is in a state of flux. As this is written in March, 1989, the new Global Positioning Satellite (GPS) system is only partially developed. Seven satellites are in orbit, allowing partial use from seven to 12 hours a day, but more are being put into orbit, and 24-hour operation is supposed to be possible by the end of 1989, with enhanced operation from added satellites in the early 1990s. Right now, this is a pretty expensive system for the private yacht owner, somewhere around $10,000 for Magnavox's multi-function MX 5400, but prices are expected to come down when the service is complete and more manufacturers get into the act. Magellan Systems Corp. has come out with a hand-held portable GPS receiver with a small antenna attached that operates on six AA alkaline batteries and sells for about $3,000. Raytheon has also come out with Raystar 920, for about $6,000.

GPS may eventually eclipse Loran, which has been the standard electronic navigation instrument for many years, but new Loran sets continue to come out. Some of them, such as Trimble Navigation's new 10x for $2,995, allow eventual upgrading to GPS capability by simply adding extra circuitry. This would seem to be good insurance in a Loran set. New advances in Loran include conversion of complicated data into easily understood graphic displays, such as the credit-card-size chart cards that can be used to imprint cruising area chart data into the memory of Raytheon's Rayplot 700L.

Micrologic's Commander Loran C has factory-preprogrammed data on more than 14,000 lights and buoys, and pressing a key for local selection shows the 20 buoys nearest to current position, complete with a full description of the buoy's characteristics. This also works for lights. Most modern Lorans claim accuracy from 50 to 100 feet in positioning. The old phrase "navigation is not an exact science," which described celestial navigation, has just about been made obsolete by GPS, Loran, and the like. Since Loran is not operational in all parts of the world, including the Caribbean, GPS may be the answer when it is completely programmed and all satellites are in place.

A relatively new wrinkle in electronic navigation is electronic charts, which can be used by themselves on shipboard computers, interfaced with Loran receivers, or in some cases with a regular television screen. For example, Loran's 2nd Mate Chart System works on either AC or DC power and is programmed with details of chart data and marina information. A Pilot Manual Program (a computerized cruising guide) gives lists of marinas and clubs, describing facilities and services, plus rules of the road, safety, first aid, tides and currents, and updates of local *Notices to Mariners*. The equipment is about $3,000 and each chart is $95. Available charts cover most of the U.S. and the Bahamas.

Most of the chart systems available can be interfaced with existing equipment such as Loran C so that a position is immediately indicated on the chart.

Obviously, this is not the cheapest way to have a supply of charts, and the manufacturers all display that familiar warning, the same one on charts printed on place mats, that these charts do not replace regular printed navigation charts from NOAA, etc.

Radar, while a safety factor, is also a navigational function, and it has become widely accepted on cruising boats, especially those whose cruising area is subject to fog. Radar has reached a fairly advanced stage of sophistication and there have been no startling innovations in recent years. The trend, through miniaturization, is to smaller, more compact sets and antennas, increasingly suitable to smaller sailboats. New radomes about two feet across, weighing as little as 30 pounds, are well adapted to small boats, and the shape is good for sailboats since it doesn't foul halyards and topping lifts.

The old circular sweep on the radar screen, so familiar for so many years, has been replaced by a raster scanning system that puts the information on the screen in a fixed picture, all at one time. It is also possible to interface radar with Loran and have the Loran position indicated on the screen. Some sets use colors to differentiate between targets. Modern radar can discriminate between targets that are close together, and for close-in navigation and feeling one's way in a buoyed channel, for example, the ability to pick up objects close aboard is important.

Radar now gives an alarm for targets approaching, helping to avoid collisions. For cruising use, it is of greater importance to have this close-up accuracy than to have extreme range. Once radar is aboard, it is important to learn all the tricks and nuances of operating it, as correct interpretation of what it shows is of vital importance. Radar can give a sense of security, but it can also be frightening at times. I was on a tanker once coming into New York's Ambrose Channel in zero fog. The captain went to check the radar as we approached the channel entrance, turned pale, and uttered a frustrated oath, as the screen looked as though it had the measles, so numerous were the targets that lay ahead of us. Instead of moving ahead, we anchored immediately.

Electronic compasses are relatively new, called flux-gate compasses. They provide extremely accurate course reading and give great help to autopilots in following a course closely. Their accuracy at any angle of heel is important for sailboat use. KVH Industries has a new integrator option that feeds Loran information into the compass mode and thereby tells an autopilot to correct for drift on a course that has been set without allowance for wind and current.

Communications

Aboard pleasure boats, the old AM radio channels have gone the way of oilskins and kerosene lamps, and radio communications are carried on by VHF line-of-sight radio, single sideband (SSB) long-distance radio, and, for properly licensed and trained operators, ham radio. VHF is the "party line" of yachting in most of the world now, with a total of 55 channels available, but most activity confined to a few standard ones, led by Channel 16 as the contacting and emergency channel. In some areas with a high density of boats, the popular channels can become so busy that it is very hard to get time on them, and special use of lesser used channels is becoming more common.

The basics have not changed much in recent years, but there is an increased emphasis on compactness, on waterproofing, and on hand-held models. Prices range widely, from under $200 for a simple hand-held to $1,000 and up for the more sophisticated installations. It is possible to have dual band monitoring on some models, which can do away with switching after initial contact, as well as a remote microphone for cockpit use, or even a second full-function station, if the installation is below decks. Another innovation is to have a liquid crystal display (LCD) bar graph below the channel display that tells whether the set is transmitting properly.

With better waterproofing, hand-helds have gained in popularity, making it convenient for the skipper to work the VHF without having to leave the wheel, a great convenience when negotiating a tight channel or involved in heavy traffic. A boat without a VHF today is like a house without a telephone. Because of the great popularity, procedure abuses can frequently be heard, and it is important for anyone using VHF to know the correct procedures.

Since VHF's range is line of sight, long-distance voyagers and boats operating out of sight of land must resort to SSB for their radio use. As long as VHF has the range to reach a shore station, long-range communication by telephone to all land stations is possible through marine operators, but beyond that, communication is up to SSB. We had one in *Brunelle* and found it was completely unnecessary in the Caribbean where we were always within range of a shore marine operator on one of the islands. SSB has been fairly standard for years, but there are a couple of innovations that are of interest, such as ICOM's, in which owners may store their own choice of channels. The ICOM also has a remote control head that sends its signals via a ⅛-inch fiberoptic cable to the main receiver box. This type of cable is small, flexible, and can be worked through oddly shaped areas, and it does not pick up interference from the vessel's other electrical systems. As many as four remote heads can be used, and they can also serve as an intercom system if the boat is big enough to require one.

Another innovation in this field is Raytheon's SSB/Telex radio in which an error-correcting telex interface provides computerized communications worldwide. SSB prices are still quite high, and special sets like these can cost more than $3,000.

For those qualified to use it, ham radio is the best way possible for keeping in touch anywhere in the world. The ham radio fraternity is a special one that speaks its own language and that forms ham-pal relationships that are quite close and friendly among people who have never met face-to-face. Sometimes they even arrange reunions, and ham operators can always find kindred souls, often people they have communicated with, when they visit a foreign country.

I was aboard a ham operator's boat in the Chesapeake and listened to him talk to friends in Madagascar and Australia, as well as his home near Boston. It is a fascinating hobby, but it is also a very effective means of communication for boats in remote areas. Quite often, a boat in trouble is able to signal for help through some ham contact halfway across the world. It is a fraternity that sticks together and looks out for its own. Anyone contemplating a long voyage should seriously think of going through the ham operator's licensing course. It is also great fun and a convenience for those whose operations are closer to home. The gear, of course, is specialized.

Another form of communications is weather reporting that is now available on such machines as Raytheon's NCR 300-A, about the size of a Loran set with keyboard controls for $1,395. Raytheon also has a JAX 9 receiver ($3,495) that produces weather satellite charts in 16 gradation levels on 10-inch paper and can be preprogrammed for reception from as many as 100 weather stations, and preset to stop and start at any chosen broadcast time, so that it can be operated unattended.

If there is concern about theft of electronic equipment, which can certainly happen in some marinas, the gear can be locked to its brackets with a devise called Yacht-Lok from International Security Services of Hermosa Beach, California. And for the other side of the radar picture—for those who want to make sure they are seen on someone else's radar—in addition to the conventional mast-mounted radar reflectors, an item called Visiball from Kestrel Electronic Designs in Annapolis gives off uniform radar echoes regardless of angle of heel, and has a mount for an antenna or masthead tri-color light.

Part III

Worldwide Cruising Areas

Now that equipment and organization are settled, where can all this be put to use? The world is full of good cruising waters, many close to population centers, others more remote and exotic. Getting to them is a matter of time and home location. Of course it is a special thrill to take one's own boat into fascinating and challenging cruising waters, but the development in recent years of the charter industry, both bareboat and professionally crewed, has truly made cruising easy in a different context from equipping a private boat.

In both bareboat and crewed chartering, the equipment and amenities are out of the charterer's hands, already taken care of. In this respect, charter boats, to stay competitive, have been equipped with an ever-increasing sophistication of gear, and professional crews are forever developing ways to make their service more attractive. In deciding whether to bareboat or to charter a crewed yacht, several factors should be considered. Cost, of course, comes first, as crewed boats are more expensive. Aside from cost, it is a question of whether to make it more of a vacation from galley duty and shipboard chores.

From a nautical point of view, experience should be a factor. Taking on too great a challenge in strange waters might put too much pressure on an inexperienced charterer, and professional help can make life a lot easier, whether with a full crew, or just a boatman who handles only the nautical responsibilities.

In many of the areas of the world chartering is available, but there are of course places where it is not. In areas where sailing is seasonal, bareboat chartering is usually available as an individual arrangement booked through a yacht broker or directly with an owner of a boat. There are fewer commercially operated bareboat fleets based in areas with short seasons.

I have personally experienced the places described in this section, with an exception or two, in the course of a number of years. Those I have not sailed in personally are given brief mention based on reports of others. My intent here is to describe what an area has to offer so the reader may gain an idea of what to expect of it as a cruising ground. Some places are remote enough to be available only to world voyagers or through chartering, while others are close enough to home to think about taking one's own boat there. The general format proceeds roughly westward from northeastern North America (in what might be called a zigzag fashion). A list of cruising guides for each area is provided in the bibliography at the end.

XIV

Northeastern North America

~~~~~~

Confined to a relatively short season by dramatic swings of seasonal weather, the upper righthand bulge of North America has an amazing wealth of cruising areas. They are taken advantage of in great numbers due to the proximity of an enormous population, which means overcrowding in some places, but the first one, Newfoundland, is remote enough to avoid this problem.

Newfoundland

This is a fascinating and challenging area that is not easily accessible, but it is well worth the effort, given sufficient time. A charter might possibly be arranged privately, but Newfoundland is mainly an area for adventurous owners to take their own boats. To get there one must be prepared for offshore passagemaking, for fog navigation, and for a good measure of self-sufficiency. The boat we cruised in, a Valiant 40, got there via an eight-day passage direct from Sandy Hook, New Jersey, mostly powering in fog. From New England ports, a week to 10 days should be allowed for a direct passage, but it is probably wise to allow more time and to break the passage by stopping in Nova Scotian ports on the way. In any event, there are open-water legs across the Gulf of Maine and the Gulf of St. Lawrence.

The big question is the weather. On the average, Newfoundland weather produces a fair amount of fog, rain, and strong winds. In the summer of 1987 we were very lucky on an eight-day cruise to have generally pleasant weather and fair winds. This was evidently an exception to the normal, as the Newfies, as they are affectionately called and who are warm and friendly hosts to visiting sailors, kept telling us to "come back. You brought us our best summer in years."

Despite the weather and the short season (late June to early September), Newfoundland (scans with "understand") has a wealth of fascinating cruising areas. The greatest number of good harbors is on the east coast, which is the farthest from routes of access.

The west coast, bordering on the Gulf of St. Lawrence, is extremely rugged, with harbors rather widely spaced, which is also the case on the south coast. The harbors there are primitive in the way of facilities and civilization ashore. The towns are mostly lonely fishing villages, but there are wonderfully unspoiled coves where those who appreciate this sort of isolation can be very happy. The French islands of St. Pierre and Miquelon, just off the south coast, offer a unique taste of "Europe" in this out-of-the-way place, bleak and lonely, but with a good harbor at St. Pierre and very Gallic ambience.

At the far southeastern tip of the island of Newfoundland, which is Canada's newest province (1949), is St. John's, the capital, a bustling city of 150,000 with sophisticated shops, hotels, and restaurants, and a busy harbor. Yachts may temporarily make do here, although it is really only a commercial port. Local yachts have a base around the peninsula on its north side at Long Pond, site of the Royal Newfoundland Y.C. The marina here is completely landlocked, and visiting yachts are made very welcome.

North of here, the east coast, which borders on the open Atlantic at about the same latitude (48° N) as Puget Sound, is indented all the way to the Straits of Belle Isle, which separates Newfoundland from Labrador, with an incredible wealth of island-studded bays that are cruising perfection. In succession northward, the bays are Conception, Trinity, Bonavista, and Nortre Dame.

They abound with isolated anchorages and, here and there, plain, utilitarian fishing villages that have a special fascination for that very reason. The distinguishing feature in each one is a cloud of wheeling, screaming seagulls concentrated over the trawlers at the fish piers, and the surrounding, almost treeless hillsides are dotted with square, plain, no-nonsense houses. There is a sense that the basics of life dominate in these surroundings. While there are no yacht facilities as such, supplies can be had at Brigus, Bonavista, Trinity, and others. The locals are invariably friendly: some boys brought us fresh codfish as a swap for a ride in our dinghy, and a man drove home and came back with three days' newspapers when I asked him where I could buy one.

Between the villages there are innumerable little coves that are perfect for quiet overnights. Bonavista, incidentally, got its Italianate name from being the first North American landfall of explorer John Cabot in 1497, who was really an Italian named Caboto who hired out to the British. It has been a fishing port since the early days of the 16th Century. Except for the Vikings, who were here centuries earlier, and for the landfalls of Columbus in the Caribbean, this coast of Newfoundland abounds with the history of the earliest European explorers and settlers of the Western Hemisphere.

An affecting phenomenon of this coast is the presence of a number of deserted villages, where empty, half-collapsed houses stand vacantly gaping at the waterfronts of harbors that were once active fishing ports. A government program in the 1960s resettled the inhabitants of these spots, accessible only by water, to more populated towns. The harbors are still attractive anchorages, and the atmosphere is an eerie one of ghost towns recalling days gone by.

Newfoundland is not easily attainable, but its special cruising attractions make it well worth the effort. North of here, The Labrador and Greenland are a challenge beyond the realm of normal cruising, ranking as an "expedition."

Nova Scotia and New Brunswick

I have never cruised in these waters, but from many reports from those who have, the Bras d'Or Lakes of northern Nova Scotia are an attractive, rewarding area, with a climate of their own that is milder and pleasanter, with less fog, than the surrounding seacoasts. There are many secluded coves as anchorages. Baddeck is the main port, with

The Bras d'Or Lakes of Cape Breton Island

full facilities for yachts. Many owners who have taken their boats to Newfoundland do it over a couple of seasons, leaving the boat at a yard in Baddeck for the winter.

The Atlantic coast of Nova Scotia is rugged and challenging, with fog an almost constant factor. There is often rough offshore work, but there are frequent harbors freighted with an atmosphere of bygone days. Halifax is a major commercial port that also has excellent facilities for yachts.

The Bay of Fundy, between Maine and New Brunswick and southern Nova Scotia, is notorious for the greatest tide ranges (40 to 60 feet) anywhere in the world, with resultant swift and tricky currents, which makes relaxed cruising difficult. The major attraction is the St. John River, a world unto itself for cruising, noted for the Reversing Falls, where the current does a spectacular turnaround, complete with overfalls, with each tide. Once these are negotiated at slack water, the upstream area affords a lovely cruising grounds in pastoral surroundings.

Maine

There are some cruising addicts who say, "I don't care where I cruise as long as it's in Maine." This deeply indented coastline, whose profile is like the hem of a torn skirt, has a loyal bunch of fanatics, "Maine-iacs" as they are called, who consider it the world's finest cruising grounds. There are so many harbors and coves that it would take a lifetime of cruising, at least during Maine's relatively short season of mid-June through September, to cover them all. In fact they are so numerous that it is still possible on occasion in these increasingly crowded days to find solitude and isolation. The old-line Maine cruising man considers it an insulting invasion of privacy when another boat comes into a spot where he is anchored.

The key phrase for cruising in Maine is "turn to port" when you leave a harbor. Eastward ho is the challenge, beginning with the approach to Maine from southern New England. The old phrase had this as going "Down East," which meant running before the prevailing southwest winds, and experienced Maine cruising people feel that the cruising gets better the farther east one gets.

Although there are hundreds of anchorages wrapped in the solitude of pine trees and rocky shores on which there is no sign of civilization, there are several busy and crowded yachting centers. These are good ports for supplies and repairs, but a peculiarity of the Maine Coast is that there are very few marinas because of the great range of the tides. What marinas there are have floats and ramps instead of piers, and several places have large harbor floats for multiple mooring because anchoring room is so tight. The tide range is part of the coastal config-uration that gives the Bay of Fundy its great range. In an area that is adjacent to the open sea and that gradually narrows toward its inland end, the funnel effect compresses the tide and forces it to increasing heights. Other examples of this are Narragansett Bay and the western end of Long Island Sound. Because of this tide range and the currents that go with it, plus frequent fog, careful navigation must always be

A quiet Maine anchorage at Minister Cove, Pulpit Harbor

kept. There are few shoals or sandbars in Maine. It is either deep water or bang on a rock.

The busy centers for supplies, repairs and service, and crew changes include Falmouth Foreside (for Portland), South Freeport, Camden, Boothbay, and some of the harbors on Mt. Desert Island (pronounced like the last course of a meal). There are many other harbors with small settlements, either fishing villages, resorts, or both, and, in between, a wide choice of isolated coves, which increases as one heads eastward to the Mount Desert area. After that the harbors are farther apart, less crowded, and continuously rewarding all the way to the Canadian border.

Maine-iacs who have seen me in some of their favorite coves have faced me with the stern admonition: "Now don't you go writing this place up," so I will honor that sentiment. In any event, they would be too numerous to mention. One of the advantages of Maine cruising is that, should the often-present fog create problems along the coast, there is still a chance to be underway by heading up some of the rivers, like the Kennebec, Damariscotta, or Penobscot, and there is also an extensive network of cuts, channels, and tideways inland from the coast that connects some of the rivers and makes progress possible while the coast is socked in.

I am giving away no secrets in reporting that thorofares such as Deer Isle and Fox Islands, and Eggemoggin Reach, all well protected amid lovely scenery, make for fine cruising, as do the entire Penobscot Bay and Mt. Desert regions. With all this as a starter, it is then great fun to explore for oneself and discover one's own "secret" Maine anchorages.

Southern New England

From Maine southward to Cape Cod, there is a great deal of local yachting in such teeming centers as Marblehead and the various arms of Boston Harbor, but this is not exactly cruising country for visitors. The locals do a great deal of in-and-out sailing from home port, and perhaps an overnight visit to a neighboring harbor, but they head Down East to Maine or down south of Cape Cod for their serious cruising. Despite its many good harbors, this area is too crowded with resident boats and too urbanized to rate as an attraction for visitors.

Once through the Cape Cod Canal, which a low-speed auxiliary should negotiate with a fair tide if possible, cruising opportunities open up in a wide variety of choices in Buzzards Bay, Vineyard Sound, Nantucket Sound, and the Narragansett Bay and Block Island area. Because this is the best cruising grounds within easy reach of the great Boston-to-New York megalopolis, it has become increasingly crowded to the extent that many popular harbors are chockablock by mid-afternoon or earlier, and marina reservations have to be made well in advance. Resident boats now take up most of the space in Buzzards Bay, Narragansett Bay, and southern Cape Cod ports, but vacant berths of permanent boats can be taken by advance reservation. Newport, the most active yachting center in the whole region, is well set up to handle its local fleet and a great influx of visitors. Its prices for facilities and services reflect the pressure of demand, but it still rates as a must stop on most cruises south of the Cape. The key attraction of the region is of course the offshore islands: the Elizabeth Islands that separate Buzzards Bay and Vineyard Sound, Block Island, Martha's Vineyard, and Nantucket.

The season is a bit longer here than north of the Cape. It can be stretched from mid-May into October with a fair expectation of good cruising conditions. Fog is an important factor, though not quite as much so as in Maine. Fog is especially probable early in the season before the water warms up. It can develop without warning and drift in quickly on the prevailing summer southwester. Three-day northeasters sometimes spoil the good part of a week, and hurricanes have historically taken their toll here over the years, but there is always plenty of warning as they follow their normal sweep up the coast from the Caribbean in late summer.

Again, a navigational check must be kept continuously, even in the seemingly most pleasant conditions, as the fog can come quickly, and the tide, while not as great as in Maine, is a factor and sets up strong currents through much of the area. There are famous spots, like the narrow cuts of Woods and Quicks Hole in the Elizabeth Islands, where the current sucks navigational buoys under, and many more places where it is a real factor. In addition, much of the area is quite shallow, with large sandbars strategically placed to embarrass the unwary. Except for the "Holes" in the Elizabeths, most of the hazards are sand, not rock. Given these caveats the general summer conditions, when the southwester is blowing its best at up to a smoky 16 to 18 knots by midafternoon, are ideal for cruising.

Because of this special attraction, Cuttyhunk in the Elizabeths, Vineyard Haven and Edgartown on Martha's Vineyard, and the main harbor of Nantucket are always crowded, and a visitor has to fight for a mooring, a marina berth, or even anchoring space at the height of the season. The local yacht clubs have given up coping with visitors. Some harbors have commercial launch service and paid moorings.

Edgartown during the New York Yacht Club cruise

Block Island gets a triple blast of weekenders from Long Island Sound and Narragansett Bay, plus transients on their way through the area, but its Great Salt Pond is spacious enough to handle a tremendous influx, and there is a lot of marina space for transients.

Despite all this crowding, with everyone seeming to have to visit the main attractions, an enterprising skipper can still root around and find a few less crowded spots.

In both Maine and Southern New England, bareboat chartering is possible, mainly of privately owned boats through yacht brokers. A couple of commercially operated fleets have joined the scene in recent years. Since both these chartering procedures undergo frequent changes in boats and people involved, it is best to check the ads in the monthly boating magazines for these services.

Long Island Sound

Between the tide-swept channel called The Race at its eastern end and the equally swift tides of the East River at City Island 100 miles to the west, Long Island Sound is a textbook example of a prime cruising area, but with two drawbacks: lack of wind and overcrowding. Because it is landlocked by highly developed areas whose rising heat tends to block the normal daily thermals, such as the afternoon southwest sea breeze, the Sound has the infamous nickname of "The Dead Sea" in summer. The afternoon breeze often takes till 4 P.M. or later to build in across Long Island's curtain of rising heat, and sometimes it never does make it. Of course there are days with breezes from other directions, and spring and fall have more days of good breeze, but, unfortunately, the reputation is well deserved.

Its many excellent harbors, especially in the heavily populated areas of the western half, are jammed with resident boats. Transient cruisers can usually squeeze into a corner of a harbor or find an open slip at a marina, but it takes luck and patience. East of New Haven there is a better chance for pleasant cruising in a few anchorages along the Connecticut shore and around the "fishtail" of Long Island into Gardiner and Peconic Bays. New London and adjacent Fisher's Island Sound has another heavy concentration of local boats, but transients can usually find good services and facilities.

City Island is built around the marine trades and is a good spot for services of every kind. The atmosphere is urban and utilitarian. Stamford, Oyster Bay, Port Washington, Port Jefferson, and the towns on Huntington Harbor have good commercial facilities, and there are also the suburban harbors like Rye, Larchmont, Greenwich and Cold Spring Harbor where the local yacht clubs dominate, but almost every harbor has some commercial facilities.

If one should choose Long Island Sound as a cruising area, it is best to avoid summer weekends, using the less busy midweek to move around. Spring and fall, from early May into June, and Labor Day to mid-October are the best times.

XV

Middle Atlantic and Florida

South of New York and Chesapeake Bay

The waters between Long Island Sound and the Chesapeake are a cruising wasteland. The New Jersey coast and Delaware Bay are just paths to better areas, with nothing to tempt cruising visitors to linger. New York City, especially Manhattan, surprises sailors from other areas with its almost total lack of facilities closer in than the outer fringes of the five boroughs. There are marina developments along the Jersey side of the Hudson opposite Manhattan, and a trip up the Hudson can be scenically and historically interesting, especially for powerboats. A great many boats are based locally in Gravesend Bay, Coney Island, Jamaica Bay, and Staten Island, and transients can usually find an empty berth in a marina. Raritan Bay, between Staten Island and New Jersey, has several good harbors and many local boats. A major facility for transients heading north and south is the municipal marina at Atlantic Highlands, New Jersey, just inside Sandy Hook. It is crowded but does make room for transients. Inland from Atlantic Highlands, the Shrewsbury River system is a dead end but does have some pleasant anchoring spots and facilities of all sorts.

The only open-sea section of the Intracoastal Waterway is the 24-mile stretch from Sandy Hook to Manasquan Inlet, which makes the Atlantic Highlands Marina such a good jumping-off place. Shark River Inlet lies between Sandy Hook and Manasquan but is not recommended for transients.

The ICW from Manasquan Inlet (and don't get caught trying to negotiate that inlet in a strong onshore breeze) to Cape May is a tortuous business. Local traffic is heavy, shoaling is prevalent, and there are bridges. Barnegat Bay and the ICW have plenty of facilities, and Barnegat even has a few spots to anchor out overnight, but the whole area from Manhattan to Cape May is mainly a base for small boats and offshore sportfishermen. In taking the offshore route for the 110 miles from Sandy Hook to Cape May, Barnegat Inlet is very treacherous and should not be entered. Atlantic City Inlet is usable and Cold Spring Inlet at Cape May is a good one. A 50-foot bridge clearance governs passage of the canal from Cape May into Delaware Bay. Boats with taller masts must go outside around the Cape.

Delaware Bay has very little to recommend it, and the wind always seems to be contrary to the tide. The tidal currents are strong enough for a slow-speed boat to play a favorable one, and commercial traffic is extremely heavy. Side rivers like the Maurice and Cohansey offer stopping places in strong tidal currents if absolutely necessary. From the upper end of the bay, the Chesapeake and Delaware Canal is the highway to the Chesapeake and an entirely different cruising world.

In its 200-mile length, this storied body of water rivals, or perhaps surpasses, Maine in the number of possible anchorages. If someone set out to design a body of water well suited for cruising, it would be hard to do better. However, like Long Island Sound, the weather conditions do not match up to the rich variety of harbors, as summer is not an attractive time for cruising here. From late June to early September, the Bay suffers from a lack of wind, a surplus of thunderstorms, and, in most years, an overabundance of jellyfish.

Spring, starting in late April, and fall, often stretching well into November, are attractive cruising seasons on the Chesapeake. Local boats are out in force, especially on weekends, and transients to and from southern waters often linger for a time, enjoying a dividend of this pleasant diversion from ICW travel.

The local boat population has reached staggering proportions in such areas as Georgetown, Gibson Island, the recently rejuvenated inner harbor of Baltimore, Annapolis (most crowded of all), the West River, St. Michaels, Oxford, Solomons, and many smaller harbors, but visitors can usually find a spot for fuel, supplies, services, and an overnight berth. And surrounding these home-base ports is an endless choice of coves and creeks for overnight anchorages in quiet surroundings. Below Solomons, the Bay is less crowded, though the boat count in local harbors has been growing in recent years. At the bottom of the Bay, Norfolk, Hampton, Newport News, and Portsmouth, bordering Hampton Roads and its great armada of naval and commercial vessels, comprise a populous network of bases for local boats, and marinas catering to transient ICW traffic.

The Intracoastal Waterway

Although the ICW technically stretches from Maine to Mexico, with a few breaks here and there, the section most often thought of when referring to the ICW is that which starts at Mile Zero off the Portsmouth Naval Hospital on the Elizabeth River branch of Norfolk Harbor and continues down the East Coast to Key West, Florida.

On this nautical highway, which man has organized by connecting many natural bodies of water bordering the coastline with canals when necessary, distances are measured in statute miles. The navigation marks, with distinctive yellow borders, are red to starboard southbound. There are times, however, when the ICW coincides with an inlet from the sea or some other natural body of water, when this system is preempted by the normal buoyage for this stretch of water. This can sometimes cause confusion if a careful check of progress is not being kept.

Many users of the ICW look upon it as purely a passage route, a nautical I-95, and they rush through it as quickly as possible. This is naturally true of commercial traffic and of professional yacht delivery crews, but it is a mistake for private users, since it offers many opportunities for relaxed exploration and cruising enjoyment. There are many areas that have more charm than pure ditch-crawling provides, especially in North Carolina. I have done both, moving along as quickly as possible when time was a factor, and taking a more relaxed approach when I could.

The canals from the Norfolk area into North Carolina waters, either

Along the Intracoastal Waterway in North Carolina

the Dismal Swamp route or the Virginia Cut, are atmospheric in their wooded surroundings, especially during the period of fall foliage. The one lock of the whole route, at Great Bridge, is a feature of this section. Once in North Carolina, Currituck Sound is limited by shallow water outside the dredged channel, but Albemarle and Pamlico Sounds are good cruising areas in their own right, worth some relaxed exploration. The Neuse River area also offers a chance for some side diversions. Many local boats base at Oriental, a major ICW stop, and New Bern, with excellent facilities. An excursion to the Outer Banks from this area can be very interesting, though the water is quite thin and continuous navigational caution is needed.

Morehead City is not only an important stop on the ICW, but it is also a recommended jumping off place for passage to the Caribbean (see Chapter IV for advice on offshore routes south). The complex of facilities in the Morehead area at Beaufort, Morehead City, and Spooner Creek offers everything for transients and local boats. It was from Morehead once, in late March, that we took a side trip to Lookout Bight at the bottom end of the Outer Banks in summerlike weather, and we had the whole vast anchorage there to ourselves, a small hint to those who complain that it is impossible to find isolated anchorages anymore.

South of Morehead there are fewer stretches of this sort of open water, and ditch-crawling sets in more solidly. There is enough in scenery, quaint little towns, and major cities like Charleston and Savannah and their satellites to offer pleasant overnight anchorages and side diversions. Screens should be used at most times along here as a pleasant, bug-free, breezy evenings can turn into a whining, humming nightmare if the wind quits.

It is of course impossible here to mention all the good stops, and the best advice is to keep referring to the *Inland Waterway Guide* (see the Cruising Bibliography) which is a must for the route. It is published yearly and is as up-to-date as any such publication can be, but even the *Waterway Guide* can be outdated on occasion, so it should not be a surprise if some marina has changed hands, closed its restaurant, started a new one, or even gone out of business. We once tied up after dark at the pier of what was supposed to be a marina-*cum*-restaurant, only to find, when daylight came, that it had burned down.

In a slow-speed auxiliary, a 50-mile day is a long one in ICW travel, though I have covered almost 85-miles pushing through from dawn to dusk in the long daylight hours northbound in May. Operation after dark is not recommended except in emergencies, and the days are of course much longer when northbound in spring than on a fall trip south. It is wise to be south of the Chesapeake by at least mid-November and not to get that far north until late April at the earliest unless your boat has an enclosed steering station.

South of Charleston and all the way into the Florida Keys, year-

Hilton Head, South Carolina

round cruising is possible, but there can be cold fronts bringing severe weather as far south as southern Florida in midwinter. Most of the ICW in Florida is truly just a "highway" with little opportunity for side junkets, although the St. Johns River at Jacksonville is well worth a few days. Some of the towns are interesting, such as St. Augustine, and there is the Kennedy Space Center. In settled weather it is sometimes possible to break the monotony of the ditch by venturing offshore between inlets, hugging the shore inside the Gulf Stream southbound, and using its boost while headed north.

Most of the bigger towns and cities, especially from West Palm Beach south, are loaded with all facilities. Fort Lauderdale is the yacht brokerage capital of the world, with many marinas and service yards as a plus to selling or looking for a used boat.

The Miami area around Biscayne Bay is lined with facilities in all sections but too urban to be a cruising area. However, the southern half of Biscayne Bay, bordered by Elliot Key and Key Largo, is a pleasant area for weekending or starting a cruise into the Keys.

Florida Keys and West Coast

Stretching 140 miles from the south end of Biscayne Bay to Key West, the Florida Keys and their barrier reef, one of the largest in the world and the only one in the continental U.S., are a specialized kind of cruising area. The sailing is limited by the water depth, which is very shallow out of the dredged channels in most areas. The main attractions are diving and fishing. Hawk Channel on the seaward side of the Keys offers open water in settled weather, and it can be an interesting junket to head out into the Gulf Stream, crossing the sharp line between the pastel inshore waters and its inky blue. This is prime sportfishing country.

Florida Bay, on the other side of the Keys, is very shallow, with a wilderness aura. Some isolated cays can be explored, and Florida Channel is a marked route across it between the Keys and Florida's west coast. Marathon, Islamorada, Tavernier, and Upper and Lower Matecumbe are among the major spots in the Keys, all as bases for sportfishing. In the Key West area there are a few anchorages tucked away in secluded spots, and Key West itself is a busy boating center and colorful community. Beyond it, the Marquesas and Dry Tortugas, isolated little cays, offer opportunities for exploring, but they are exposed in bad weather, especially winter northers. In the opposite season, late summer hurricanes should be monitored in all of southern Florida. North of the Keys, Florida's west coast offers surprisingly good opportunities for cruising. At the southern end, the Ten Thousand Islands and Everglades are a unique wilderness best explored by small powerboat with a guide who knows the region. It is extremely easy to become lost in the trackless maze of waterways throughout the area, and depth is a problem. The little settlement of Flamingo is a base for this sort of expedition and for fishing trips.

Above this area of swamps, lush vegetation, wildlife, and confusing waterways, the mainland west coast is a much better cruising area than might appear from a casual look at a map. The open Gulf affords passage between the inlets, called passes here. As wide open as an ocean, it has a different aspect in that there is seldom an underlying groundswell. In pleasant weather it is docile, but it can be treacherous when weather makes up. The seas become short and steep and very choppy.

Marco Island, the first harbor going north, is an elaborate resort with a marina, but the entrance depths should be checked carefully, as shoaling can occur. From here up to Naples there is no section of the ICW, and the open Gulf is the way, which is actually the case up to Fort Myers. From Fort Myers north, the ICW is well marked and maintained, connecting the many coastal bays and sounds that line the coast from here to well north of Tampa. Fort Myers is at the western end of the Okeechobee Waterway which crosses the waist of Florida. Its limits for auxiliaries are a bridge clearance of about 49 feet, which can vary according to water levels, but it is a good shortcut between the coasts if it can be negotiated.

Between Fort Myers and Tampa Bay there is good inland cruising in the Port Charlotte area and such pleasant stops as Gasparilla, Captiva, Venice, Sarasota, Siesta Key and Longboat Key. There are several passes offering the choice of going offshore for a while in settled weather. Tampa Bay, heavily developed as it is, still has a choice of cruising anchorages and a host of marinas. The Manatee River leading to Bradenton is an attractive area with many yards, and St. Petersburg and environs teems with marinas and yards. North to Clearwater and its many facilities, and to the Anclote Keys and Tarpon Springs, marks the end of cruisable waters on the west coast, as it is mostly mangrove swamp north and west to the Panhandle, Panama City, and Pensacola.

Spring and fall are the best seasons. Winter weather, normally warm and pleasant, can be disrupted by fog and cold blustery northers. In summer, there is very little wind, heat and humidity predominate, and thunderstorms are an almost daily feature, especially in late afternoons.

XVI

Offshore Islands

~~~~~~

The Bahamas

Fifty miles from Florida across the challenging turbulence of the Gulf
Stream lie the Bahamas. Hundreds of islands, ranging from large land
masses to tiny croppings of coral, stretch over 5,400 square miles of
the Atlantic from 27°N latitude at Walkers Cay to 21°N at Great Ina-
gua. Many books have been written on the cruising opportunities here
(notably the annually issued *Yachtsman's Guide to the Bahamas*—a
must while cruising there), and it is only the intention here to give an
overall picture.

The weather is suitable for cruising year round, with a caveat or
two. Hurricanes must be monitored in late summer, which is also
more unsettled as a rainy season. Winter northers, tempered by the
Gulf Stream, still manage to blast their way across to the islands, losing
force and gaining in temperature the farther south they get. Sometimes, though, they are robust enough to carry all the way to the northern tier of Caribbean islands, the Greater Antilles. In one January in
the central Bahamas, we experienced eight northers of varying viru-
lence, most of them strong enough to keep us in port for a day or two.

The usual cycle of a norther is for the prevailing east-to-south-east
trades to clock into the south and increase in strength. As the southerly
increases, it is a warning that the front preceding a norther is getting
close, marked by a bank of fast-moving clouds, and sometimes by
thunderstorms. There can be strong squalls with rain as the front hits,
followed by a shift to northwest or north and a strong wind in the 20-
to- 40-knot range. This usually blows for about a day, then gradually

swings into the northeast and east. Sometimes this cycle takes a week or more in the winter, but in a period of fast-moving fronts, as in the January when we saw eight, it can happen within two or three days. This feature is usually confined between mid-December and mid-March, and some winters have seen stable periods of steady trades, with relatively few fronts. In 1977, though, one of these fierce northers actually brought snow showers to Grand Bahama for the first time in recorded history.

Another caveat concerns security. Since the '70s there have been incidents of violence against visiting yachts, including one well publicized double murder in the Exumas. Rumors exceeded incidents, but there was enough of a problem to scare away many visiting yachts. The drug trade was evidently the cause of many of the problems, but local "piracy," really just plain robbery afloat, was also a factor. Local officials were often felt to be less than vigorous in preventing or following up such crimes. The last time we cruised in the Bahamas (1979), there was very little evidence or rumor of this sort of crime. We never experienced any problems ourselves. Evidently, from latest reports, things have smoothed out, and tales of such troubles are not frequently heard.

In any event, the Bahamas offer magnificent cruising in the lay of the islands. Bareboat charter fleets and professionally crewed yachts have had trouble operating in the Bahamas due to problems with government officials, but private boats are there in good number. Visitors must obtain a cruising permit at a port of entry, and the length of stay is limited and should be noted.

In their vast spread across the Atlantic (contrary to an oft-repeated misconception, they are not in the Caribbean), the Bahamas are divided into several distinct areas as far as cruising is concerned. Northwest and Northeast Providence Channels, deepwater passages that cut across the enormous Great Bahama Bank, separate the central and southern Bahamas from Grand Bahama and the Abacos. These latter are on the Little Bahama Bank and are a separate world unto themselves. Grand Bahama has few good harbors, and these are built up as resort centers, but the Abacos are a fine cruising area, especially in late winter and spring. Because of their location, they are particularly susceptible to winter northers. Between the big island of Abaco and the string of islands off its east coast, Abaco Sound is well protected, though quite shallow with many fine stopping places, such as Green Turtle Cay, Man O'War Cay, Elbow Cay, and Marsh Harbour on Great Abaco. This is the only area where bareboats are available in the Bahamas.

Across Northeast Providence Channel, Nassau on New Providence is the capital and only Bahamian city, a bustling, tourist-jammed island with a good harbor, several marinas and all the services and supplies. Everywhere else is known colloquially as the Out Islands, though the official name for them is the Family Islands. Nassau is the hub, strategically located at the elbow of the adjoining deepwater Northwest and Northeast Providence channels. To the north, the Berry Islands offer a few attractive anchorages. To the west, the deep Tongue of the Ocean separates New Providence from Andros, the largest land mass

Nassau, Bahamas

in the Bahamas and the least developed, with few harbors to attract cruising boats. West of it, the Great Bahama Bank spreads westward 60 miles to Bimini and Cat Cay on the edge of the Gulf Stream, just 50 miles from Florida. They are sportfishing centers, teeming with activity and host to many boats crossing from Florida for the fishing and the chance to "go foreign." The Great Bank, which spreads southward almost to Cuba, is a challenging area where the pure sand of the bottom is always eerily in sight in the 8- to 12-foot depths of the crystal clear water, where unpredictable currents make piloting tricky, and where strong winds can kick up a wicked short sea. Too wide for a daytime crossing by a slow-speed auxiliary, it is an area that must be respected and carefully planned for.

The Great Bank swings back up to the north across the bottom of the Tongue of the Ocean all the way to Nassau, and on out eastward to the Exumas. This 130-mile string of cays stretching southeastward 35 miles southeast of Nassau is the prime cruising area in the Bahamas with a succession of ideal anchorages for most of its length. Approaching it from Nassau is another eerie experience with the bottom ever in sight. A straight course to Allan's or Highborne cays is possible for six feet of draft, though a lookout should always be kept for occasional coral heads, and deeper draft vessels should take a dogleg course to avoid possible heads.

Highborne Cay has become quite developed with a real marina but many of the anchorages are still in an unspoiled, natural state. Norman's Cay, off-limits for a few years because of presumed drug activity, is reportedly open again, and from here a host of fine anchorages string down to the prime area of the Exumas, Pipe Creek. This well protected channel winding through flats and little cays ends just north of Staniel Cay, a meeting place for yachts, with a marina and restaurant, and often the turnaround point for boats operating out of Nassau. Below here there are fewer anchorages and more isolation. To get to George Town, Great Exuma, a favorite port at the bottom of the chain, a 20-mile jaunt in the deep, open waters of Exuma Sound, often quite rough, is needed. George Town, on magnificent Elizabeth Harbour, is an attractive little town with resort clubs, restaurants, and supplies.

Pipe Creek, Exumas

Across the harbor, there are excellent anchorages on Stocking Island.

From here on out, the Bahamas are more scattered and lonely and much less visited by cruising boats, which are much more on their own down this way. A real feel for the old-time Out Island lifestyle can still be gained in such places as Cape Santa Maria and Clarence Town on Long Island, and seldom-visited spots like Rum Cay, Crooked Island, Acklin's, and Mayaguana. Anyone interested in the controversy as to the true landfall of Columbus can check it out at San Salvador, for many years presumed to be the place, or lonely Samana 20 miles north-northeast of Acklin's, which recent research points to as the more likely spot.

The loneliness of these remote islands is compensated for by generally more settled weather.

For an ambitious cruising skipper to take in all of the Bahamas would use up the better part of a lifetime.

Turks and Caicos

Physically very much like the Bahamas, and once a part of them, the lonely archipelago of the Turks and Caicos, east of the Bahamas and north of Hispaniola, is a world unto itself in many ways. Now a crown colony of Great Britain, they are enough out of the way that casual cruisers and people with a limited amount of time fail to get that far. They have been developed as a resort area to some extent in recent years, but there is no highrise glitz, and the atmosphere is one of remote isolation. The Turks and Caicos are 100 miles from Crooked Island, with only Mayaguana as a possible stopover in between, and Hispaniola is 100 miles to the south.

The major developed area is on Providenciales, invariably called Provo, where there are a couple of marinas. The Third Turtle is the major one. Provo is on the western edge of the vast Caicos Bank, a prime bonefishing area, and loaded with conch. There is an airport near the Third Turtle, and a few small out-island-type resorts perch on the cays along the fringing reef. Off to the east, across Caicos Bank and 20-mile wide Turks Island Passage, Grand Turk has a small settlement and harbor at Cockburn town and is the closest jumping-off place for the passage to the north coast of Hispaniola. Interesting in themselves, the Turks and Caicos are also important as a way station on the "thorny path" route to the islands.

The Virgin Islands

From Puerto Rico, which has many good cruising harbors itself, eastward for 90 miles to Anegada Passage is a cruising area unmatched for its combination of fine weather, wide choice of anchorages, and facilities. The main components are Culebra Island, 20 miles from Fajardo, the big yachting center at the east end of Puerto Rico, the American Virgins, and the British Virgins. The only drawback is that the area is such a fine cruising grounds that it is very popular, and "splendid isolation" is virtually impossible.

About the best chance for finding some isolation is at Culebra. Its main harbor, Dewey, is often crowded with boats from Puerto Rico, especially on weekends, but a deep indentation on the eastern side, Ensenada Honda, has several quiet coves. It is also a favorite hurricane hole, but it suffered badly in Hurricane Hugo. There are also small islands and coves around Culebra with good diving, good beaching, and a chance for some solitude. The ambience on shore is Hispanic. A sister island to the south, Vieques, has a few good anchorages and beaches, but much of it is taken up with restricted military areas.

St. Thomas lies 20 miles east in the American Virgins. Its capital and main port, Charlotte Amalie, is the base for hundreds of charter and private yachts, and it is a place to cruise *from*, not *to*. St. Thomas's Lagoon and Red Hook harbors are also crowded and busy yachting bases. Neighboring St. John has, in contrast, many fine harbors on both its north and south coasts. Much of it is a national park so a good part of the island is undeveloped and in a natural state. There is excellent diving in many places, and an easily followed, marked underwater trail for snorkelers in Trunk Bay. St. Croix, another Hugo victim, 30 miles to the south across the open Caribbean, is a world unto itself and not often visited by boats operating in the northern Virgins. It has no anchorages that are especially attractive to cruising boats.

To go between the U.S. Virgins and the British Virgins it is necessary to clear and enter customs and immigration at both ends, which is something of a nuisance but usually accomplished fairly easily at Cruz Bay, St. John, and at West End or Jost Van Dyke or Nanny Cay on the BVI side. Charlotte Amalie, and Road Town, capital of the BVI, are ports of entry, but more formal, busy and fussy.

The British Virgin Islands are a paradise for cruising boats, given the understanding that there are always a lot of them around. There are about 30 overnight anchorages and a few more lunch stops within the 25-mile scope of the chain, so an anchorage is always close at hand throughout the area. There are major marina and yard facilities at

Cooper Island, British Virgin Islands

West End, Nanny Cay, Road Town, and Virgin Gorda, all services and supplies are easily available, and there is a wide choice of places to have dinner ashore. Food shopping is easy in American-style supermarkets (U.S. dollars are the BVI currency), and the rule here, as in all of the Caribbean, is that booze is cheap and food expensive by stateside standards. Beer and wine are not the bargains that liquor, especially rum, is. Diving opportunities are numerous and good, either directly from the boat if properly equipped, or via special dive-boat excursions that pick up divers right from anchored boats.

Two major attractions for lunch stops are the caves at Norman Island, reputed to be the inspiration for Stevenson's "Treasure Island," and The Baths at the southern tip of Virgin Gorda. The caves make for interesting dinghy exploration and snorkeling. The Baths are a fantastic jumble of building-size granite boulders heaped upon one another, with pools hidden underneath them. A lovely beach sits among the

Sprat Bay, Peter Island, British Virgin Islands

boulders and snorkeling is excellent just off the rocks. This is such a popular spot that 50-plus boats are the norm anchored here on a good day. There is almost a gridlock of dinghy traffic to and from the beach. Overnight anchoring is no go because of a constant surge that can be enough on some days to prevent anchoring or landing.

Speaking of beaches, the one at The Baths and its neighbors along that shore are about the best in the BVI, as there are not very many. A northerly surge, which can develop rapidly and almost without warning in the winter months, can make the few beaches on the north side of the BVI untenable. A small islet, Sandy Cay, just off Jost Van Dyke, has a beautiful beach and a nature trail and is another popular lunch stop.

Road Town is the metropolis of the BVI, with a forest of masts ringing its shores in several marinas, and it is a must stop for food and supplies. The cruising highlight of the whole Virgin Island area is landlocked, scenic Gorda Sound at the northeast tip of Virgin Gorda. It is the site of several resorts, such as Bitter End Yacht Club, a favorite target for the cruising fraternity, Biras Creek, Drake's Anchorage, and Leverick Bay. A good procedure for cruising the Virgins is to work to windward to Gorda Sound in the first days, relax and explore there for a day or two, and then have a downwind slide to the harbors to leeward on Drake Passage and the main charter bases. The low, lonely island of Anegada, 18 miles to the north, is off-limits to bareboats because of its complex of reefs. For crewed and private boats, the attractions there are its isolation, its beaches, and the fishing and diving.

My own experiences with the BVI go back to 1964, when we had Gorda Sound all to ourselves for two days, in dramatic contrast to today. In many subsequent cruises, including 12 seasons of keeping our own boats there, I have not found any other cruising area, given the sizable population of boats, that puts it all together 12 months a year (with a bit of extra rain in the fall) for easygoing, rewarding, albeit far from hairy-chested, cruising, any better than the BVI.

The St. Martin/Sint Maarten Area

On my first visit, in 1958, to the binational island of St. Martin/Sint Maarten, shared amicably for centuries by France and Holland, there was not a single craft afloat in Philipsburg's bay, not even a canoe, and the town stringing along one narrow dirt road, was a sleepy village. Now large hotels rim the shore, and the street is still narrow but is lined with jewelry, electronic, and clothing stores and boutiques and restaurants. The once empty bay now has two large marinas protected from a constant surge by jetties, a boat yard, and normally more than 100 boats at anchor. Cruise ships unload passengers daily, and a busy airport has jet service direct from the U.S. and Europe, and connections to other Caribbean islands.

From something of a no-man's-land in the cruising world of the early '60s, St. Martin has become a hub for bareboat and crewed charters and private yachts. Philipsburg has all services including haulout and off-season boatkeeping, and Marigot on the French side has developed from a scruffy fishing village into a resort reminiscent of the French Riviera. There are excellent restaurants (at a price), and there is good shopping for French foods, perfume, and so forth.

Its development as a cruising center has been relatively recent because of its isolation from other popular Caribbean areas. It is 80 miles of rough going across capricious, unpredictable Anegada Passage from the BVI, a passage not to be taken lightly, as conditions can change rapidly, and nasty seas are the norm. It is another 87 miles southeastward to Antigua, often a thrash to windward. Statia, St. Kitts, Nevis, and Montserrat lie between but are off the rhumb-line course and have only open roadsteads for anchoring. If island-hopping instead of opting for a through passage, the end result is usually to be over 40 miles dead to leeward of Antigua. Island-hopping is an easier route when northbound. This double dose of tough conditions tended to keep boats away and slowed development at St. Martin.

But St. Martin, after its late start, has caught up with the rest of the Caribbean as a cruising haven. It does suffer from a lack of all-weather harbors. Philipsburg is wide open to the south and southwest, and Marigot is exposed to the north. Oyster Pond on the east coast is land-lockerd and secure, but the entrance is often impassable because of strong onshore trade winds and seas. *Brunelle* spent a secure summer there in seasonal layup, but it is not wise to enter Oyster Pond in winter. Simson Lagoon, which takes up much of the center of the island, is completely landlocked but access is hampered by a drawbridge with infrequent openings. There are several other anchorages around St. Martin for pleasant overnighting. Nearby St. Barts, until recently a colorful and seldom visited smugglers' hideaway, is now perpetually crowded with yachts and tourists on shore, but well worth a visit. Anguilla, six miles north of St. Martin, is desperately trying to hold onto its unspoiled charm, and is noted for miles of gorgeous beaches, but it, too, is undergoing development. It still does afford a glimpse of a Caribbean lifestyle of other days. Saba, 30 miles south of St. Martin, is a fascinating, unique island that is best visited by plane from St. Martin, as it only has a tiny, artificial boat basin for a couple of vessels that is often untenable in surge conditions. Very recently, and way behind the other islands in the area, St. Kitts and Nevis have instituted developments that should make them much more attractive to the cruising fraternity than they have been, with a new marina at Basseterre, St. Kitts, and other facilities planned. Nevis was devastated in 1989 by Hurricane Hugo.

Antigua

Antigua is where the yachting boom first hit the Caribbean. The Nicholson family, en route from England to Australia in the schooner *Mollihawk* for a new life after World War II for retired naval officer Vernon Nicholson, his wife, and two teenage sons, stopped at the Dockyard in English Harbour, colonial base for Lord Nelson's fleet,

English Harbour, Antigua

194

St. James's Club, Antigua

for rest and repairs. They ended up providing daysailing charters for guests at the Mill Reef Club and never left the island. Vernon's sons are now carrying on the family charter business in the second generation. English Harbour, a wonderful collection of old naval buildings, had been in complete ruins, but over the years, at first through the efforts of the Nicholsons, and later with the formally organized Friends of English Harbour, it has gradually been restored. The semicircular stone quay remains, old cannons are embedded as bollards, and the old brick buildings have been put to modern use as an inn, shops, repair facilities, and offices. A full-service yard is located on the east side of the harbor across from the Dockyard quay, and the area is jam-packed at all times with yachts of every size, description, and hailing port. All kinds of charter yachts are based here, as well as many private ones, some in dead storage moored to the bordering mangroves. The confined anchorage is always full and Freeman Bay, just outside the entrance, is also crowded. In fact, the whole area has become so busy that there is an overflow to neighboring Falmouth Harbour, home of Antigua Yacht Club. There is plenty of anchoring room here in a wider, breezier area than the confines of the Dockyard.

English Harbour, the best natural harbor in the eastern Caribbean both for defense of Lord Nelson's fleet and for modern yachting operations, is a gathering place for world voyagers as well as short-term charterers and private boats needing service, and the island of Antigua is itself a rewarding cruising area. Strangely, in contrast to the crowding in English and Falmouth Harbors, many of its anchorages are lightly populated, perhaps because so many boats have come for the facilities between distant ports.

We have used Antigua as a base for a month or two at a time on several different occasions and have used it as a cruising ground several times. There are about a dozen anchorages on both coasts of its 20-mile length, as well as the satellite island of Barbuda, 20 miles to the north. Barbuda has no facilities and its resort does not welcome visiting yachts, but its beaches are fabulous, and the diving is good.

A second chartering and service base for Antigua has been developed at Parham Sound on the northeast coast, and the capital city of St. John's has a good natural harbor, with handy shopping, but is made quite unattractive by pollution and commercial use.

XVII

Lower and Western Caribbean and South America

~~~~~~

The Lower Caribbean

From Antigua southward in the Lesser Antilles, the islands of Guadeloupe, Dominica, Martinique, St. Lucia, St. Vincent, the Grenadines, and Grenada have developed into a very active cruising area, with charter fleets and many locally based private boats, especially in the French islands of Guadeloupe and Martinique, which are departments of France, not colonies. There is a distinct culture change from island to island, and the scenery varies from the dramatic peaks of the big islands, including volcanoes, to the sea-swept beauty of the comparatively low-lying Grenadines.

The sailing conditions vary, too. The passages between the five northern islands are from 30 to 40 miles in the open sea, reaching across the trades and the big, deep-sea rollers sweeping in unimpeded all the way from Africa. Once in the lee of the mountains of the high islands, the wind plays capricious tricks. Sometimes the trades accelerate down the leeward slopes in wild gusts, as at the south end of Dominica or under St. Lucia's Pitons. At other times there can be a fresh backwind from the west, or there may be large cones of complete calm and stray catspaws. Another leeward-side problem is the presence of a multitude of fish pots for as much as five miles offshore. A watch for them must be kept at all times, and night passages must be made

Mayreau, Grenadines

far enough out to the west to avoid the pot area.

Once boisterous Bequia Channel, five miles of current-tossed turbulence, is crossed between St. Vincent and Bequia (pronounced Beckwee), the Grenadines offer quite different conditions and some of the best sailing and cruising opportunities in the lower Caribbean. For much of their 60-mile north-to-south length, the sailing waters of the Grenadines are protected from the open sea by reefs and their eastern islands, and the islands are not high enough to impede the trades. There are a few open stretches where the deep-sea rollers can be felt, but only for a few miles, and the rest of the chain has protected waters and an attractive choice of anchorages. The weather changes little throughout the year, and it is relatively hurricane-free south of St. Lucia.

Heading south from Antigua, the major transient stops are Deshaies, (Guadeloupe), Les Iles des Saintes, Portsmouth (Dominica), Fort de

Marigot Bay, St. Lucia

France and Anse Mitan (Martinique), Rodney Bay, Marigot Bay, and Soufriere (St. Lucia), and Cumberland Bay, Wallilabou Bay and Blue Lagoon (St. Vincent). In the Grenadines, Elizabeth Harbour in Bequia, Union and Petit St. Vincent islands, and Tyrell Bay in Carriacou are the stopping spots, with many more delightful anchorages to choose from at Mustique, Cannouan, Mayreau, and the highlight of the whole area, the Tobago Cays. This idyllic group, protected as a national park, which we had all to ourselves in 1962, has become so popular that up to 100 boats, including small cruise ships, can be found there in season, the price of popularity that is being paid all through the Caribbean. Its beaches and diving reefs cannot be topped. At the bottom end, Grenada has made a strong comeback from its political troubles of the '70s and early '80s and it is well set up for visiting yachts. The marina in the picturesque city of St. George's is being updated, and on the south coast, L'Anse aux Epines (Lansapeen to locals) is an attractive harbor with services and some pleasant nearby anchorages.

Beyond Grenada, Barbados, 90 miles to the east, and Trinidad and Tobago, nestled against South America, are not recommended as cruising stops except for personal convenience. They are isolated from the rest of the area. Barbados has poor harbors, and the Trinidad-Tobago climate is too hot.

Venezuela and the San Blas Islands

Off the coast of Venezuela there are many islands, with Margarita being the largest and most developed as a tourist mecca, and an atoll called Los Roques the most interesting spot for a cruising visit. The smaller islands closer to the coast have plenty of places to anchor, and there are major marinas, chockablock with local boats and complete with all services, along the mainland coast near LaGuaira, the port of Caracas. Offshore, the open waters of the Spanish Main, where the trades blow with authority, make for rugged conditions, and working eastward must be done as much as possible in the protection of the islands. A big plus in this area is the fact that it has been hurricane-free over the centuries, and it would be rare indeed to experience one here. For this reason, knowledgeable owners in the Caribbean often bring their boats to the Venezuelan islands for the hurricane season farther north, enjoying the quiet anchorages in the process. Drawbacks are the language difficulty for non-Spanish-speaking sailors, and the lack of readily available services and supplies in the offshore islands.

Colombia, Venezuela's neighbor to the west, has been a no-man's-land for visiting yachts since the drug trade developed, and it is impossible to get insurance coverage for cruising there.

This makes a long jump of almost 600 miles westward, but at least downwind with the trades, to get to friendly waters again. And friendly is only a comparative term, as the next stop is Panama, where the question of how things are for visitors, especially Americans, is a touchy one.

For those who want to take the chance and who go to the trouble to check things out ahead of time as to the situation at the moment, the San Blas islands, home of the Cuna Indians, are a tempting area for the adventurous cruising addict. They string for miles along the Caribbean coast of Panama in an idyllic setting of tiny cays and fringing reefs. The Cuna Indians, attempting to maintain their almost unspoiled pre-Columbian society, have had the modern world impinge on them with the arrival of cruise ships at the westward end of the chain, and there have been unpleasant incidents of violence against visitors in other parts of the islands, so a visit here should be carefully checked out beforehand.

The same applies to transit of the Panama Canal, which is bound to become more of a problem for world-voyaging yachts as American control of the area gradually fades. It is no longer an easy, hospitable place for yachts on their way through.

The Bay Islands and Belize

There is a great cruising area in the Western Caribbean, with all the physical attributes one might ask for, but the political problems of Central America in recent years have been a drawback and a deterrent to pleasure boats. A burgeoning charter industry has suffered, and private owners have become leery of the situation, especially given the considerable distance to get there from the States or the Eastern Caribbean.

Belize, with its magnificent offshore barrier reef, said to be second in size only to Australia's Great Barrier Reef, is not as much bothered by political uncertainty as the other Central American states, and there is some activity there in cruising and diving. Belize City is, to put it politely, a dump, and not a good base for yachts, with the incredible pollution in its harbor, but some smaller mainland ports can be used. The major attraction is to get out to the reef and explore its many facets. Several islands, such as Lighthouse and Turneffe have anchorages and opportunities to explore ashore, and there are other small islets that host booby bird and frigate bird hatcheries and resident iguanas.

The boobies do not mind visitors and sit calmly while inspected at close range, but the frigates actively resent intruders with noisy dive-bombing attacks.

The top attraction while cruising in Belize is the incredible Blue Hole, far off in a maze of shallow reefs and approachable only by eyeball navigation from up the mast. Surrounded by this vast reef the Hole is 490 feet deep, perfectly circular, and several hundred yards across. Its walls are lined with caves containing all sorts of sea life, and hammerhead sharks laze around without, apparently, bothering divers. Divers from the schooner crew I was with reported it as some of the most fascinating diving they had ever done. The fabulous reef world makes Belize an area well worth contemplating.

Offshore in the Gulf of Honduras, the Bay Islands, centered on the main island of Roatan, are a compact area with many excellent harbors, and a native population that still shows its descent from English settlers of centuries ago, although Queen Victoria ceded the islands to Honduras in mid-19th century, a deed still actively resented by the inhabitants. Their accent is reminiscent of the Bahamas.

Roatan's south shore is lined with good harbors that are well protected, but the reef-lined north shore has fewer anchorages, and winter northers should be guarded against. Anthony's Cay, an active diving center, is the best harbor on the north.

Satellite islands, including the peaceful Cochinos, halfway to the mainland on the south, make a fine place to visit after a good reach across the prevailing trades, and the isolated groups of the Utilas off the western end and Guanaja at the east, are both well worth a look. If Central America ever settles down politically, this area could make a good comeback as a prime cruising attraction.

North of Belize, the Yucatan Peninsula shelters the popular Mexican island ports of Cozumel and Cancún. Not so much cruising attractions in themselves, these are active sportfishing centers with a big fleet of local charter boats for visitors. Diving is also very popular in this area.

XVIII

Inland

Lake Champlain and the Great Lakes

~~~~~~

While most of the cruising is in coastal areas, North America is blessed with two of the most extensive freshwater cruising areas to be found anywhere: the Great Lakes and Lake Champlain. In addition, while the canal and river network in North America cannot begin to approach the amazing canal systems of Europe, there are areas that are attractive for cruising under power, The Hudson River-Erie Canal system between New York City and the Great Lakes is one, and there can be rewards, as well as hazards, in cruising the Ohio, Mississippi, and Missouri river systems. The Trent and Rideau canal systems in Canada are used by a lot of power cruisers, and the St. Lawrence River, leading from the Great Lakes to the sea, has some stretches that cruisers visit, though the conditions are often marginal because of swift currents and commercial traffic. The most attractive part of the St. Lawrence is the Thousand Islands area just east of Lake Ontario between upper New York State and Ontario, Canada.

Lake Champlain

Whimsically called "the west coast of New England" by Vermonters, 118-mile long Lake Champlain, which flows northward to the Richelieu River and the St. Lawrence, is a prime cruising area, with many special attractions, especially its mountain-girt scenery. Home base to a huge local population of yachts, it can also be reached by visitors from either south or north. The Champlain Canal runs from the Erie Canal and Hudson River confluence near Albany to the south end of the lake, with locks to traverse, and sailboats must have masts on deck, as bridges are fixed. There is a 55-foot bridge clearance limit on the northern approach from Canada.

Because it is the water supply for all the towns and cities around it, Champlain must be kept pollution-free, and there is therefore strict control of discharge from marine toilets. All boats must be equipped with holding tanks, and there are many pump-out stations around the lake. Visiting them is as routine a function as taking on water and fuel. The state of Vermont operates some free pump-out stations, and most marinas are so equipped and charge a fee of about $10. There are strict fines for failure to obey the regulations for this.

Champlain is a border lake between Vermont on the east and New York on the west, and its northern end extends a bit into Canada. Much of the visiting boat traffic comes from Canada, with the great population complex of Montreal so close-by to the north. On the Vermont side there are several main bases for yachts at Charlotte, Burlington, and Mallett's Bay. With less population on the New York side there are fewer facilities there, but the lake is becoming more and more popular, and therefore more crowded, a cause of concern to longtime local residents.

Perhaps the main attraction of Champlain is its scenery, with graceful hills along its shores and a backdrop of the Green Mountains to the east and the Adirondacks to the west. In addition to being handsomely scenic, the mountains are also a weather factor, a breeding place for sudden, dramatic wind shifts and thunder squalls. The winds tend to funnel north and south along Champlain's valley, which means that the waves they produce can attain good size in the long, relatively narrow, sweep. Freshwater waves tend to be steeper than their saltwater counterparts, so a strong wind on the lake means a steep chop. Few of the lake's anchorages have all-round protection, and a snug anchorage of the moment may become a wide open lee shore in a very short

Stave Island, Lake Champlain

time. The choice of anchorages on both shores is a multiple one, with plenty of variety for several weeks of cruising.

In addition to the actual scenery, the geology of the area can be a fascination, and there is plenty of history to absorb. Oddly, Champlain is the birthplace of the U.S. Navy, which is proudly proclaimed at Whitehall, New York, a small town on a creek off the head of the lake. It was here in 1776 that Benedict Arnold (still loyal to the American cause at the time) had a fleet of small ships built with which he faced the British at Valcour Island, halfway down the lake. It was a standoff for quite a while before the British prevailed over the roughly built little fleet, but it delayed the British long enough so that they did not gain control of the lake that year, which contributed to the American victory at Saratoga in 1777.

In this northern location at the Canadian border, the sailing season is fairly short—mid-June to mid-September as a rule—and the area is ski country in the winter. While the season is on, Lake Champlain is a rewarding, challenging and exciting place to cruise.

Lake Ontario

The whole Great Lakes complex is an incredible feast for cruising sailors, hampered only by the shortness of the season. Each of HOMES (the acronym for the lakes, in case you are not a crossword puzzle addict) has its own special features and attractions. For the statistically minded, the Great Lakes have a water surface area of 94,710 square miles. The highest lake, Superior, is 600 feet above New York City's sea level. The lakes drop gradually in elevation as their drainage heads to the sea via the St. Lawrence, and Ontario is only 245 feet above sea level. The drop in elevation accounts for the locks in the Soo canals from Superior to Michigan and Huron, the swift current in the Detroit River, and the largest descent of all, the 326 feet the Niagara River drops between Erie and Ontario, including the cataract of Niagara Falls. Only Lake Erie, much the shallowest, has a lake bed that is above sea level. For that reason, and because its east-west axis is along the path of the prevalent weather-system movements, Erie is particularly susceptible to the fluctuations in lake level known as seiches, in which water is piled up by wind force at one end of the lake. All of them have this effect in some degree, but Erie has the most pronounced. The lake levels also fluctuate seasonally and through the effects of periods of drought or extra rainfall. All these phenomena affect cruising conditions, so the favorite harbor of one season may be the run-aground special of the next one.

Ontario, though the smallest, is well equipped with cruising areas, particularly at its eastern end. On the west, the urban sprawl of Toronto and its satellites makes a major sailing area, though it is not cruising country. Sailors from here head east in Ontario, or back up the other way to Lake Huron, when they become serious about cruising.

Inland

At the eastern end of Ontario, the Thousand Islands offer some special attractions, with innumerable anchorages and good facilities in some of the towns, such as Alexandria Bay and Clayton. Also on the New York shore, the area around Chaumont has good harbors and bases and is home to a great amount of activity. Main Duck Island, in the middle of the lake, is a favorite target for cruisers, though it is small and access is restricted, but the major cruising area of Ontario is the Bay of Quinte on the Canadian side at the northeast corner of the lake. Amid graceful hills, a winding bay provides a choice of anchorages in such spots as Prinyers Cove, or the comparative urban atmosphere of Picton, a pleasant town at the head of the bay. At the other end, Kingston is an active yachting center with some interesting sightseeing available on shore.

Lake Erie

Erie, the second smallest of the lakes, has less to offer in cruising grounds than the others, but is by no means a washout. The eastern part, with rather straight shores and not too many harbors, dominated by big cities, including Buffalo at the extreme eastern end, has locally based yachting but is not an area to attract cruisers. Erie makes Pennsylvania and New York the only states to have ports on tidewater and the Great Lakes. The urban complex of Cleveland takes up a good portion of the featureless south shore, and the Canadian side is almost the same, with none of the breaks and indentations that make for interesting cruising.

Only at the western end, marked off by two peninsulas, Pelee on the Canadian side and Catawba Island in Ohio, with a string of islands in between, is there the kind of configuration that provides good cruising. The islands center on Put-in-Bay, and there are some pleasant cruising stops in the area.

Lake Huron

Huron is the star of the Great Lakes from the cruising fraternity's point of view, particularly in Georgian Bay and the North Channel, which line its north shore. This is one of the treasured cruising areas in America, a magnet in midsummer for sailors from every one of HOMES. It is a configuration reminiscent of Maine, or perhaps Puget Sound, with hundreds of islands and coves for the cruising sailor to explore, an inexhaustible supply that also manages to provide seclusion for those who seek it ardently, though the area has become so popular that its afloat population from early July to mid-August or later is growing larger each year. Manitoulin Island, indented with hundreds of covers and surrounded by smaller islands, is the heart of the area, with Little Current as the "must visit" port, and such spots as Killarney, Blind River, Thessalon, and Cockburn as just a few of the names that ring with a special meaning to Great Lakes sailors.

Lake Michigan

Michigan and Huron are of a level, without swift rivers or series of locks between them, and the North Channel area is a major attraction for sailors from Chicago, Milwaukee, Sheboygan, Muskegon, and other down-lake ports. Where the lakes meet, Mackinac Island is a famous resort, a special target for cruising sailors, and the apex of the two distance races to it from Chicago and Detroit. After the hundreds of boats that take part in these classic races finish up at Mackinac, many of them switch hats to the cruising mode and take off for North Channel.

Lake Michigan itself has long, straight coastlines for much of its length, and cruising along either of its shores is mainly a matter of port-to-port passages to none-too-glamorous harbors, mostly in the process of getting to or from the more attractive areas up north. However, at the north end of Michigan, there is a change in the lay of the land, and there are areas that are well worth some relaxed cruising. The Green Bay area of Wisconsin, a deep indentation off the main lake, separated by the Door County Peninsula, has some attractive cruising stops, and good service ports like the twin ones of Marinette, Wisconsin, and Menominee, Michigan. Ephriam, Egg Harbor, and Sturgeon Bay on the Door County side are some of the spots worth a visit. Out in the lake, the Manitou Islands and the group around Beaver Island are a separate world, and Beaver has special interest as the onetime realm of "King James," who established a Mormon colony in the mid-19th century that led to all sorts of complications, followed by an attempt by "King Ben" of the House of David to duplicate the "kingdom" in the 1920s, but with meager success. Beaver, a sizeable 13-mile island, and its town of St. James, originally founded by you know who, make a colorful stop, as do its surrounding islands of Garden, High, and Hog if conditions are right.

Back of the Manitous, steep islands off the Michigan shore, Traverse Bay, Lake Charlevoix, and Little Traverse Bay, provide some interesting stops, either as a target in themselves or as a pleasant interlude to break the trip to and from North Channel. My own experience of this area has been in passing through it in a Chicago-Mackinac Race and in some daysailing in Green Bay, but friends who have sailed here report that it has very worthwhile attractions.

Lake Superior

I have not sailed Lake Superior. My knowledge is confined to views from an airplane, but it has a reputation of being the wildest and least civilized cruising area in all the Great Lakes, calling for good preparations, careful planning, and good seamanship in the execution. There are many areas on Superior where the cruising man is entirely on his own, with no shore facilities and no direct contact with civilization, rewarding cruising for rugged individualists. The major attractions for cruising are the Apostle Islands off Chequamegon Bay and Ashland, Wisconsin, and sizeable Isle Royale on the Canadian side of the lake, where wildlife abounds. In its wide open areas and the severity of the weather that can sweep across it from the northern plains, Lake Superior, much the biggest of the Great Lakes, demands complete respect from the cruising sailor. Seas can build up to match anything on the wildest stretch of ocean, and its great rewards of wilderness isolation, scenery, and wildlife must be earned by the most careful kind of cruising preparations.

XIX

The West Coast

Baja to British Columbia

~~~~~~

The long, rugged West Coast, stretching from Mexico to Alaska, is a very different proposition from the East Coast, with its many indented bays and string of sounds behind barrier beaches. The West Coast cruising areas are widely separated, with long stretches of virtually harbor-less coast presenting cliffs and a straight shoreline to passing vessels, and boats making passage between the cruising areas must be thoroughly prepared and equipped for open sea work. Once reached, some of the cruising areas have very special atmosphere and attractions.

Mexico

My only sailing in Mexico has been between Ensenada, just south of the border, and Southern California, and some daysailing out of Acapulco. For Southern California yachtsmen, who really only have weekend cruising in home waters, Mexico is a lure despite the distances involved. The long seaward side of Baja California is not very hospitable, and one of the prices to be paid in negotiating it to get to good cruising in the Gulf of California inside it is that the return trip to California is a long, tedious slog to windward. From Cabo San Lucas at the tip of Baja, in and around to the Gulf, there are many fine cruising anchorages, mostly in primitive surroundings, and such towns as Mazatlan, Guaymas, and La Paz for supplies. Diving and sport fishing are excellent, and the Mexican government has recently changed its tune and allowed establishment of charter operations of foreigners. The Moorings is now running a bareboat operation in the upper gulf, which has made enjoyment of this area much easier for visitors. Baja cruising is a winter proposition. Heat and the likelihood of hurricanes rule out summer cruising here.

Southern California

The stretch of coast between Santa Barbara and San Diego, at the Mexican border, supports an enormous boating population, with the bulk of it, naturally, in the Los Angeles and Newport Harbor area. Unfortunately for all these people, local cruising, as mentioned, is confined to weekending to a few offshore islands, or possibly down to Ensenada and the off-lying Coronado Islands. There are islands off Santa Barbara, but much of the area is restricted by government activity or private ownership, and there are no really secure harbors. The bulk of the pressure falls on Catalina Island, a little over 20 miles off the Los Angeles area, and cruising people accustomed to easy-come-easy-go in most parts of the country would be amazed at the regimentation here, and in all Southern California ports. Catalina's many coves on its north side, facing the mainland, are all controlled by clubs and local authorities. Mooring is by permission only, at least on busy summer weekends, and the harbors are literally a city gone to sea. One does not just drop in on clubs and marinas in Southern California's jammed harbors. There is almost nowhere that anchoring is possible, and advance arrangements must be made for berthing at a marina or club.

Catalina is fine until a Santa Ana, locally nicknamed Santana, starts to blow. It is a hot land breeze from the desert that can take over the scene in a matter of minutes when it pipes up, often without much warning. With gusts up to hurricane strength, and hot, heavy air from inland, it makes the normally well protected coves on Catalina into lee-shore traps very rapidly, and there can be all kinds of excitement as everyone tries to leave at once and head back to the protection of the mainland.

San Francisco Bay

For the cruising sailor who is not partial to long offshore passages, the only protected water between Los Angeles and Puget Sound, far up in the Pacific Northwest, is in the confines of the San Francisco Bay area, which also includes the delta of the Sacramento River. San Francisco Bay itself is heavily populated along all its shores, and cruising here mainly consists of marina-hopping to the various cities. Much of the local activity centers on the Golden Gate, with its swirling tides and frequent fogs, and some amazing contrasts in weather conditions within a few miles. The Gate can be rough and breezy, with a raw, cold fog sweeping in from the open Pacific making foul weather gear very much in order, but a brief jaunt through Raccoon Strait behind Angel Island can bring warm sun in the 70s and T-shirt sailing in the northern reaches of the bay.

At the head of the bay, the delta region extends inland for many miles, a unique area for exploring by boat. In addition to the main river, there are sloughs and canals lined with reeds, locally called tules, in a network of waterways that is a world unto itself. Much of the land is below sea level, with dikes and levees keeping the waterways under control. There are quiet little towns and backwaters, and tying up is possible as the spirit moves. Surprisingly, it is possible to do a fair amount of sailing here, and it is like coming out of the wilderness to emerge from the Delta back into the civilized welter of the Bay. Escape to the delta is an effective "safety valve" for those who feel somewhat confined in the bay's busy bustle, but it is often extremely hot in summer.

Puget Sound

As if to make up for the lack of cruising areas on most of the ocean coastline of the west, Puget Sound and adjacent waters, at the far northwest corner of the country, makes up in spades for lack of opportunities south of it. This is a cruising dreamworld, with the only drawbacks the possibility of an extra allotment of rain, perhaps with fog, and a noticeable dearth of wind in the summer months. The lack of wind becomes especially evident when negotiating some of the narrow passes between the islands, where tidal currents can build up broad-shouldered heft. Reliable power is needed in spots such as Deception Pass.

There is an unlimited choice of coves and harbors, and while the boat population is extremely heavy, it is still possible on occasion to find a quiet corner. Although there are harbors all the way down the sound to Tacoma, and such surroundings spots as Vashon Island, the major target for cruising here is the San Juan Islands and the Gulf Islands north of them. They are found inside the Strait of Juan de Fuca that leads to the Pacific from Puget Sound between the Olympic Peninsula to the south and Vancouver Island to the north at the U.S.-Canadian border.

To an Easterner used to a steady diet of sand dunes and low bluffs along much of the Atlantic Coast, the scenery of Puget Sound is a spectacular plus, something like Maine with real mountains. The immediate foreshore is rock and evergreen, and the islands have some fairly good-size peaks, but these pale beneath the distant views of Mt. Rainier back of Tacoma, Mt. Baker farther to the north, and the Olympic Range on the west side of the bay and along Juan de Fuca. These majestic mountains are always snow-clad, and a constant wonder as a backdrop to marine activities.

The San Juans, on average, have slightly better weather conditions than surrounding areas, as the weather systems blowing in from the Pacific seem to separate inside Juan de Fuca, leaving the islands as an enclave of sunnier, milder weather, although this is far from guaranteed. Some of the highlights of Puget Sound cruising are Orcas Island, the Penders, and Roche Harbor in the San Juans. Port Townsend, Washington, once a scruffy and rundown lumber port, has been "gentrified" and made more picturesque in answer to the boating boom. Vancouver Island, with its main port of Victoria, is a tourist spot that maintains an atmosphere suggested by its name. Anyone interested in cruising traditions will enjoy the small maritime museum here that contains *Tillikum*, the converted Indian canoe in which Captain Voss did a circumnavigation in the wake of the fuss made over Joshua Slocum's voyage in *Spray*, and John Guzzwell's tiny sloop *Trekka*, in which he circumnavigated as a young man.

The west coast of Vancouver Island is a primitive, undeveloped area that is a real challenge as a cruising grounds, and a rewarding one for those undaunted by its rigorous demands.

Strait of Georgia and Desolation Sound

North of Puget Sound, the Strait of Georgia, a 100-mile-long landlocked sound, up to 20 miles wide for most of its length, is a gorgeous cruising area in itself, and also the pathway, for those who have the time, to the special pleasures of Desolation Sound at its northern end. From the top of the Strait, the Inside Passage leads on to Alaska.

Vancouver, British Columbia, is the hub of the area, a population center of 2 million people just north of the border at the southeast end of the Strait of Georgia. Perhaps the most beautiful city in North America, Vancouver is a busy yachting center with many good anchorages, marinas, and facilities, and well worth a visit. It has easy access to the Gulf Islands and the San Juans if desired, and the area north of it all the way to Desolation Sound is prime cruising country. With Mt. Baker an awesome fixture to the south visible for up to 100 miles in clear weather, a snowcapped ridge running up the spine of Vancouver Island, and more snowcapped peaks on the British Columbia mainland, the scenery here is a constant feast for the eye. The British Columbia mainland coast is known as the Sunshine Coast (at

Refuge Cove, Desolation Sound, British Columbia

least in contrast to some of the other areas) and in addition to the harbors on both sides of the Strait, Howe Sound and Jervis Inlet, leading to Princess Louisa Inlet, are deep indentations into the mainland that offer great cruising opportunities. Visitors can find charter boats in the Vancouver area and some of the neighboring harbors.

Highlight of the whole region is Desolation Sound at the top of the Strait of Georgia. It was named by George Vancouver in a fit of depression while exploring the untouched wilderness there in 1792. He had no success finding a northwest passage, saw few living things and felt lonely and desolate, but today it does not live up to its name for the cruising fraternity. In summer it is an area of rather gentle weather, gorgeous scenery, and a choice of a multitude of attractive anchorages. Although civilization does not impinge here, there is a handy supply base, with fuel, water, ice, and a well-stocked market at Refuge Cove. A lot of the traffic in and out from southern areas is by seaplane, with

Prideaux Haven, Desolation Sound

people making crew changes this way. If a day is spent in one of the many idyllic anchorages, like Tenedos Bay, Prideaux Haven, or Teakerne Arm, there is plenty of exploring to do by dinghy and by hiking ashore, oysters to be picked off the rocks at low tide, and clams, mussels, and salmon to be gathered in (with a fishing license for salmon). The water is cold for swimming, but in many spots there is a lake not far inland with much warmer water. All in all a delightful area.

North of here, the adventurously self-sufficient can explore areas that are wilder than the well-visited Desolation Sound region. Offshore from Prince Rupert, the Queen Charlotte Islands are a wildlife wonderland and a major salmon fishing area, with all sorts of little islands and coves, but not for the timid, which also applies to the waters on to the northwest to Alaska. The "tail" of Alaska, around Ketchikan, Sitka and Juneau, has a maze of protected waterways threading through islands, with strong tidal currents, and the beginnings of glacier country. Like the Labrador on the East Coast, this is an area for "expeditions," not easy cruising as most people pursue it.

XX

The Pacific Islands and Southeast Asia

〜〜〜〜〜〜〜〜〜〜〜〜〜〜〜〜〜〜〜〜〜

The vast reaches of the Pacific have long had a fascination for dedicated voyagers, and more and more of them have been following its legendary sea lanes of recent years. The magic ring of names like the Marquesas, Tuamotus, Iles sous le Vent, Tonga, Fiji, and the lands beyond have lured more and more sailors to make the long passages to them, and it is now possible for those with less time to jet to many of the areas and charter, either crewed boats or bareboat.

Hawaii

My Hawaiian sailing has been confined to daysailing out of Honolulu. While the islands look like a tempting cruising grounds from a cursory look at a map, they are actually not in the best formation for easy cruising. There is a great amount of exposed water between the islands, and there is not a wide choice of good harbors. Handling the strong trade winds and big seas of the open interisland passages is demanding work. Honolulu is a natural target and haven for long-distance voyagers bound from the States to the farther reaches of the South Pacific, and there is always a colony of transients in Ale Wai Yacht Harbor. For the dedicated cruiser who likes open sea work, the outlying islands offer spectacular scenery, some pleasant coves, tradition, as in the old whaling port of Lahaina, and a good taste of trade wind sailing.

219

Routes to the Islands

The North Pacific is a vast oceanic wasteland as far as the cruising sailor is concerned, with little in the way of cruising targets except Hawaii, but south of 10°N latitude and on down south and west the procession of archipelagoes is an endless temptatation to the long-range cruising sailor. From California and the Pacific Northwest, the natural route is via Hawaii. Sometimes that is as far as anyone gets when the realities of long voyages and getting along with shipmates have been experienced, but for those who continue on, the next step is usually the 2400-mile leg to Tahiti and Les Iles sous le Vent. It is about the same distance to Samoa for those who want to be farther west. Now that French Polynesia does not permit foreign boats to stay more than six months, there may be more of a tendency to head to the westward, but the Society Islands (Iles sous le Vent) and Tuamotus are still such a magnet that most long voyagers want to take them in.

From Panama it is 4,493 nautical miles to Tahiti, and this is the route of many circumnavigators. Question marks hang over the transit of the canal nowadays. I have not been there for a few years, but reports are that transient yachts are not treated hospitably by officials or the local clubs, and one of the prime meeting places for world voyagers has lost much of its appeal. As local control increases, this problem could increase.

Out of Panama, it is a tough push to get through the calms, squalls and doldrums of the Gulf of Panama. I have made two transits of it and saw these conditions both times. Once these have been worked through and the southeast trades have been found, it is a glorious slide across the equator with the wind broad on the port quarter. I made this passage in a subchaser on our way to New Guinea during World War II, and day after day I sat on the bridge looking at the procession of little white clouds and whitecapped seas marching up on our quarter longing to be on a sailboat instead of inhaling the diesel exhaust the wind wafted up to me. It should be classic sailing, with a dividend of fantastic sunsets over the bow each night.

Moorea, as seen from Tahiti

The majority of voyagers head for the Marquesas as a first stop, 1,000 miles short of Tahiti. There used to be a time when the Galapagos would be a stop on the way, and this unique group of islands on the equator is about as fascinating and unusual a cruising area as could be imagined. My view of them was via a three-day visit in the four-masted barque *Sea Cloud* after a passage from Easter Island (which has no harbor, incidentally, and is not a good cruising stop, aside from its total isolation). Months could be profitably spent in the Galapagos exploring the extensive archipelago and reveling in the wildlife and weird geology, but the Ecuadorian government, in an effort to preserve the fragile ecology here, has severely curtailed access for cruising yachts.

It is the work of months to get a permit to stop there, and then all movements must be under the control of government officials.

The Marquesas, from reports, as I have not been there, are strikingly scenic, interesting culturally, but are known by cruisers to have rather difficult harbors because of surge. From reports I have had, those who stop there are glad they have. The same applies to the Tuamotus, which are low-lying atolls that require extremely careful navigation and ship handling. Vagrant currents and the low profiles of the atolls make landfalls tricky, and negotiating the passes into the lagoons can be hair-raising because of extremely powerful currents.

The Society Islands (Les Iles sous le Vent)

Papeete, capital of French Polynesia, long the romantic symbol of South Sea island glamor and the object of cruising sailors' dreams, is now a depressing sinkhole of commercialism, although the scenic splendor beyond the urban blight of the city itself remains. The waterfront of Papeete is one long quay skirted by a boulevard and has traditionally been a rendezvous point for voyagers from all quarters of the globe. With the new regulations about foreign boats having to move on, it is not quite what it used to be, but it is still a striking panorama of all kinds of passage craft, many in a shocking state of disrepair, and many, also, with "A Vendre" (For Sale) signs in the rigging telling a sad story of the end of a cruising dream. The 4,400 miles from Panama has often been the end of what started out as a happy cruising partnership.

The best sailing and conditions are away from Papeete, sous le vent (to leeward), where Raiatea, Tahaa, Bora Bora, and Huahine lie in a cluster 100 miles northwest of Tahiti. In between, Tahiti's satellite, Moorea, is one of the world's most scenically striking islands, with two excellent harbors. Twelve miles from Tahiti, it used to be a complete world apart, but in recent years it has adopted some of the commercialism of Tahiti. It's beauty is still intact, however.

A thriving charter industry now operates out of Raiatea, including a

Bora Bora Yacht Club

branch of the worldwide operations of The Moorings, and French companies as well. The four islands make a delightful cruising area. Raiatea and Tahaa share a mutual lagoon inside one big, encircling reef, and there are many fine anchorages between the two islands, all, unfortunately, sharing the characteristic of all the anchorages here of being very deep, usually between 80 and 100 feet. The town of Uturoa on Raiatea gives a glimpse of modern Polynesian life without too much influence of tourism, a busy, modern little center for the island's economy and government. In contrast with this is the jungle-girt peace of the little Faaroa River, worth a dinghy expedition into its other-world atmosphere. Tahaa is the least developed of these islands, with an agrarian economy and very little evidence of tourism. Off to the east about 25 miles, Huahine is another example of present-day Polynesian lifestyle in its sleepy little main port, where the single street is lined with stores operated by Chinese. A cruising highlight here is Port

Inside the reef, Bora Bora

Bourayne, an almost totally landlocked bay, reached by a narrow cut, in the middle of its mountains. When we were there a few years ago we had the whole place to ourselves on a night of moonlit peace.

Most publicized of these islands is Bora Bora, which is 25 miles to the west of Raiatea and Tahaa, and a fine open ocean sail to its only pass, Teavanui. Bora Bora's distinctive double peak is a picture post-card image of the South Seas, so striking and photogenic that I found myself taking repeated shots of it when I probably had more than enough already. Going around it inside the lagoon presents constantly chang-ing perspectives on its fabulous contours.

Bora Bora is the most developed of these islands, with sophisticated hotels, a Club Med, many restaurants, and a yacht club (commercial) that is a gathering place for sailors from all points. All the islands but Tahaa have airline service to Papeete's jet airport and are easily accessible for hotel visitors. On Bora Bora there is not so much of an "away-from-it-all" feeling as on the other three islands, but the anchorages inside the lagoon, the brilliant water colors, the diving and swimming, and the trade wind sailing are all very much a part of the scene, and the stuff that the fulfillment of cruising dreams is made of.

Tonga

On out in the Pacific, almost 1,500 miles beyond Tahiti and across the international date line, the Kingdom of Tonga is a unique cruising destination for long-distance voyagers and charterers. Consisting of three groups of islands on a northeast-southwest, 200-mile axis at 18°S latitude, its northern group, Vava'u, is the major cruising area out of the well-protected harbor at Neiafu. It is a compact area, perhaps 20 miles by ten, all within a fringing reef, and with 42 anchorages spelled out on the cruising chart given to charterers at Neiafu. With everything so close, there is a constant changing of perspectives and vistas and always something to look at while enjoying trade wind sailing. Diving and swimming are excellent, and there are caves to explore. We had a mix of absolutely isolated anchorages off lovely curving beaches with visits to small villages, scrupulously neat and parklike with their cropped grass, flower beds marked off by borders made of upended bottles, and well-tended bungalows. Tongans are very religious, very proud of their life-style, friendly, and outgoing, and the cares of the world seem a million miles away in a Tongan village. Tonga has been a kingdom since long before the advent of white explorers. It has been a protectorate of Great Britain, but is now independent again, the only kingdom in the Pacific islands. Of all the places we have cruised, this stands out as the most "away from it all."

Air travel to Tonga is through Samoa, and it was a disheartening contrast to compare the neat, litter-free atmosphere there with the sloppy, garbage-strewn litter and unkempt look of Samoa. Pago Pago Harbor in Samoa is a layover spot for cruisers during the hurricane season, and the inner end of the long narrow harbor there, with its almost ever-present curtain of rain clouds, sees quite a few boats in wet storage for the season, moored to bulkheads with a cat's cradle of lines.

Fiji

This storied archipelago a couple of hundred miles west of Tonga may very well be the cruising area of the future. It has all the natural attributes in a host of small islands gathered around big ones, a completely enclosed "sea within a sea" in the Koro, which is ringed by Fiji's islands and reefs, and interesting local atmosphere. The political troubles of a few years ago seem to have given way to a desire to attract more visitors, including yachtsmen, and a charter industry is in the development stage. Fiji has long been a favorite stop of sailors due to the civilized facilities at Suva and an active yacht club, but it does have a problem with vulnerability to hurricanes, so cruising here is largely seasonal over the austral winter. I was first struck with the fascinations of Fiji, and its potential for cruising, coming through there in my subchaser in 1943, and I had another taste of it in a three-day cruise out of Suva in 1962 into the fringes of the Koro Sea. In recent years, there has been a charter industry of "head" boats, mostly power, but now the New Zealand company, Rainbow Yacht Charters, is opening a new service in the Yasawa group off the northwest coast near Nadi airport, the big jet field. Chartering is being done on a flotilla basis as a starter.

For private boats on their way through, the many islands around the Koro Sea, the Yasawas, and Suva itself all make interesting stops, well worth considerable time.

New Zealand

Probably no country in the world is more boat-minded than New Zealand. Per capita ownership is the highest anywhere, and the whole island nation is ideally set up for using boats. On a summer weekend, Auckland Harbour looks as though all 3 million Kiwis are out there sailing, and there are many more harbors full of boats. Their record in international sailing in events like the Admiral's Cup, the various round-the-world races, and, who could forget it, the America's Cup, has been far out of proportion to the size of the country. New Zealand yacht designers and boat builders have worldwide reputations, and cruising Kiwis can be found in most of the popular centers around the globe.

At home they love to cruise, too, and they have wonderful waters for doing it. The South Island, famous for rugged alpine scenery and rather severe weather, is a challenging area for the hardy, but from Auckland north on the North Island there are cruising attractions aplenty. The Huraki Gulf outside Auckland, dotted with islands and enclosed by several big ones off to the eastward, is a handy area close to home for Aucklanders. The prime area lies close to 100 miles farther north in The Bay of Islands. This enclave, tucked in behind the imposing headland of Cape Brett at 35°S latitude, is ideally set up for relaxed cruising. It was discovered and named by Captain Cook on his first voyage of exploration in 1769. Its place names reflect a mix that is typical of New Zealand's history and blend of cultures. Anglo-Saxon names like Brett, Roberton, and Russell, recalling early explorers and settlers, mix with liquidly tripping Maori names from New Zealand's Polynesian heritage, long antedating European explorations. Opua, Motukiekie, Urupukapuka, Whangamumu, Motorua, and Motoroa take a while to come easily off English speaking tongues, but they help to add to the atmosphere of an attractive, exotic area.

It is not quite subtropical at this latitude, though much of the vegetation has a look of the tropics, and the water is quite cool for swimming and diving. In late summer, a sweater or light windbreaker felt good after sundown, but the atmosphere is so clear and unpolluted that the sun has a special brilliance that burns like a tropical one. We were there in late February and early March, corresponding to late summer in the Northern Hemisphere, and the weather was exceptionally bright and clear, with cloudless early mornings and evenings, and

Opua, Bay of Islands, New Zealand

a parade of fair weather clouds marching in on the prevailing northeast breeze during the day. The winds were mostly light, and we had just a few sprinkles of rain in two weeks after what had been classed as a very wet and rainy summer.

The Bay Islands are not a big area, stretching only about 15 miles east to west and about the same north and south. The islands offer a dividend of heading out into the open Pacific around Cape Brett to some harbors on the outside when the weather permits. Most interesting of these outside harbors is Whangamumu, a well protected cove that was the home of a whaling station until the mid-1930s. Its ruins now make an atmospheric setting for exploring on shore in an area that can only be reached by hiking trails. A striking feature of the passage around Cape Brett is a rocky pinnacle of an island off it with a hole through it big enough for tourists' powered sight-seeing catamarans to pass through when there is no ocean swell. On our rounding, there was a surge of at least 10-foot swells from a distant Pacific storm, and a kayak would have had trouble in Hole in the Rock.

On the inside of Brett, the islands lie close together, sheltering a series of coves on the mainland, and there is a choice of anchorages every mile or two, many with lovely beaches and hilltop trails for hiking. The islands are only a few hundred feet high at most, but there are wonderfully panoramic views for those who climb them. Pipis, soft clams that are steamed and eaten, can be picked up on many of the beaches, and the fishing is generally good throughout. This was where Zane Grey made his record marlin catches back in the '30s, operating out of Deep Water Cove just inside Brett. Nothing is left now of the thriving camp that was the fishing base then.

Hole in the Rock, Bay of Islands

Everything is so close together that it is no trouble to duck back to the town of Russell, New Zealand's first capital in 1841, for more supplies or a meal ashore, as this is the only "civilization" in the area. An interesting small museum there, a memorial to Captain Cook, chronicles his explorations and is also a record of the Maori culture and European settlements of the region. The Bay of Islands, compact and atmospheric, ranks as one of the fine cruising areas of the world despite its small scope.

Australia

New Zealand's Down Under neighbor is another boat-minded land, though perhaps not in quite the same ratio to population as the Kiwis. In its vast spread, roughly equivalent to the continental United States, there are a few fine cruising areas, but they are widely separated. Sydney, the major metropolis, is perhaps the most boat-oriented big city I have ever seen. Its magnificent harbor teems with pleasure boats of every size and description, and it is big enough for a few days of cruising strictly within its confines. Many arms extend from it back into the hills, offering quite a choice of anchorages, though nothing in the way of isolation, and sailing around it is a constant delight of watching the marine traffic, both pleasure and commercial, and taking in such landmarks as the Opera House and the Harbour Bridge, or the imposing cliffs known as the Sydney Heads at the relatively narrow entrance. The coastline outside does not offer many cruising stops except for Pitt Water, a system of sounds and rivers some 30 miles north of the Sydney area. This is home to a big hire-cruiser business of U-drive motorboats that are popular for family vacations. Tasmania, south of the mainland of Australia, has some beautiful scenery and interesting bays and villages but it is quite far south. Since tempestuous Bass Strait must be crossed to get there, Tasmania is only for the adventurous.

Australia's major cruising area is in the semitropical and tropical northeast, up the Queensland coast, inside the phenomenon of the 1,200-mile-long Great Barrier Reef. There are sportfishing centers, such as Cairns, many "out island" resorts on the islands that dot the area, and a prime cruising grounds in the Whitsunday Islands. Getting there from Sydney is comparable to a New York-Miami trip in the States, so there is not a lot of private cruising. World voyagers do pass through here enjoying the protected water and the unusual surroundings, and there is a big charter industry both crewed and bareboat, mostly out of Shute Harbour.

The Whitsundays, another discovery of Captain Cook, and also named by him in 1770, a year after his adventures in New Zealand, are comparable to the Virgin Islands in scope and layout with two major differences. They are a largely unsettled national park, and the tide range is considerable, as much as 16 feet. They are hilly, in fact almost mountainous, with steady southeast trades in the winter season, gorgeous beaches that are hardly touched by human feet, and a wide choice of uncrowded anchorages close together. The only civilization is a scattering of island resorts, informal and water-oriented. Most of them welcome yachtsmen for meals ashore, and we had a couple of congenial visits doing this. The summer season is not recommended for cruising, as cyclones (local for hurricane) threaten, and heat and humidity are high.

The absolute highlight of the area, lying 40 miles offshore at 20° South latitude, is the Great Barrier Reef itself. Charter boats are restricted to the Whitsundays and not allowed to go out to the reef, as navigation is extremely tricky and tidal currents are strong, and anyone on their own would be advised to have good local knowledge before giving it a try. It is available, however, by seaplane. A small one with four passenger seats picked us up from our dinghy, after reservations were made by radio ahead of time, aiming to be on the reef at low tide, which was 8 a.m. in our case. At high tide, everything is at least six feet under.

The plane landed in a lagoon on the reef after a wonderful glimpse of the fantastic color contrasts, and we were taken off in a glass-bottom launch left out there on a mooring. Our pilot was a naturalist, explaining some of the features of the reef and warning us of the dangers, such as fire coral, and asking us not to step on any live coral. We were wearing sneakers (sand shoes in Australia) and were equipped with a

Whitsunday Islands, Australia

glass-bottom viewing bucket. The sea was mirror calm, and it was a unique experience to be 40 miles at sea and walking across the wonderland of the reef and its myriad forms of life.

With the tide on the make, the last part of the trip was a run in the launch along the edge of the reef where it fell away into the lagoon, with an excellent view of the thousands of fish, large turtles, and one shark that flicked its tail and shot away from under our shadow. Although we did see people on other boats swimming over the side, and that was the only shark we glimpsed, we did not do any swimming in these waters.

Southeast Asia

A look at a map of the world of islands above Australia would make one think that there should be all sorts of cruising opportunities in this great spread, but the fact is that not too many boats venture into the area between New Guinea and the Philippines for security reasons and lack of facilities. Piracy is perhaps more imagined than actual, but there are areas where it still does exist.

My experience of New Guinea was all under the auspices of the U.S. Navy, and I have had a hankering, as yet unfulfilled, to get back there in more peaceful circumstances. The north coast of Papua, and islands like New Britain and the Admiralties, had a fascination that would have been different if they hadn't been harboring Japanese dive bombers, etc., at the time. The scenery was magnificent, the weather was hot and humid with lots of rain, but seldom stormy, and there seemed to be all sorts of places to explore. I understand that there is some cruising there, but that there are problems with security.

For cruising people bound around the world or at least to the Indian Ocean, there is the question of which route to get from the Pacific to the Indian. The standard one most followed is to cross the top of Australia, negotiating the treacherous tides and reefs of Torres Strait with great caution, then the Arafura Sea to Darwin, Australia, and on through the Timor Sea to Christmas Island and the Cocos in the Indian Ocean itself. From there it becomes the basic choice of Red Sea or Cape of Good Hope, both of which present special problems.

Lately, with more political stability and security in Indonesia, some passagemakers go north of the Timor Sea to the islands east of Bali and then head up north of Java for Singapore before breaking out into the Indian Ocean. I have talked to a few people who have managed this route without feeling threatened by possibilities of piracy.

Normal cruising operations have become relatively commonplace in the area from Bali up to Singapore and on to Thailand, depending on the monsoon season. In the northeast monsoon, the west coast of

Thailand on the Andaman Sea, an arm of the Indian Ocean, has become an active yachting area. In the southwest monsoon, the boats shift from western Thailand down to Singapore and Bali or into the Gulf of Siam. Although there is a limited choice of good harbors, and supplies and services are hard to come by, Bali is popular as a base because of its scenery and the glamor of its reputation. Boats also come up here from the west coast of Australia around Perth and Fremantle to escape the winter season there.

Yachting activity on the west coast of Thailand is centered on the Andaman Sea island of Phuket (pronounced Poo-ket, in case you wondered—the "h" is silent, as in Thailand). It is 32 miles long north to south, at 8° North latitude, and a bay called Phang Na separates it and the mainland. About 30 boats are in the charter trade here, all professionally crewed, as there are no facilities as yet for bareboating. World voyagers have been stopping here more and more in recent years to gird for the long Indian Ocean passage, or to recover from it if eastbound. The island, which has jet connections with Bangkok and Europe (about 10 hours away) is connected to the mainland by a causeway and it has become an "in" winter resort for the so-called jet set from Europe. Some of its hotels, all on beautiful beaches, are first-class luxury ones, and there is also an unbelievable honky-tonk area at Patong on the west coast.

We were there in the northeast monsoon season in mid-February sampling three of the charter boats, including the classic maxi *Stormvogel*. The weather was hot, with no rain for the 10 days of our stay, and quite humid. The northeast monsoon would blow with some authority from just after dark into the next morning, gradually fading at noon, to be replaced by a soft sea breeze in the afternoon. This would fade at sunset and the northeast monsoon would start the cycle again soon after dark.

This is the most exotically different area I have ever cruised in, starting with the scenery. Phang Na Bay is full of islands that look as though they were shaped by a mad sculptor as backdrops for a Gothic fairy tale. Thin and tall, of limestone, their bases are all eroded by the sea, with weird patterns of stalactites hanging down in the recessed

Phang Na Bay, Phuket, Thailand

areas. There are many caves in the cliffs, and sometimes a tunnel will lead through to an interior lagoon in the center of the island, a steep-walled enclave of eerie silence, broken only by the frantic skittering of little fish alarmed at the intrusion of a dinghy. Occasionally, a monkey can be seen scampering along a ledge on a foraging expedition. On the water, pale green garfish skip along the surface in undulating flight. The water color ranges from deep indigo where the bay joins the sea, to a muddy brown near the head of the bay fed by rivers. In between, away from the influence of the river mud, it is a pale green.

As strange as the scenery are the local boats. All through the area, the native inshore fishing boats are long, low canoes with a strange form of outboard motor. The motor, whether gas or diesel, is on its side near the stern, and the propeller shaft extends at a shallow angle a dozen or more feet aft of the boat. They are called "longtails," they are ubiquitous, and they make an ungodly roar as they charge along throwing a great rooster tail. The offshore boats are equally exotic. The fishery is for squid, mostly, and the boats, which have sampan-type hulls and pagodalike deckhouses several tiers high at the stern, are equipped with long outriggers that hold strings of lights. They go out at night, and the offshore waters look as though a city has gone to sea.

When the northeast monsoon quits sometime in April as a rule, the west coast of Phuket, lined with half-moon bays that are good anchorages in the northeast period, is exposed to open sea surf and the yachts depart, as mentioned, for Singapore, Bali, or the Gulf of Siam. Those who choose to stay behind usually ride out the season at anchor in Ao Chalong, a bay on the east side of Phuket.

XXI

The Mediterranean World

It is a long jump from the Andaman Sea to the Aegean Sea, but the reaches of that long jump are mostly devoid of cruising opportunities and of interest mainly to world voyagers who must negotiate the Indian Ocean and a route into the Atlantic. The Seychelles, a large island group southwest of India, between it and Madagascar, have often been looked upon as a last resort by skippers who have grown bored with the more popular and accessible cruising grounds. I have heard charter captains in the Caribbean, vexed with a run-in with red tape or the growing impingements of civilization, mutter, "On to the Seychelles, that's the last answer," but very few have actually carried out this threat. Political problems have beset the Seychelles in the '80s, and an unstable government and comparative lack of facilities have been enough to deter most dreamers.

My own experience of the Indian Ocean west of Western Australia and the Andaman Sea has been at 30,000 feet, though I have read many manuscripts, published and unpublished, about crossing it, and have listened to the tales of those who have. The big choice, as already stated, is whether to head for the Red Sea and the Med or to go down around South Africa. Both choices happen to be a bit daunting, and if I had ever in my own wildest dreams contemplated a circumnavigation, I think the problem of this choice would have been a strong deterrent to anything beyond dreaming.

The South African route means a very long passage, with only an island or two to break it, rugged conditions getting around Good Hope, and long uninterrupted legs up through the South Atlantic afterward.

One has to be a passage fanatic to contemplate this route with pleasure.

The Red Sea choice means facing two problems: weather conditions and the very real danger of unfriendly locals. My only view of the Red Sea was at its northern end in very pleasant weather in February from the deck of a ship, but the tales of beating up it against strong northers, plus the trickiness of reefs along both shores, and the physical danger from piratical inhabitants, make it sound like the toughest section of all in a complete circumnavigation. If at all possible, it is best to cruise in company with another boat until the Suez Canal and the Med are attained.

The Aegean

This storied sea, so rich in history and legend, and in the modern attractions of its unique surroundings, is one of the great cruising grounds of the world. From the legends of Odysseus through the centuries of history to World War II and the modern era, it has attracted seafarers and been enriched by their tales and traditions. Today, the Aegean is the scene of a thriving charter industry of crewed and bareboat yachts, and private boats from all over the world have come here to taste its special atmosphere. There are prices to pay for its pleasures. The season afloat runs from May into October; winter is a time of storms and cold. During the sailing season, the summer months bring severe heat, and the peculiar "trade wind" of an Aegean summer, the *meltemi*. This is a giant thermal that sweeps down from the great land masses to the north and, under a clear blue sky, blows at gale-force strength down the center of the Aegean, gradually weakening as it fans out into the open Mediterranean. A sail through a full-force *meltemi* is a memorable experience, accentuated by the fact that the Aegean is quite cold, and being doused by its spray is a forceful reminder. July and August are therefore months to be avoided if possible. In addition to the *meltemi* and the heat, there are hordes of tourists in all but the most remote islands, and visits to the famous landmarks of antiquity

Patmos, Greece

are in crowded conditions. And the antiquities are one of the main reasons for cruising here. It is a special thrill to visit one such as the Temple of Poseidon at Sounion on its magnificent promontory, site of the legend of how the Aegean got its name. King Aegeus stood watch at Sounion for the return of his son, Theseus, from dealing with the Minotaur in Crete. Theseus had promised to use white sails if he was returning in triumph, and black sails if in defeat, but he forgot his promise, and, though victorious, still had black sails set when Aegeus sighted the returning fleet. Distraught at the implication, Aegeus threw himself into the sea, giving it its name in his death.

Almost every cape and island has a story like this to tell. There is Santorini, with the reminder of the eruption of its volcano in 1500 B.C. now the crater that serves as its harbor; Kos, with the ruins of the world's first hospital, the Aesclipion of Hippocrates; Ios, the supposed burial place of Homer; Crete and the restored ruins of Knossos; Patmos, with the cave where St. John the Divine dictated the Apocalypse; Delos, birthplace of Apollo and Artemis, and long a holy shrine; Rhodes and the ancient capital at the acropolis of Lindos; and many, many more. Jane majored in Greek at Smith, which fostered a real and learned interest in archaeology, and it was a special thrill for her to combine the pleasures of sailing on the bright blue Aegean, even in the *meltemi*, with visits to such antiquities.

The yacht harbors around Athens are the hub for Greek cruising. There are two busy, bustling yacht harbors at Piraeus, the port of Athens, Mikrolimano and Zea. The shores of the Bay of Phaleron to the east of Athens are lined with marinas and yacht harbors as well, including a major one at Vouliagmeni. There is startling contrast between the large power yachts and big schooners of the Greek shipping magnates and the smaller caïques and family cruising boats. Greeks have been seamen throughout history, and there is still a great love of the sea in modern Greeks. Nearby islands such as Hydra, Aegina and Poros provide easy weekending and are visited by a constant stream of tourists on hydrofoils and ferries. Farther out, the islands of the Cyclades and Dodecanese, the latter close against the Turkish coast, are targets for longer cruises with a wide choice of places to visit. In recent years, the government has established fuel and water supply spots in some of the harbors, and there is a great variety in the life of the islands, from the frenetic tourism of Mykonos to the peace of tiny fishing villages. Mykonos, stepping-off spot for a visit to uninhabited Delos, is the most heavily developed of all the islands and also happens to be in the path of the strongest *meltemi*. It is not unusual for boats to be weathered in there for days at a time. If operating during the *meltemi* season, it is often possible to make quick passages between islands at dawn and in the late afternoon, when the wind tends to slacken off some, but middays see it at its most blustery.

In the northern Aegean, the Sporades make another attractive cruising area, and these are especially popular with organized flotilla cruises, which is the way a great many Europeans cruise in Greece. The boats, usually small auxiliaries about 30 feet or a bit smaller, are bareboats, but the whole group of boats is shepherded by a mother ship with a guide aboard, and also a mechanic or handyman / trouble shooter. In this way, navigation and language difficulties are simplified, and it is a very good way to cruise an area that might otherwise be a bit daunting. Flotilla bookings are run through agencies that specialize in this in England and France, particularly.

Rhodes, at the southeast corner of the Aegean, is also an important yachting base, both for crewed charter yachts and private boats, as it has easy access to the Turkish coast, which is as fascinating a cruising area as the islands. Antiquities such as Ephesus abound on the Turkish mainland, and there is a wealth of harbors and coves, some developed, some unspoiled. The south coast of Turkey is an area that has seen minimal development and is reportedly a wonderful place to cruise for the adventurous. I have only been there by ship. Because of the age-old political animosity between Turkey and Greece, regulations for cruising between the two countries are sometimes subject to change, and the latest developments should be checked before visiting the area.

Most dedicated cruising people feel that their experiences are not complete without a cruise in the Aegean.

The Ionian and Adriatic

The "other side" of Greece, across the Peloponnesos to the Ionian Sea, is quite a contrast to the Aegean, with its stark, dun hillsides, occasional cypresses bent to the wind and silvery olive groves. Here is a greener landscape, reached from the east via the Corinth Canal and the Gulf of Corinth, where are found such historic islands as Ithaca, and Corfu (Kerkyra to the Greeks). A popular jet-set resort for Europeans, graceful Corfu has an Italianate look in its hills and groves of trees, and cruising here, strictly a private proposition, can be very pleasant and relaxing.

Opposite Corfu on the mainland, the forbidding ramparts of Albania are a wasteland for visitors. This most isolated of all European countries does not welcome visitors, or even let them land, and it makes something of a no-man's-land out of the approach to the Adriatic and the very real and worthwhile cruising attractions of the Dalmatian Coast of Yugoslavia. Approaching from the south, it is advisable to head over to the heel of Italy's boot to such ports as Otranto or Brindisi before heading north to the east side of the Adriatic and the very real charms of the Dalmatian Coast. At its southern end, the Gulf of Kotor is an area of spectacular scenery, with steep cliffs giving right down to the water, impressive mountains as an inland backdrop, and picturesque little villages along the shores.

Until recently, cruising in Yugoslavia had to be done by private boat or in charters based in Greece or Italy, but there have been recent moves to run flotilla cruises there. Considering it is a communist country, it is wide open to visitors, one of the areas of Europe most visited by tourists in the summer. The tourism centers on large, modern, luxury hotels sitting on seafront hillsides with tiers of balconies towering over the landscape, but there is also a lot of camping on the offshore islands, and it is a common sight to see inflatables with German or Austrian flags zooming between the islands of the offshore archipelagos.

Medieval cities like Zadar, Split, and Dubrovnik offer an idea of what the Adriatic was like when Venice controlled the commerce of the area and they were important city-states on the route to the treasures of the Middle and Far East. A walled city like Trogir offers a journey back to medieval times, and offshore such islands as Vis, Hvar and the Kornati archipelago have a timeless quality in contrast to the modern tourism of the mainland.

One drawback here is that summer winds are fickle. In my two experiences of ranging this coast the weather was delightful, but deficient in breeze for most of the time. However, there can be periods of strong northers or southerlies sweeping the narrow length of the Adriatic with considerable force, calling for caution.

Sardinia and Corsica

The Mediterranean west of Italy has many interesting cruising areas, but my own experience has been confined to the area where these two mountainous islands face each other across the Strait of Bonifacio. Sicily has interesting harbors, teeming with antiquities, and such colorful resorts as Taormina, under the shadow of Mount Etna. Malta, due south of Sicily, one of the smallest independent nations in the world, and a symbol of independence in many ways with its long history of invasion and change of ruling powers, is a favorite of Mediterranean-based cruising boats, many of whom lay up here for the winter. The adventurous can head off for Pantelleria and Lampedusa and the African coast at Tunis, and there are harbors worth visiting on up the west coast of Italy, with Capri, Ischia, and the Bay of Naples as worthwhile targets. Off to the west, the Balearics provide many cruising ports, and the Riviera from the northwest coast of Italy westward into Monaco and France is a very crowded and busy yachting area, where the harbors are jammed with local and visiting boats, and summer crowds on shore. This is not getting away from it all by any means.

Out in the middle of the Med, some 100 miles west of the mainland of Italy, Italian Sardinia and French Corsica (where many natives would like to have their independence) provide an interesting cruising area that is a major target of summer activity from the mainland ports of France and Italy, as well as visiting yachts from farther away. The major fixture of the region is the area known as the Costa Smeralda, a 30-mile-long enclave on the northeast coast of Sardinia, developed as a prime resort in the late '60s by the Aga Khan. It has two major yacht harbors, Porto Cervo, site of an enormous marina, yacht club, hotel, and service complex, and Cale di Volpe. There are several luxury hotels, golf courses, and a controlled architectural theme that has produced harmonious structures fitting in with the contours of the hills and the lay of the land. Costa Smeralda is a base for many of the most luxurious yachts in Europe and a cruising target for boats from the mainland, and it is gateway to an area that is excellent for relaxed cruising in interesting surroundings.

Between the Costa Smeralda and Corsica, 40 miles to the north, the Strait of Bonifacio, a busy sealane for commercial traffic, is speckled with dozens of islands that provide good cruising anchorages, one sizeable town in La Maddelena, and easy access to Corsica. The French and Italians sensibly had no customs or immigration procedures when we were there in 1977, but this should be checked out for any recent developments in this age of terrorism and international tensions.

Approach to Corsica across the strait is impressive, with great white cliffs, perpendicular from the sea, stretching northwestward from Cape Pertusato at Corsica's southern tip, backed by towering interior mountains. They loomed mistily out of rainsqualls as we made an approach to Bonifacio on a passage from the south side of the strait, where we had spent a night in lonely splendor in a cove called Porto Puddu, surrounded by stark Sardinian hills rising to impressive inland peaks. We were headed for the port of Bonifacio. Few towns have a more dramatic setting than this ancient one, whose houses cling to the sheer cliffs, looking as though they would tumble into the water at any moment, though some of them have probably been there since the place was founded in 875. The harbor entrance is also dramatic, tucked in behind the cliffs and not visible from the sea until right opposite it. Then it is a narrow two-mile cleft between the cliff-hanging houses and inland mountains, with a quay around its inner harbor jammed with boats and lined with taverns, shops, and restaurants. It was crowded in June when we were there, and the height of the season must see a real jam, with everyone stern-to the sea wall in Med-moor fashion. Corsica has good harbors along its coasts and is a favorite target for those adventurous enough to break their anchors out of the tangle of Med-moors in Riviera ports and head out for some cruising.

XXII

Northern Europe

England, France, the Netherlands, Germany, and the Scandinavian countries all have tremendous boating populations, and, despite the vagaries of summer weather in these northern latitudes, they head off for vacation cruising in great numbers. The prime target is Scandinavia, which is the only locus of my own northern European cruising, though locals do move about the coastal ports of England, Ireland, and France in great numbers. From reports of friends who have been there, Irish cruising is rewarding, given a good amount of cold rain, wind, and fog, and the islands of Scotland offer very much the same conditions. One advantage in June and July is almost endless daylight. English Channel ports in England, France, and Belgium are picturesque in atmosphere, but the same cautions pertain to weather conditions, and the tides are something very much to be reckoned with. Many channel ports are bare and dry at low tide, with boats resting on the "putty." This makes bilge keels popular, and some boats set up "legs" to prop them up when the water deserts them. Some harbors, such as St. Malo in France, a very popular haven, have tidal gates that keep the water inside when the tide goes out, but movement in and out is confined to half tide and up.

River and canal cruising is popular in Europe. I have been on canal barges on the Thames in England, the Loire region of France, and the lowlands of Holland. It is a wonderful, relaxed way to see the countryside, and many owners of masted vessels put their spars on deck and venture through the canal systems. A popular route is across Brittany by canal from the Channel to the Bay of Biscay, avoiding the rugged conditions rounding the Ushant (Ile d'Ouessant) at the western tip of

France. This route is also close to the lovely bay of the Mourbihan in northwest France. From the Gironde, further down the Bay of Biscay, the Canal du Midi is a much-used scenic route to the Mediterranean, with the excitement of going through tunnels on occasion, and a real taste of the unspoiled countryside. The long way around the Iberian peninsula is a demanding trip, and the Bay of Biscay can be one of the most unforgiving bodies of water in the temperate regions. There are good harbors, along the coasts of Spain and Portugal, but the open ocean stretches are quite long.

Denmark

As I have said, Scandinavia is a target for summer cruising for boats from all over Europe, and the harbors of Denmark, Sweden, Norway, and Finland sport a colorful array of ensigns in their crowded confines. Closest to the rest of Europe is Denmark, and it receives a great influx of boats in July and August, while supporting an enormous population of local boats. It is virtually an all-island nation, with only the Jutland peninsula as part of the mainland, and the traffic between islands is steady and voluminous, both in cruising yachts and in ferries and commercial vessels.

Copenhagen is of course the permanent base for many of the local boats, and the string of harbors northward from the commercial port of Copenhagen along the Oresund displays an amazing array of boats. Danes can cruise north from here to the west coast of Sweden and the southeastern coast of Norway, or head around into the Baltic, but there is also excellent cruising in the area between Zealand, the big island that Copenhagen occupies, and the Jutland peninsula off to the west. The islands in here are known as the Fyn archipelago, and it is a gracefully relaxed cruising area, with a wide choice of harbors among the "skipper towns" of the area, old ports that provided Denmark with most of its seafarers. In contrast to the rest of Scandinavia, there are no mountains here. The highest point in Denmark is 300 feet, and the cruising waters are lined with sandy bluffs and alternating stretches of farm fields and forests. To me, it was reminiscent of the atmosphere of Chesapeake Bay. Much of the water is shallow, and navigation is often in channels marked by stakes topped by brooms, with the broom either up or down at the top of the stake to show which side it should be passed on.

In various visits to Denmark, I have seen blowy, rainy, changeable weather, but our cruise in the Fyn archipelago at midsummer was graced by warm, sunny weather and good breezes. It was even sunbathing weather some of the time, but a sweater or light jacket felt good in the evening or when the sun was not out. Scandinavian twilights are long and lingering in midsummer, and there are many hours for cruising.

It is a peculiarity of the area that no one ever seems to anchor out. The anchor on the 27-foot charter boat we were on had never been used. We had no dinghy but did not miss one, as we tied up every night in a system of marinas known as *lystbodhavns*—pleasure boat harbors, equating "lust" to "pleasure." An amazing number of boats seemed to shoehorn into each one every night, with a predominance of German boats on vacation cruises from the Kiel Canal area, which is only about 50 miles away to the south. There were Dutch, Belgian, French, and English ensigns in evidence too, and the whole population of Denmark seemed to have taken off in small cruising sloops of the Folkboat type with their children along. When everyone had snugged down in a harbor in late afternoon, the area between the slips would come alive with towheaded youngsters in little rubber boats or Optimist prams having a fine time while the parents had their *schnapps* hour and got dinner ready. To get to know the area better, we ate ashore every night and had some interesting adventures in the little towns.

Each *lystbodhavn* has a wash house with showers and toilets and a laundry area, and the mornings would see a parade of families heading up the path to the wash house.

Some things we learned about cruising in Denmark are that liquor is extremely expensive and it is wise to stick to local *schnapps* (aquavit) and beer, and that ice is very hard to come by except at fish piers.

Although we were told that "everyone in Denmark speaks English" we found that this was not so in the islands, but, when we would enter a harbor looking for berthing instructions, a clearly proclaimed "I only speak English" would always bring someone who would direct us to a berth.

The Swedish Skerries

If imaginable, there is an even busier cruising area up the Oresund and the Kattegat from Denmark on the west coast of Sweden. In Sweden's population of 8 million, there are 800,000 pleasure boats, and, as in Denmark, most of them seem to be on the water in the short summer cruising season. All of Sweden takes a holiday in July, and this is the most crowded time. At 58°North latitude, equal to northern Labrador in the Western Hemisphere, there are very long hours of daylight, from about 3 a.m. to 11 p.m., and a vague twilight instead of complete darkness after that, and everyone takes advantage of this contrast to the long, dark hours of winter. Weather can be iffy, and I have experienced both warm, delightful sun and breezes, and some rather blustery cold in three cruises along this coast.

Gothenborg, Sweden's main west-coast port, is the base for much of the cruising activity, and the area north of it as far as the Norwegian border is ideal for protected cruising. The whole coast is a series of inland waterways, protected from the open sea by a network of skerries, rocky islands of varying size. It is an amazing maze of channels with unlimited choice of stopping places, and, as in Denmark, there is very little anchoring, though there are some harbors where it is done, and there is also frequent use of the Scandinavian moor. In this procedure, an anchor is dropped close to shore and then a line is taken ashore to a tree, or sometimes to iron rings that have been set into the rocks by commercial sailors. Often, boats raft up in this sort of setup, and there is a great deal of cruising in company.

Although the channels in among the skerries look like a nautical

I-95 on most days, there are so many places to stop that it is not too hard to find isolation if desired. The water is too cold for swimming by any but the hardiest polar bears, but many of the towns have a public bathhouse with pool, used by all and sundry. The towns offer civilization and a chance to eat ashore and to shop, and there are certain ones, like the island towns of Smögen and Marstrand, that are a magnet for all, with a perpetual party atmosphere in season. Boats jam into a place like Smögen in amazing numbers, mooring fore-and-aft to the quay, squeezed together like so many sardines, and a general atmosphere of jollity and friendly cooperation prevails.

As in all Scandinavian countries, charter boats are available, usually as bareboats.

My only experience of the Baltic side of Sweden, and Finland, has been by ship. The Stockholm area is alive with boats and surrounded by islands and coves providing fine anchorages. A string of islands, literally thousands, across the Baltic to Finland, reportedly offers wonderful cruising, with the main problem being to keep track of one's position in the endless profusion of look-alike islands.

Norway

Norway does not have the population of Denmark or Sweden, but per capita it is as boat-minded, and it, too, has some fine cruising grounds to enjoy during the short season. Long, scenic Oslofjord is the base for much of it, with some cruising harbors along its shores, but the main thrust is southward, away from the city, in the cruising season. The Royal Norwegian Yacht Club shifts its activities down the fjord to Hanko, near the southern end, and the cruising fraternity heads that way, too. There is a choice of cruising down the Swedish coast among the skerries just described (the Norwegian ensign is seen in many harbors there and on down to the Fyn archipelago), or to stay on the southeastern Norwegian coast across the Skagerrak from Sweden. Actually, boats often work both coasts in the course of a vacation cruise, as it is about

Misingen, Oslofjord, Norway

60 miles across the Skagerrak, easily accomplished in good weather given the long hours of summer daylight.

This section of Norway is also a network of inland waterways behind off-lying islands, and it is seldom necessary to move into open water in working up and down the coast. Again, there are anchorages galore, though not as many "managed" harbors as in Denmark and Sweden, and it is possible to find complete isolation, or to enter into a community of boats, as the spirit moves. There are sizable towns, like Larvik, Kragere and Kristiansand, and many smaller ones loaded with atmosphere. Anchoring is very often by Scandinavian moor to trees on shore, and again, the whole population, complete with kids in dinghies and prams, seems to be on the water in midsummer.

Around the corner from this coast, out into the North Sea to Stavanger and Bergen and the striking scenery of the fjords all the way up

A Scandinavian moor, on the south coast of Norway

the west coast to the North Cape, far above the Arctic Circle, conditions are much ruggeder in exposed water on the treacherously unpredictable North Sea. My sailing cruising stopped in the Skagerrak, but I have been out to Bergen and into fjord country by ship, and it is a scenic wonderland of majestic proportions. Cruising here by sailboat takes careful preparation and a readiness for all sorts of conditions, as well as a measure of self-sufficiency. The fjords, with sheer cliffs towering thousands of feet straight up from deep water, would be a difficult area to operate a cruising boat, as the winds are very varied and unpredictable, and anchoring would be a chore in many areas. Well-prepared boats have gone up this magnificent coastline for its entire length, but, again, this rates more as an expedition than a normal cruise. One way to see this coast without the problems of handling a cruising boat is to book on the mail steamer that runs from Bergen to the North Cape and takes passengers. Those who have taken it report that this is a marvelous way to see this unmatched display of dramatic scenery.

Crossing to America

Anyone who has spent some time in Caribbean harbors might get the impression that there are very few cruising yachts left in Europe, judging by the number that have come across. There was a time when sailors who crossed the Atlantic received awards and wrote books about their experiences, but today it is a common milk run, and there is an impression that anything from an orange crate with a diaper for a sail on up can make the passage. This is not so, and it is not a trip to be undertaken casually, but a tremendous number of boats are doing it, and there is now an annual cruising race each fall from the Canaries to the Caribbean that attracts upward of 200 boats.

There are several choices of route, with the basic purpose to end up in the northeast trades at about 16° North latitude for the couple of thousand miles to the West Indies. Columbus took this route some time ago, stumbling on a trade wind pattern that was unknown at the time, and it remains a classic to this day. He went from southern Spain along the African coast to the Canaries and then across. This is perhaps the most popular route, but there are those who like to go through the Azores, some prefer beautiful Madeira, and some even go down as far as the Cape Verdes to get the best advantage of the trades and the shortest distance of open sea. Coming back, incidentally, to avoid the trades, which Columbus and whose who followed him in the Spanish fleets finally discovered, it is best to head north around Bermuda and then circle along the northern edge of the Azores High, an almost permanent mid-Atlantic pressure area, to the Azores.

From the Mediterranean, boats about to take off gather in Gibraltar waiting for a break in the weather, and from Northern Europe the Bay of Biscay must be braved. If possible, it is wise to get through it fairly early in the fall, but there is no time when it is guaranteed that there will not be severe weather here.

My experience of this passage was a particularly pleasant one on the aforementioned four-masted barque *Sea Cloud* on a route from Marbella, Spain, to Gibraltar, Casablanca, Lanzerote in the Canaries, and, in 14 days, sailing during the day and powering at night, to Martinique. It was a wonderful way to experience this classic passage, and back we were in the familiar waters of the Caribbean.

Cruising Bibliography

This is a short list of publications about cruising grounds throughout the world. Prices and publishers' addresses change frequently, so prices have not been included, nor have all addresses. For most of the books below, and for additional titles, inquiries can be made of the following:

Armchair Sailor Bookstore, Lee's Wharf, Newport, RI 02840

International Marine Publishing Co., Inc., Blue Ridge Summit, PA 17294

Book Dept., *Cruising World* Magazine, 5 John Clarke Rd., Newport, RI 02840

Northeast North America

Newfoundland Information from Government of Newfoundland and Labrador. Dept. of Development and Tourism, Box 2016, St. John's, Newfoundland, Canada, A1C 5R8.

Nova Scotia *Cruising Cape Breton. Spray* Magazine, Suite 102, 1127 Barrington St., Halifax, Nova Scotia, Canada B3H 2P8. *Cruising Guide to Nova Scotia.* International Marine Publishing Co., Inc.

New England *Cruising Guide to Maine,* by Don Johnson. Vol 1, Kittery to Rockland, Vol. 2, Rockland to Eastport. Wescott Cove Publishing Co., Box 130, Stamford, CT 06904.
Cruising Guide to the New England Coast, Including Hudson River, Long Island Sound, and the Coast of New Brunswick, by Robert F. Duncan and John P. Ware. Putnam Berkeley Group Publishers, New York.

Atlantic Coast *Inland Waterway Guide.* Annual regional editions: Northern, Middle Atlantic, Southern, and Great Lakes. Inland Waterway Guide Communication Channels, Inc., 6255 Barfield Rd. Atlanta, GA 30328.
Cruising Guide to Chesapeake Bay, by Fessenden Blanchard and William T. Stone.

The Intracoastal Waterway, by Jan and Bill Moeller.
Cruising Guide to North Carolina, by Claiborne Young.
Cruising Guide to South Carolina, by Claiborne Young.

Bermuda, Florida, Bahamas, and Caribbean

Florida   *Eastern Florida*, by Claiborne Young.
   Florida Keys, by Captain Frank Papy.
Bermuda   *Yachtsman's Guide to the Bermuda Islands*, by Michael Voegeli.
Bahamas   *Yachtsman's Guide to the Bahamas*, Meredith H. Fields, editor.
   Tropic Isle Publishers, Inc., Box 610935. North Miami, FL 33261.
   Cruising Guide to the Abacos and Northern Bahamas, by Julius M.
   Wilensky. Wescott Cove Pubs.
Virgin Islands   *Yachtsman's Guide to the Virgin Islands*, Meredith H. Fields,
   editor. Tropic Isle Publishers.
   Cruising Guide to the Virgin Islands, by Simon Scott. The
   Moorings, 1305 U.S. 19 South, Suite 402, Clearwater, FL
   34624.
Eastern Caribbean   *St. Maarten / St. Martin Area + St. Kitts and Nevis*,
   William J. Eiman, editor. VIP Charters, 239 Delancey
   St., Philadelphia, PA 19106.
   Sailing Guide to the Windwards, by Chris Doyle.
   Yachtsman's Guide to the Windward Islands, by Julius M.
   Wilensky. Westcott Cove Publishers.
   Street's Cruising Guides to the Eastern Caribbean, by
   Donald M. Street Jr. Vol. 1, *Introduction*; Vol. 2, *Anguilla
   to Dominica*; Vol. 3, *Martinique to Trinidad*; Vol. 4,
   Venezuela. W. W. Norton & Co., 500 Fifth Ave., New
   York, NY 10110.
   South to the Caribbean, by Bill Robinson. W. W. Norton
   Publishers.
   Caribbean Cruising Handbook by Bill Robinson. Putnam
   Berkley Publishers.
   *Cruising Guide to the Caribbean and Bahamas Including
   North Coast of South America, Central America, and
   Yucatan*, by Jerrems Hart and William T. Stone. Putnam
   Berkley Publishers.
   Cruising Guide to the Bay Islands, by Julius M. Wilensky,
   Wescott Cove Publishers.

Inland

Lake Champlain *Cruising Guide to Lake Champlain*, by Alan and Susan McKibben. Lake Champlain Publishing Co., 176 Battery St., Burlington, VT 05401.

Great Lakes *Cruising Guide to the Great Lakes and Their Connecting Waterways*, by Marjorie C. Brazer.

West Coast

Baja *Baja Sea Guide*, by Leland R. Lewis.

Pacific Coast *Sea of Cortez*, by Dix Brow.
Cruising the Pacific Coast, Acapulco to Skagway, by Carolyn and Jack West.

Pacific Northwest *Gunkholing the San Juans*, by Al and Jo Bailey Cummings.
Gunkholing in the Gulf Islands, by Al and Jo Bailey Cummings.
Pacific Yachting's Cruising Guide to British Columbia. Vol. I, *Gulf Islands*; Vol. 2, *Desolation Sound*; Vol. 3, *Sunshine Coast*; by Bill Wolferstan. Vol. 4, *West Coast of Vancouver Island*, by Don Watmough. Pacific Yachting Publisher, 202-1132 Hamilton St., Vancouver, BC, Canada V6B 2S2.

South Pacific

Polynesia *South Pacific Handbook*, by David Stanley.
Landfalls of Paradise, by Earl R. Hinz.
Cruising Guide to Tahiti and the French Society Islands, by Marcia Davock. Westcott Cove Publishers. *Cruising Guide to the Islands of Tahiti and French Polynesia*, The Moorings Publishers.

New Zealand *New Zealand's Bay of Islands*, by Claire Jones. Port of Opua Trading Co. Ltd., Opua, New Zealand.

Australia *100 Magic Miles of the Great Barrier Reef, The Whitsunday Islands*, by David Colfelt.

Papua / New Guina *Papua New Guinea*, by Tony Wheeler.

Europe

Turkey   *Cruising Guide to the Turquoise Coasts of Turkey,* by Marcia Dav-
  ock, Wescott Cove Publishers.
  Turkey and the Dodecanaese Cruising Pilot.
Mediterranean   *Mediterranean Cruising Handbook,* by Rod Heikell.

Index

Index

Index

Index

Index